HOPE FOR
COMMON GROUND

HOPE FOR COMMON GROUND

Mediating the Personal
and the Political in a Divided Church

JULIE HANLON RUBIO

Georgetown University Press / *Washington, DC*

Library of Congress Cataloging-in-Publication Data

Names: Rubio, Julie Hanlon, author.
Title: Hope for common ground : mediating the personal and the political in a divided church / Julie Hanlon Rubio.
Other titles: Moral traditions series.
Description: Washington, DC : Georgetown University Press, 2016. | Series: Moral traditions series | Includes bibliographical references and index.
Identifiers: LCCN 2015024220 | ISBN 9781626163089 (hardcover : alk. paper) | ISBN 9781626163065 (pbk. : alk. paper) | ISBN 9781626163072 (ebook)
Subjects: LCSH: Christian sociology—Catholic Church. | Christian sociology—United States. | Social ethics—United States. | Church and social problems—Catholic Church. | Church and social problems—United States. | Christianity and politics—Catholic Church. | Christianity and politics—United States.
Classification: LCC BX1406.3 .R83 2016 | DDC 261.80973—dc23
LC record available at http://lccn.loc.gov/2015024220

♾ This book is printed on acid-free paper meeting the requirements of the American National Standard for Permanence in Paper for Printed Library Materials.

17 16   9 8 7 6 5 4 3 2 First printing

Printed in the United States of America

Cover design by Kara Davison, Faceout Studio. Cover image © Shutterstock.

*For Steve and Fran Hanlon
and
Hector and Marilyn Rubio
with deep gratitude*

CONTENTS

ACKNOWLEDGMENTS

I approach this work with gratitude to the many others who have worked for common ground among Catholics, especially all those involved with the Catholic Common Ground Initiative inspired by Joseph Cardinal Bernardin of Chicago and his consistent ethic of life. I am especially grateful for the witness of two of my theologian heroes, Elizabeth Johnson, CSJ, and Charles E. Curran. Each paid a price for prophetically challenging the church, and yet both remained committed to working within it and serving it. Both give gracious witness of humility and openness to dialogue.

I am thankful for engagement and friendship with many scholar friends with whom I have both substantial agreements and serious differences. Thanks for many conversations in conference hotel bars and college recreation rooms to Emily Reimer Barry, Jana Marguerite Bennett, John Berkman, Charlie Camosy, Holly Taylor Coolman, Dana Dillon, Brian Flanagan, Jason King, Reid Locklin, Bill Mattison, and Kari-Shane Davis Zimmerman.

I owe a debt of gratitude to my publisher, Richard Brown, who believed in this project even though he knew it was guaranteed to offend almost everyone who read it; to the anonymous reviewers, who offered essential critical feedback; and to my editor and friend, David Cloutier, who encouraged me to make my best attempt to speak across the lines that unnecessarily divide the church.

This book is dedicated to my parents, Steve and Fran Hanlon, and to my in-laws, Hector and Marilyn Rubio. They formed me and my husband Marty as people of faith and citizens in very different modes. I grew up in a house church called "Spes Nova," whose members were involved in protests in support of the United Farmworkers and against nuclear war. Marty's family has been deeply involved in the pro-life movement, including sidewalk counseling at abortion clinics and protesting with Operation

Rescue. Yet somehow, in the fall of 1986, Marty and I were able to find our way to each other and see that we had plenty in common. The last thirty years have provided many opportunities for all of us to seek understanding across political and religious divisions. I know that my work as a theologian would not have been the same without the strong foundation and love that my parents gave me or the challenge and support given me by my in-laws. If I am able to contribute to growing common ground among Catholics, I owe it to all four of them.

Last, I want to thank my readers. I have tried my best to write for a broad audience, but I know that my efforts at inclusivity will inevitably fall short. I am conscious that readers from different perspectives will have concerns and objections that I did not anticipate or could not address. I look forward to hearing about these challenges, and I hope conversation will continue among both academics and ordinary Christians—at conferences, in parishes, in classrooms, and at family dinners, where we all can recognize one another as members of the Body of the Christ.

INTRODUCTION

Reasons for Hope in a Divided Church

During the months preceding the 2012 US presidential election, American Catholics commanded public attention. Two Catholic vice presidential candidates were competing for office. The cost-cutting budget plan of one of these candidates, the Republican Representative Paul Ryan, was the subject of intense public debate. Pundits discussed the complexities of Catholic Social Teaching (CST). Theologians appeared in the media to explain the nuances of the concept of cooperation with evil.[1] The "Nuns on a Bus" crisscrossed the country to drum up support for antipoverty programs.[2] Bishops in some areas offered advice for Catholics to take to the voting booth.[3] It was most certainly a Catholic moment—one when the public square was not, to use the late Richard John Neuhaus's famous phrase, a "naked square" but rather a fully clothed space, full of theological discussion and religious imagery.[4] Everyone, it seemed, was talking about Catholics and their theological debates.

Yet Catholics themselves were not exactly enjoying their moment in the sun together. Though Catholics have long been divided on political issues, division has perhaps never been so intense.[5] Public opinion polls during the campaign showed stark divisions among ordinary Catholics.[6] Catholic organizations lined up on opposite sides, both claiming justification for their choices in the Catholic tradition. Theologians entered the public debate in a new way through blog posts and signed public statements.[7] Candidate Ryan's claims to have been influenced both by the objectivist, atheist philosopher Ayn Rand and the tradition of CST confounded most theologians. How, they asked, could someone adhere to both Randian individualism and a Catholic commitment to the option for the poor? Theologians such as Vincent Miller and Daniel Finn publicly criticized Ryan, suggesting that he was much more indebted to Rand than to CST.[8] Hundreds of Catholic theologians signed a statement questioning Ryan's claim to have put forward a Catholic budget.[9] But a law professor, Robert George, and other Ryan supporters shot back with criticism of the statement, asking why Catholics necessarily had to agree on the scope of government's role in providing a safety net for the poor, and lauding Ryan's pro-life credentials.[10] How, they asked, could Catholics in good conscience support a candidate like the Democratic Party's incumbent vice president, Joe Biden, who studiously avoided issues such as abortion that are of central concern to the Catholic hierarchy? Debate became quite pointed, as some theologians articulated their frustration with what they saw as the co-optation of the language of CST in support of conservative politics favoring "makers" over "takers."[11] Still, others worried that most liberal Catholic academics had allowed their political allegiances to override their loyalty to the church's essential teachings on the dignity of life.[12]

In the summer of 2014, Catholics again found themselves in the limelight when the Supreme Court decided not to force Hobby Lobby, a closely held corporation, to comply with the contraception mandate of the Affordable Care Act because doing so would have violated the religious liberty of this family-owned business.[13] Although the members of the family that owns Hobby Lobby are evangelical Christians who objected to what they believe are the abortifacient effects of four forms of contraception, all five justices who supported the ruling are Catholic and just one of the four dissenting justices is Catholic. As Leslie Griffin pointed out in *America* magazine, Justice Samuel Alito's opinion made reference to the Catholic principle of cooperation with evil and cited a classic of Catholic moral theology, Father Henry Davis's 1935 manual, *Moral and Pastoral Theology*.[14] A group of sixty-seven conservative Catholic scholars filed an amicus brief, arguing that the religious liberty interests of Hobby Lobby had been violated because family members rightly believed that by providing health insurance coverage for the four contraception methods, they would be engaged in moral cooperation with evil.[15] Notably, the list of scholars who signed the brief did not include any of the major liberal Catholic theologians who have done serious work on the principle of cooperation with evil, which suggests that theologians would be deeply divided on this issue. Early reactions among the public were also highly polarized.[16]

In both popular and academic Catholic circles, politics has become a very uncomfortable space. One side favors reducing the size and scope of government, but the other side cannot imagine how government funding and programs would be replaced. Some see dignity-of-life issues as absolutely central, but others characterize social justice commitments as the most vital ones. Catholics are more divided than at any point in their history, and in this they mirror society rather than providing an alternative to it.[17] From the high point of Catholic consensus in the early 1960s, after the election of the Catholic John F. Kennedy as president, division among the faithful has spiraled to the point where one can justifiably speak of many divergent Catholic approaches to social problems.[18] It is not only that Catholics disagree on abortion, same-sex marriage, and taxes, but also that they disagree on what the major social problems are and how to approach them.

In this context of divergence, the principles of CST do not seem to provide much help, given that commitments to human life and dignity, the family and community, human rights, solidarity, subsidiarity, the dignity of work and workers, and stewardship of the environment can be honored by both liberals and conservatives with very different political commitments and thus do not often bridge the gulf between them.[19] The divide seems impossible to overcome.

Perhaps the division itself is not the problem. Some would argue that the more significant issue is the misinterpretation or misapplication of CST. Thus the solution is to convince those who are misguided of the weaknesses of their position. Or perhaps Catholics should simply agree to disagree and work with people outside the church who are more sympathetic to their various worldviews.

In my view, division itself is a serious issue because it weakens the Body of Christ. When so many feel that they cannot understand or be understood by Catholics on "the other side," the church is not simply diverse; it is fractured. Moreover, the inability of Catholics to unite on a common cause weakens their influence in the public sphere. Though not all moral solutions occupy the mean between two extremes, there is often much to gain from listening to the best points of one's opponents, especially those with whom one shares foundational faith commitments. With the current stalemate in the pews, among theologians, and in politics, little progress can be made in solving important social problems.

This is why it is encouraging to know that, despite Catholics' continuing divisions, it is still possible to find common ground among them. Most share a realistic hope about the potential of politics, concerns about avoiding what the tradition calls "cooperation with evil," and a desire to identify community-based solutions that result in beneficial outcomes. If this unacknowledged common ground can be further developed in the local realm—in the space between the personal and the political—the church could offer a great deal of wisdom to public debates, instead of serving as a poster child for the culture wars. Although the foundations for common ground are sometimes difficult to see, they are discernible to those who look beyond labels and rhetoric—for three main reasons.

First, most Catholics maintain a hopeful realism about politics. At a time when many despair that politics is useless because the entire system is corrupt, Catholics affirm the importance of political participation. The US bishops write that "responsible citizenship is a virtue, and participation in political life is a moral obligation."[20] Although admitting that politics is "the art of the possible," the Catholic tradition insists on calling the government to remember its role as protector of the vulnerable. It does not, however, seek to make illegal everything it sees as immoral, and it accepts the reality that "incremental improvements in the law" are sometimes all that is possible.[21] Sometimes, a prophetic witness is called for; and at times, citizens on both the right and the left engage in it. However, different strategies are appropriate for different problems, and many on both the right and the left would agree that it is imprudent for churches to place too much faith in politics while giving less than due attention to other methods of social change.

Second, there is a widely shared, if implicit, recognition of the problem that the Catholic tradition calls cooperation with evil. Most US Catholics have moved into the economic, social, and political mainstream, and thus they are more aware of their power to shape society. More people worry about how their difficult socioeconomic and political choices, which could involve cooperating with evil—for example, whether to buy products made in unjust situations or by companies with problematic political connections, whether to vote for candidates who hold positions to which they object, whether to live in wealthy or transitional neighborhoods, whether to give to charities that engage in activities to which they object, and whether to visit cities with unjust laws—affect the lives of others.

During the last two decades, the US Conference of Catholic Bishops (USCCB) has more frequently invoked the principle of cooperation with evil. This principle is drawn from manuals of moral theology that were developed in the nineteenth and early twentieth centuries to help priests determine the sinfulness of various actions. The USCCB has questioned whether it is morally legitimate to vote for candidates who do not hold pro-life positions, arguing that the voter enables the politician, who in turn enables abortion clinics or the health care plan that includes free contraception. Although holding that intrinsically evil acts (i.e., acts that are always evil, regardless of intentions or circumstances) deserve special consideration, they raise concerns about possible cooperation with evil, while leaving specific political decisions to the consciences of individual Catholics.[22]

Although there has been a great deal of controversy about the particular arguments made by the USCCB, many on both the right and the left worry about how actions they aid with their money or votes may be immoral. There is increasing interest in examining the social implications of everyday choices and in seeking to discern better ways to avoid cooperation with evil and, even more important, increase cooperation with good.

Third, many Catholics are, like many other Americans, becoming increasingly frustrated by partisan divides and thus are more and more interested in focusing on outcomes that can be achieved at the local level. Although those who belong to political parties are more divided than ever, party disaffiliation is a growing trend, especially among young adults.[23] No matter how good a solution sounds or which party it comes from, many people simply want to know if it works. In the field of social ethics, theologians are increasingly employing social science to provide evidence for solutions to moral problems. In universities, professors are assessing student learning in order to see if particular pedagogical approaches are helpful. In political science, the use of evidence to assess the value of various approaches to social problems is increasing. In health care, researchers are studying best practices and encouraging their widespread use. Along with a shared concern about cooperation with evil and a realistic approach to politics, the new willingness to work on practical solutions, especially at the local level, suggests that there is reason for hope. Perhaps Catholics, led by a less polarized new generation, can move past bitter divisions to the common ground of evidence-based, participatory solutions.

In this book I argue that the potential for seeing and developing common ground is particularly strong if we focus on what can be done in the "local" sphere—that is, in the space between the personal (i.e., the individual) and the political (i.e., the governmental).[24] The much-discussed Catholic principle of subsidiarity privileges local action but does not repudiate either systemic political change or an individual's change of heart.

However, it recognizes that individual, bottom-up efforts are often insufficient and that top-down government programs are not always effective. Legislative efforts are crucial, but they can only accomplish so much, as the history of race relations in the United States shows. Conversely, though personal efforts are essential, supportive communities and social structures are also necessary.[25] Efforts to transform households, neighborhoods, and communities are not all that are needed, but they are key factors in social change.

Focusing energy on the local level need not mean returning to nostalgic ideas about simpler ways of life, whether they were organized on the basis of worker guilds (as in early CST) or urban farms (today). It does not mean neglecting the role of personal efforts or opting out of political campaigns. It does mean placing emphasis on communal efforts, including local church initiatives. If Catholics can begin to get along better, they might be able to inspire in others a similar commitment to developing more robust spaces for common life, within which problems can be solved.

In the local sphere, Catholic "liberals" and "conservatives" should be able to find common ground in the balance advocated by CST. Some believe that we should stop using the terms "liberal" and "conservative" altogether.[26] In my view, these labels are problematic but necessary. They describe distinct perspectives and commitments that persist, even among younger Catholics. Although I argue in the pages that follow that common ground exists between the sides (sometimes because the sides are not are clear-cut as we might think), I remain convinced the labels are a useful shorthand, as long as they are employed with charity and an awareness of their limitations.

This book is structured in two parts. In part I, I describe the wisdom that the Catholic tradition offers on faithful citizenship, cooperation with evil, and local problem solving. In each area, I pull out the best of the tradition and suggest how these areas of strength and common ground could be further developed. In part II, I apply this framework to four social issues that divide Americans (including Catholics): the family, poverty, abortion, and end-of-life care. Of course, I could have chosen many other issues (e.g., war, racism, immigration, the death penalty, contraception, artificial reproductive technologies, and stem cell research). However, the four issues I have chosen seem both especially intractable yet also especially amenable to the kinds of solutions I propose. In each chapter I argue not for abandoning the political or personal but for developing a third space for social action. Although I hope that this book's approach can also be applied to other issues, the four issues with which I begin strike me as the best possible cases. Using these issues, I argue that the local level is a fundamentally important space for gathering people of different perspectives who are realistic about the limits of politics but are still convinced of their connection to social evil and their responsibility to act for the common good. In the often-neglected "space between" the personal and the political, common ground is possible to find, and progress might not be as far-fetched as one thinks.

NOTES

1. Grant Gallicho, "'The Daily Show' with Cathleen Kaveny," *Commonweal*, March 2, 2012, https://www.commonwealmagazine.org/blog/daily-show-cathleen-kaveny.

2. See Network: Nuns on the Bus, http://www.networklobby.org/bus2015.

3. Joshua J. McElwee, "Bishops Step into the Election Fray with Focus on Abortion, Same-Sex Marriage," *National Catholic Reporter*, October 5, 2012, http://ncronline.org/news/politics/bishops-step-election-fray-focus-abortion-same-sex-marriage.

4. Richard John Neuhaus, *The Naked Public Square: Religion and Democracy in America*, 2nd ed. (Grand Rapids: William B. Eerdmans, 1988).

5. Stephen T. Mockabee, "The Political Behavior of American Catholics: Change and Continuity," in *From Pews to Polling Places: Faith and Politics in the American Religious Mosaic*, ed. J. Matthew Wilson (Washington, DC: Georgetown University Press, 2007), 81–104.

6. Pew Forum, "Trends in Voter Preferences among Religious Groups," November 5, 2012, http://projects.pewforum.org/2012-presidential-election-candidate-religious-groups/#catholics.

7. See, e.g., Charles Camosy, "Is the 'On All of Our Shoulders' Statement Partisan?," October 12, 2012, http://catholicmoraltheology.com/is-the-on-all-of-our-shoulders-statement-partisan/; and Julie Hanlon Rubio, "A Wide Space for Prudence," October 15, 2012, http://catholicmoraltheology.com/a-wide-space-for-prudence.

8. Vincent J. Miller, "Unfair to Ryan? Questions for Robert George," *America*, October 17, 2012, http://americamagazine.org/content/all-things/unfair-ryan-questions-robert-george-0; Daniel Finn, "Dear Prudence: Translating Moral Principles into Public Policy," *Commonweal*, October 10, 2012, https://www.commonwealmagazine.org/dear-prudence.

9. "On All of Our Shoulders: A Catholic Call to Protect the Endangered Common Good," http://www.onourshoulders.org/.

10. Robert P. George, "The Catholic Left's Unfair Attack on Paul Ryan," *First Things*, October 2012, http://www.firstthings.com/web-exclusives/2012/10/the-catholic-lefts-unfair-attack-on-paul-ryan.

11. Ben Craw and Zach Carter, "Paul Ryan: 60 Percent of Americans Are 'Takers,' Not 'Makers,'" *Huffington Post*, October 5, 2012, http://www.huffington post.com/2012/10/05/paul-ryan-60-percent-of-a_n_1943073.html.

12. R. R. Reno, "Paul Ryan and the Angry Catholic Left," *First Things*, April 2012, http://www.firstthings.com/web-exclusives/2012/04/paul-ryan-and-the-angry-catholic-left.

13. *Burwell v. Hobby Lobby*, 2014, http://www2.bloomberglaw.com/public/desktop/document/Burwell_v_Hobby_Lobby_Stores_Inc_No_13354_and_13356_US_June_30_20.

14. Leslie C. Griffin, "Catholic Moral Theology at the Supreme Court," *America*, July 2, 2014, http://www.americamagazine.org/content/all-things/catholic-moral-theology-supreme-court.

15. See the Becket Fund for Religious Liberty, http://www.becketfund.org/amicusbriefsupportinglsp/.

16. Michael Sean Winters, "The *Hobby Lobby* Decision," *National Catholic Reporter*, July 1, 2014, http://ncronline.org/blogs/distinctly-catholic/hobby-lobby-decision.

17. I am characterizing in broad strokes here and leaving out significant overlap which I later explore, but even more nuanced portraits show enduring divisions in people's responses to questions about the size of government. See Pew Research Center, "Beyond Red vs. Blue: The Political Typology," June 26, 2014, http://www.people-press.org/2014/06/26/the-political-typology-beyond-red-vs-blue/. Of course, church history is full of conflicts. My claim here is about polarization on social and political issues in the US Catholic Church.

18. Matthew J. Streb and Brian Frederick, "The Myth of a Distinctive Catholic Vote," in *Catholics and Politics: The Dynamic Tension between Faith and Power*, ed. Kristin E. Heyer, Mark J. Rozell, and Michael A. Genovese (Washington, DC: Georgetown University Press, 2008), 93–112.

19. The USCCB provides a brief summary in "Seven Themes of Catholic Social Teaching," http://www.usccb.org/beliefs-and-teachings/what-we-believe/catholic-social-teaching/seven-themes-of-catholic-social-teaching.cfm. Other lists include equality, participation, the common good, and subsidiarity. I have added subsidiarity to the USCCB's original seven.

20. USCCB, *Forming Consciences for Faithful Citizenship: A Call to Political Responsibility*, no. 13, http://www.usccb.org/issues-and-action/faithful-citizenship/upload/forming-consciences-for-faithful-citizenship.pdf.

21. Ibid., no. 32.

22. Ibid., nos. 31–37.

23. "Partisan Polarization Surges in Bush, Obama Years," Pew Research Center, June 4, 2012, http://www.people-press.org/2012/06/04/partisan-polari zation-surges-in-bush-obama-years/. There are more independents today than at any point in the last seventy-five years. A recent survey by Pew found more independents than ever before. See "Party Identification," Pew Research Center, http://www.pewresearch.org/data-trend/political-attitudes/party-identification/. Postpartisanship should not be overexaggerated. See Harvard University Institute of Politics, "Survey of Young Americans' Attitudes toward Political and Public Service, 23rd Edition," http://www.iop.harvard.edu/sites/default/files_new/spring _poll_13_Exec_Summary.pdf. Those young adults who identify with a party are becoming more partisan, but a growing number are independent or "tuning out" of politics altogether. Most young adults "report having friends from another political party, . . . [and] know that good people exist across the aisle [and] work- ing together does not mean selling out." The report identifies growing disenchant- ment with politics as a challenge. It is also an opportunity.

24. Of course, the terms personal and political are highly contested. I use them here in their plainest sense (i.e., pertaining to individuals and government). Throughout the book, I hope to show that approaches to social change in the local sphere combine aspects of personal and political problem solving. In the growing field of political theology, there are important theoretical discussions about the precise nature of politics, the church as a political body, etc. Here, I am interested in the more practical project of opening a space between the two options that are most often discussed and so often occupy space in conversation and imagination.

25. See Bryan Massingale, *Racial Justice in the Catholic Church* (Marynoll, NY: Orbis, 2010). Massingale shows the inadequacy of efforts to deal with racism through friendship and personal conversion, but, while advocating for political participation, also speaks to the necessity of confronting racism at the social- cultural level.

26. See Matt Malone, SJ, "Pursuing the Truth in Love: The Mission of 'Amer- ica' in a 21st-Century Church," *America*, June 3–10, 2013, http://americamagazine .org/issue/pursuing-truth-love.

PART I

Foundations for Common Ground

CHAPTER 1

Faithful Citizenship

Is There Hope for Politics?

In the summer of 2012, the US Conference of Catholic Bishops (USCCB) announced its opposition to what it saw as the Obama administration's assault on religious liberty. Its anger was directed at recent decisions to hold church social service organizations to new federal regulations, to block church care for immigrants, and, most important, to insist that Christian organizations abide by the Affordable Care Act, which originally required religious employers to include in their insurance plans provision for free contraception.[1] In response, the bishops called on Catholics to join a campaign of prayer, study, fasting, and public action. Meanwhile, women religious were traveling the country with a protest movement of their own, hoping the prospect of seeing "Nuns on the Bus" would bring crowds to hear their criticism of Representative Paul Ryan's budget plan and a defense of the federal government's duty to provide a safety net for the poor.[2]

The USCCB has been criticized for failing to live by the rules of a pluralistic society in which religious groups are free to practice their faith but not to bypass the law. Some argue that though the bishops are claiming to be victims of discrimination, in seeking to impose their moral vision on all their employees (Catholic or not), they risk violating the religious liberty of others. Opponents recall the Supreme Court's ruling in *Employment Division v. Smith* that the government needs only a rational basis to uphold a law, even when it conflicts with a citizen's religious practice.[3] Supporters of the USCCB cite the Restoration of Religious Freedom Act, signed by President Bill Clinton in 1993, along with a host of examples of accommodation of religious practice, to undergird the need to extend special protection to religiously informed actions.[4] They argue that religious freedom must extend beyond parishes to religiously affiliated schools and hospitals and their particular missions and practices.

Like the USCCB, supporters of women religious who advocate on behalf of the poor at a time when public sentiment is running in the opposite direction claim the same right to question the supposed cultural consensus out of loyalty to their religious faith. Both groups hold similar positions on the legitimacy of religious departures from social norms, but they remain divided over which issues call for dissent and how much toleration the government ought to extend to dissenters.[5]

The debate over religious liberty raises perennially controversial questions: How should religious believers approach politics? Should they compromise deeply held values for the sake of civil peace? Must they check religion at the door? Or is there room for religiously informed political speech and action? How much should believers expect of the government? What measure of optimism should they bring to public life? How important ought the government be to a religion's social agenda? Can progress toward the Kingdom of God come about through the state, or is the church the better space for actualizing the justice and peace of which Jesus spoke?

In this chapter I argue that political action flows naturally out of fundamental faith commitments, entangling people of faith in complicated situations requiring a combination of prophetic witness, political realism, and intellectual humility. Optimism about citizenship as a means for securing the common good is justified, but so too is recognition of the limits of what any government can achieve and of what any individual or institution can justifiably seek to impose. The Catholic tradition is perhaps better known for its confidence regarding the rights of the church to argue for political change using its social teaching as justification, and for its optimism about what might be achieved in the political realm, than it is for realism and humility. However, I hope to show that realism and humility are also present in the tradition. Moreover, I argue that the current context should engender even more skepticism about politics. When one considers the suspicion that many people (especially young adults) bring to religiously informed political discussion, the real possibility of failure, and strong theological voices calling Christians to opt out of politics altogether, it is clear that though optimism about what faithful citizens can do remains important, political advocacy cannot be the sum total of Christian social strategy. Although contemporary Catholics can and do enthusiastically affirm their responsibility for the common good, I argue that all Catholics—those on the left, the right, and in the middle—ought to continue to pursue social change through political means while giving greater priority to local action.

MOVING FROM FAITH TO POLITICS

The political implications of the Christian faith are inescapable. In *A Public Faith*, Miroslav Volf claims that Christians have a duty to offer society a prophetic vision of human flourishing that comes from the heart of their tradition. At its core, Christianity is a prophetic faith that seeks to transform the world rather than escape it.[6] Like the adherents of other prophetic faiths, Christians cannot fail to share the wisdom of their tradition with the world. Thus, "if we believe that God is love and that we are created for love, . . . we will care for our neighbor's well-being. . . . Compassion and help for those whose lives do not go well—for the vulnerable, the weak—will then be an essential component of leading *our* lives well."[7] In *Law's Virtues* Cathleen Kaveny likewise affirms, from a Catholic perspective, the inescapable social implications of the Christian faith.[8] She roots political commitment in the virtue of solidarity, which requires Christians to "meet the basic needs of each person," "recognize the nature of each person as essentially social," and "provide vehicles through which all persons can contribute to the community."[9] Because people are understood to be fundamentally social or connected to others, it is a duty to work for the good of all through communities and institutions.

This sense that my flourishing is not simply about my right to adopt the life of my choosing but is instead also tied up with the flourishing of others is central to Catholic Social Teaching. According to Pope Benedict XVI in *Caritas in Veritate*, love of neighbor entails not simply feeling for others but also *acting* for the common good. "To love someone," the pope argues, is not simply to have goodwill toward another but also "to desire that person's good and to take effective steps to secure it."[10] In families, parental love for children involves the provision of education, introduction to a religious community, and the establishment of practices in the home that contribute to good moral formation.[11] Spouses love each other not only by showing affection but also by supporting each other's work, parenting, and personal growth. Similarly, the pope claims that loving neighbors who live outside one's home entails involving oneself in "the life of society, juridically, civilly, politically, and culturally, making it the polis or city."[12] No one who claims to love others, then, can avoid responsibility for creating and sustaining a society wherein people can pursue the good. Christians who are called to love of neighbor are also called to social concern. They cannot eschew politics, because the social goods necessary for flourishing must be available to all, especially the most vulnerable.

What do Christians have to offer to political dialogue? For Volf, Christianity offers first and most important a vision of human flourishing centered not in needs satisfaction but in love of God and others.[13] I would put it similarly; the strength and heart of Catholic Social Teaching is its anthropology, which characterizes human beings as profoundly and inescapably social, fulfilled in their connections to others and in the practice of self-gift, in both the personal and social realms.[14] This is where Christians bring something distinctive to public discussion, an alternative to the idea of the isolated individual and to a version of human flourishing focused on freedom, happiness, and success.

The Catholic tradition in particular also brings to the table a long history of moral reasoning about the role of government in society. The virtue of solidarity suggests the necessity of paying attention to the ways in which laws, social structures, and cultural constructs shape people's lives, especially those of the most vulnerable.[15] The government, according to Catholic Social Teaching, has a responsibility to enable the flourishing of all citizens, though it does not shoulder this responsibility alone. As Pope John Paul II says in *Centesimus Annus*, "the State and all of society have the duty of defending those collective goods which ... constitute the essential framework for the legitimate pursuit of personal goals on the part of each individual."[16] Many forms of government are possible, as long as the dignity of the person, fundamental human rights, and a preference for solving problems at the community level are recognized.[17] The key is the insistence that because we are all in this together, laws, institutions, and norms ought to be directed to the good of all.

The Catholic social tradition includes a wide range of positions on social issues that begin with the foundation of this general vision, including particular teachings on war and peace and on economic justice.[18] The tradition distinguishes between the authority of its more particular conclusions and general principles.[19] However, both principles (e.g., human dignity, solidarity, subsidiarity, the universal destination of material goods) and the historical record of attempts to apply principles to concrete situations (e.g., How do the right to health care, the right to life, and the principle of solidarity shape the evaluation of health care plans? Can the use of drones fit within the just war tradition?) are valuable gifts to be brought to the public sphere.

Finally, the Catholic tradition recognizes both the importance of the law and its limits. The tradition draws its vision of the law from Saint Thomas Aquinas, who sees a relationship between human laws and the natural law. For him, Kaveny rightly points out, the law does more than act as a "police officer" who stops citizens from harming each other. The law also has an important role in "teaching virtue."[20] For instance, Kaveny argues, the Americans with Disabilities Act establishes rules to accommodate people with disabilities; but in its language and its framing of the issues, it also teaches respect for and the equality of persons with disabilities.[21]

However, the law is not always capable of teaching virtue. Aquinas recognizes that lawmakers can only judge external actions, the law cannot forbid all evil, and the law must be framed for the majority, which means that we need to take cultural customs and consensus into account.[22] For Aquinas, formulating good laws involves a delicate balancing act between what is right and what is possible, so he accepts that there will be variation and development.[23] Kaveny argues that taking Aquinas seriously means recognizing that when the virtue of citizens is not sufficient to ensure the enforcement of a law, citizens "must proceed incrementally in their efforts to inculcate virtue; otherwise, their efforts will backfire. Even in matters of life and death, human lawmakers can only impose burdens and restrictions that the population can bear, both practically and morally."[24] The law is one important means of working for the common good, but it is not the only one, and reasonable people will differ at the level of strategy. This nuanced view of the law, along with a tradition of moral reasoning about the common good and a vision of human flourishing, are gifts Christians offer to the public dialogue.

Some worry that explicitly Christian arguments do not belong in the public debate. However, many scholars today contend that religious people should be welcome at the table of public discourse along with everyone else and should be accepted on equal terms.[25] Christians ought to be allowed to contribute to these complex discussions about the law, which are also always discussions about the common life of a society.[26] Excluding their moral judgments simply because they are rooted in religious beliefs would be tantamount to allowing their understandings of reality to be counted as false while allowing secular views to be considered true.[27] Like the leaders of many religiously inspired movements throughout US history, Christians have the right to argue that their moral views should be adopted by the larger society, though like everyone else, they must present their tradition in convincing ways to a diverse populace and know that their view will not always win the day.[28]

An important part of making good, religiously informed arguments in public is recognizing that the law and morality are connected, though they are not identical. In public debate, some imply that there are straight lines between moral imperatives and the law, but others maintain that the law has virtually no connection to morals. However, Kaveny convincingly argues that both these extreme positions are flawed. In a pluralistic society we cannot make illegal everything we believe to be immoral, and even if we could, we could not assume "that by passing a law we can bring about a desired state of affairs instantaneously, without any effort, cost, or abuses."[29] However, the law by its nature does more than merely allow or stop harmful actions. First, because citizens can disagree about what constitutes harm and about how best to diminish it, decisions about what to allow or not allow involve judgments. Second, laws "routinely encourage some life choices while discouraging others," as we can see, for instance, in regulations about marriage and home mortgage tax deductions. Third, even in criminal law, we make judgments about the relative harm of different kinds of killing.[30] Making good laws involves making moral judgments about how we can best live together.

Christians need not communicate their moral judgments in only secular terms. Although a policy of using neutral language may seem attractive, it may be more honest and fruitful to allow everyone to present the reasons that compel their advocacy.[31] Some faith-based claims may be easily translatable, while others are less so yet ought to be welcome just the same. The Catholic tradition generally uses a combination of religious and philosophical language in its public discourse and asserts the compatibility of faith and reason. It recognizes that some Catholic reasoning will be difficult for others to understand as reasonable, and yet it asserts Catholics' right to make their case. For instance, in debates about end-of-life care, Catholics have argued against the growing cultural emphasis on the autonomy of the patient and in favor of the value of persons who are dying and of the dying process itself.[32] Kaveny contends that arguments such as these are not inherently incomprehensible to nonreligious people, especially if they are linked to the virtue of solidarity with the vulnerable, but they are distinctive. Yet religious people are not alone in not being able to present their arguments in terms that are perfectly accessible to everyone else or are empirically justifiable. Often, untranslatable reasons shape our views most profoundly. Allowing these views need not stop public conversation. In fact, a secular scholar of religion, Jeffrey Stout, claims that disallowing nonrational claims is unhelpful, because "reasons held in common do not get us far enough toward answers to enough of our political questions."[33]

"Real respect for others means taking seriously the distinctive point of view *each* other occupies," says Stout, who believes that conversation and even agreement are possible when differences are fully recognized. When I can acknowledge what truly moves me, I bring my full position to the surface, yet I am also free to try to find reasons that will move the other in his or her distinctiveness.[34] Stout argues that rather than being a conversation stopper, religion can be a source of better dialogue.[35] Even when arguments are made in religious terms, they can be persuasive to those who do not share the same faith.[36] Speaking from where we really are is both a right to be claimed and a basis for more fruitful public dialogue. Contrary to the arguments of some who worry about religious speech, healthy pluralism does not require the privatization of religion.[37]

In fact, it is unthinkable for many religious people to ignore the religious motivations and justifications for their positions. Though the philosopher John Rawls famously asked citizens to imagine themselves behind the "veil of ignorance" (i.e., pretending they did know their gender, class, race, or religion), many others since have convincingly argued that no one can escape particularity; we all come from somewhere and cannot pretend otherwise.[38] It is simply impossible to ask people of faith to leave this particularity behind. To forget their convictions would be like cutting off their arms, for faith is essential to their identity and their reasoning.[39]

Moreover, religious voices in public debates are vitally important to democracy. The legal scholar Stephen Carter argues that precisely because being religious means answering to a higher truth, religious people are often more able to offer prophetic critiques than those wedded to the secular order.[40] In US history, religious groups have been at the forefront of the abolitionist, civil rights, antiwar, pro-life, and anti-death-penalty movements. Of course, as critics such as Christopher Hitchens have reminded us, their public influence has not been uniformly positive.[41] Still, by daring to question the status quo and by declaring the laws of the nation-state to be unjust when they contradict the law of God or nature, religious people have often led the way to important social change. This willingness to question is crucial to a healthy nation, as long as it is balanced by a strong recognition that faith does not require opposition to all morally deficient laws.[42]

In sum, in the Catholic tradition concern about politics is rooted in compassion for others, especially the most vulnerable. Compassion lies at the heart of the tradition, and discipleship within this tradition requires action. Although political activity is not the only form of action one can take on behalf of others, because laws shape social structures, they cannot be ignored. Catholics bring to the public sphere a vision of human flourishing rooted in a social understanding of the person, a tradition of moral reasoning about the common good, and a nuanced view of the law that recognizes both its power and its limits. Practicing faithful citizenship involves healthy respect for the pluralistic nature of modern democracies, but it does not require Catholics (or any other religious or nonreligious people) to hide the true motivations or justifications for their political positions.

If this justification for mixing religion and politics sounds like a recipe for endless argument, it need not point in that direction. Laws are always connected to some vision of the common good. Whenever people advocate for one law over another, they are aiming to convince others that their vision of the common good is worth considering. If we are honest about this, "we might find that we share more broad-based (although by no means unanimous) agreement about core elements of some virtues and vices than combatants in the contemporary 'culture wars' admit."[43] Those who take up the challenge of faithful citizenship have good reason to hope that their contributions will sometimes find a sympathetic hearing among those with different religious or nonreligious convictions. They can justifiably hope that political advocacy will sometimes lead to better laws and a better common life. However, as I argue in the next section, faith-based political action is not without its problems.

THE CONTEMPORARY CONTEXT: THREE REASONS FOR SKEPTICISM

Suspicion of Religious Involvement in Politics

Although there are good reasons for people of faith to enter political dialogue and work for social change through political channels, many people, particularly younger generations of Americans, are suspicious of religion in public. In their recent book *American Grace: How Religion Divides and Unites Us,* Robert Putnam and David Campbell discuss the growth of the "nones," that is, those who are unaffiliated with any official religion.[44] According to their studies, in the United States 16 percent of adults and 25 percent of young adults are in this category.[45] More recent surveys show the upward trend continuing, with nearly 23 percent of all adults and 36 percent of young adults now identifying as unaffiliated.[46] Although the young have always been less affiliated than older generations, this generation is more disaffiliated than any previous generation has ever been.[47] The nones include not only atheists but also agnostics, as well as people who consider themselves spiritual, believe in God, and pray.[48] What turns them away from religion? In part, they are repelled by religious intervention in politics. In particular, they associate religious bodies with attempts to impose conservative views on homosexuality especially and, to a lesser extent, other social issues.[49] Moreover, "this generation seems unwilling or unable to distinguish the stance of the most visible, most political, and most conservative religious leaders from organized religion in general."[50]

Advocates of faith-based political action such as Volf and Kaveny specifically warn against uncompromising religious engagement in public and rule out culture war–style political campaigns, but their call for any public engagement at all will be controversial among a good many young adults, who are increasingly alienated from religion and suspicious about religion in public. What does appropriate intervention look like to this new generation? I have taught a course called "Faith and Politics" for nearly a decade. By the end of the course, I hope that more of my students will consider a moderate approach that values religious contributions to public discourse while not ignoring the complexities of moving from faith to politics in a pluralistic society or the necessity of compromise. In the second half of the course, we read theo-political arguments on a diverse set of issues: abortion, capital punishment, same-sex marriage, and war. In their papers, students must write about two issues—one that is traditionally the concern of liberals, and the other that is traditionally the concern of conservatives—and must articulate a single, consistent principle that applies to both. Most students find this exercise very frustrating. One kind of argument seems entirely plausible, while the other is infuriating. And almost always, they worry about imposing faith-based values on those who do not share their convictions.

Many would be happy to leave faith out of politics altogether and do not see why so many authors describe this as impossible. Beginning one's analysis of every social issue from a faith stance is much more difficult for them to imagine, and they are not at all sure that attempting to do so would be worthwhile. Although Volf's suggestion that the most important thing religious people have to offer is a vision of human flourishing and Kaveny's claim that Catholics should bring human dignity and solidarity to the fore are far less provocative than the kinds of religious-political advocacy with which students are much more familiar, they have difficulty believing that many religious people actually think this way. Thus, reasoning from any faith stance at all to politics remains uncomfortable, especially when someone they disagree with is doing it.

In short, the younger generations seem even less disposed to faith-based political conversation and advocacy than previous generations. They have seen bad faith-based advocacy both at home and abroad; this is what has driven many of them away from both religion and politics. It may not be possible to find a model of public faith that would be compelling rather than alienating for them. In light of the younger generations' strong distaste for uniting faith and politics, it may make sense for Christians to consider alternative strategies for social change.

Can We Take Pluralism Seriously?

Of course, moderate advocates of faith-based political action argue that Christians can be politically engaged while respecting the pluralistic nature of American society. Volf contends that Christian faith malfunctions both when it is idle and ignores the world and when it coerces and attempts to rule the world; good public engagement must avoid both.[51] Though Christians have no doubt been involved in coercive attempts to impose their views, Volf insists that the problem has been not too much faith but too little: "'Thin' but zealous practice of the Christian faith is likely to foster violence; 'thick' and committed practice will generate and sustain a culture of peace."[52] Because peace is essential to Christianity, faithful Christians will approach politics, as everything else, nonviolently. With this move, Volf attempts to draw Christians into a kind of faithful politics that can answer the concerns of those who are disturbed by the religious political advocacy they see.

In the Catholic tradition, the work of John Courtney Murray in *We Hold These Truths* (1960) plays a similar moderating role, in calling Catholics to political involvement, limiting the scope of political hopes, and calming the fears of skeptics.[53] At a time when the church still taught that the unity of church and state would be ideal, Murray argued for toleration. The state, he held, was "under God," that is, it was devoted to far less lofty goals than the church—it did not aim for salvation but for peace; it sought not love but justice; its goals were worthy but not ultimate.[54] Catholics should have "modest expectations" for politics, avoiding utopianism, while knowing that, through political action, "we could limit the warfare and we could enlarge the dialogue. We could lay down our arms, . . . and we could take up argument."[55] Catholics were able to participate in the argument along with everyone else, as long as they did not seek to make illegal all that they held to be immoral.[56] They could work for a minimally just and peaceful society but would solve their most important problems by other means.

Although Murray's sensible limitation of the goals of the state is crucial, he is sometimes criticized for leaving insufficient room for Christians to challenge the law. Though he harbors no illusions about the United States ("It is not a church. . . . It is simply a civil community, whose unity is purely political"), he emphasizes the compatibility of Christianity and the American experiment ("The theory of a free people under a limited government . . . is recognizably part of the Christian political tradition").[57] However, his critics contend that in fact the state is profoundly unjust and the goals of the United States are not simply less than what Christians want but are fundamentally opposed to any substantive Christian vision of the common good.[58] Moreover, some argue, the state does require far-reaching allegiance, including the right to kill in our names and to use our tax dollars to do a great many things that many Christians oppose in conscience.[59] Though correct in his concern to minimize expectations for what nations might accomplish, Murray perhaps understated the potential for conflict between the church and even a limited version of the state. Since Murray, other Catholic theologians and public intellectuals have tried to get the balance right, holding in good tension prophecy and humility, faith and citizenship.[60]

The problem, of course, is that Christians in the political sphere do not always embody humility and noncoerciveness in their political conversations or actions. Whether on the left or the right, many tend to sound a lot more strident. Zealous advocacy makes some sense because fundamental convictions about love of God and neighbor move Christians to engage with questions of how the public sphere can contribute to human flourishing.[61] Just anger can be a virtuous response to violations of human dignity. In the face of innocent suffering, compromise seems an insult, and civility seems a violation of duty. There is an undeniable responsibility to witness to the faith, even when it is at odds with the cultural consensus. This is what the heroes of the Christian faith—Oscar Romero, Martin Luther King, Dorothy Stang—do: They speak the truth, even when it is unpopular, ineffective, and costly.

And yet, at their best, they ought not coerce. Having been convinced of the power of love, even love of enemies, and having also been convinced of their own limitations, they ought to speak a language of prophecy laced with humility. A Christian anthropology suggests that to be human is not only to be social or connected to others but also to be limited, dependent on others, and even vulnerable. Christians believe that in Jesus, God embraces human vulnerability (Phil 2:7), giving them an example of what it means to love.[62] This understanding of human beings should inspire in Christians humility and a commitment not to coerce others to believe and act as they feel called to do.

This profound theological truth claim can inform Christianity's complex relationship with culture. H. Richard Niebuhr famously categorized Christian activity in public life as falling into five camps: Christ against culture, the Christ of culture, Christ above culture, Christ and culture in paradox, and Christ transforming culture.[63] However, none of these categories fully captures the complexity of being a Christian in a pluralistic society, for, as Volf notes, "Christian identity in a culture is always a complex and flexible network of small and large refusals, divergences, subversions, and more or less radical and encompassing alternative proposals and enactments, surrounded by the acceptance of many cultural givens."[64] Religious people are formed by their traditions but remain in dialogue with culture, sometimes playing the role of prophet, but at other times profiting from movements more advanced than their own.[65] Christians in particular acknowledge both with the wisdom of their tradition and the reality of human sinfulness, from which the church does not have immunity. This means that if a debate is lost or a campaign fails, it may be time to walk away and figure out other ways to work for the kind of social change that is called for by the Christian faith.

But if theologians can affirm the importance of humility, it is rare to see this sort of commitment to nonviolence, this broad an acceptance of compromise, in Christians who engage in political action. Thus, we need to ask, "If their theology *should* point Christians toward noncoercion in the public square, why are so many Christians unable to embrace it? Is there something about politics itself that brings out a certain kind of violence?"

Should We Opt Out?

Many scholars argue that the challenges of noncoercive, political action are so serious that Christians should leave the public realm to others and should instead concentrate on living out their faith in their own families, communities, and churches. Stanley Hauerwas, in decades of writing on this theme, reminds theologians that Christian ethics is for Christians. The first responsibility of theology is to help fellow Christians to "be the church," that is, to embody in their way of life the radical love of Jesus Christ.[66] It is in being the church, Hauerwas insists, that Christians can help the world understand what it is and can be. Christians "do politics" through witness, which is not withdrawal but engagement in a different key.[67] This sort of engagement is so wedded to noncoerciveness and non-cooperation with evil that it does not judge means by effectiveness but by faithfulness.[68] It requires acceptance of the possibility, if not the inevitability, of failure and the placement of all trust in God.

The modern nation-state, some Christians who sympathize with Hauerwas argue, is simply not capable of taking us where we need to go. According to William Cavanaugh, the prevailing idea that the state is "the potential solution to any given social ill" is deeply problematic.[69] Unlike Kaveny, who is somewhat more optimistic, he insists that "the nation state is simply not in the common good business."[70] Rather, it is a "bureaucratic order," "a false order," "a kind of parody of the church."[71] At its best, it may "provide goods and services that contribute to a certain limited order."[72] The task of the church is not to turn to the nation-state for help with the common good but "to demystify the nation-state and to treat it like the telephone company."[73] The real hopes of Christians should instead be vested in the church, which, though always imperfect, nonetheless offers a more promising space where they can construct community and organize advocacy. Here, Christians acknowledge that God rules, and thus it is not their responsibility to make everything come out right.[74] In the end, Cavanaugh remains deeply pessimistic about the potential of nation-states to make significant progress toward the common good. He criticizes Hauerwas for failing to articulate a positive vision of how the church can do more than witness against the state. However, though Cavanaugh does say that Christians should be "participating in other networks of connectivity that leave the imagination of the dominant society behind," and he engages in promising conversations with advocates of radical democracy, he is not much more specific in his articulation of a constructive alternative.[75]

It is, of course, possible to affirm the church's role as witness or as a "contrast society" and still believe that being faithful also means pursuing ways of "healing the world" that require public engagement.[76] While acknowledging the importance of ongoing efforts in politics, it seems prudent to consider the worries of theologians who see the church getting lost in politics, along with the fears of thinkers who see the limits of government action. If these theologians have not been specific enough in describing alternative strategies, sympathizers should take up that work. Perhaps it is time for at least some Christians to abstain from political advocacy for a season so that they may pursue other ways of working for the common good.

PUBLIC FAITH IN "THE SPACE BETWEEN": REALISM AND HUMILITY

Emphasizing "the space between" does not mean leaving politics behind, but it does mean approaching it differently. The prophetic edge of religion does not easily bend toward compromise, yet most moderate advocates of faith-based public action insist on the acceptance of limits.[77] The key is to accept very possible, if not inevitable, failure. Certainly, Christians of various political views have experienced failure in their attempts to support policies on stem cell research, immigration, war, and capital punishment. Because Christians know that they cannot always win the battles of public life, and because they know that doing so would not guarantee a just society, they should be free to put forth their best efforts, knowing they might well lose. "For comprehensive change," Volf writes, "a global revolution would be necessary. As a consequence, Christian communities must learn how to work vigorously for the limited change that is possible, to mourn over persistent and seemingly ineradicable evils, and to celebrate the good wherever it happens and whoever its agents are."[78] The only way to engage in politics noncoercively is to learn to advocate peacefully and accept failure graciously.

The nuanced understanding of the place of religion in public life advocated by Kaveny and Volf is optimistic in what it claims about the right and duty of religious people to bring forward a vision of the good, and yet realistic and challenging in what it counsels them to leave behind. Although Cavanaugh seems incredulous that anyone could think that the United States could achieve even partial peace and justice, Kaveny offers many examples of laws that teach virtue, including the Americans with Disabilities Act, the Affordable Care Act, and the Family and Medical Leave Act.[79] The law, she claims, can teach solidarity, and sometimes does so. Catholics can bring their own strong tradition of solidarity to the table and try through persuasion to move the law toward greater solidarity.[80]

Like Kaveny and Volf, I am reluctant to follow Hauerwas and Cavanaugh all the way down the path of nonparticipation in politics. I am deeply appreciative of efforts to raise up the duty of Christians to contribute to the healing of the world while avoiding accommodation, idleness, or coerciveness.[81] With Volf, I affirm that "Christian difference should always remain *internal* to a given cultural world."[82] There is no real escape from culture. Within contemporary culture, Christians will need to be content with being "just one of many players," but they can choose to accept some elements of culture while transforming or rejecting others.[83] I agree that "to become a Christian means to divert without leaving."[84] Christians can cultivate a multifaceted engagement that is personal, social, and political.[85] They can work within and outside the culture for social and political change.

How are they to do this? Volf offers a praiseworthy method. Christians ought to share wisdom by "pointing to a way of life in which they themselves participate," by acting as "channels through which God imparts wisdom," which is a way of practicing "neighborly love."[86] As givers of wisdom, Christians are not to be tyrants or merchants but "witnesses" who are always ready to receive and forgive.[87] Public engagement for Christians involves speaking in their own idiom and accepting "pluralism as a political project."[88] Although not specifically political, this sounds like a prescription for good, humble political dialogue. And this is certainly what is typically meant by "public faith."

Others share Volf's sense that Christians should stay involved in politics while changing their tone and scaling back their hopes. The political columnist E. J. Dionne claims that religious people ought to be more ready than most to embrace compromise because they believe in human sinfulness and call humility a virtue.[89] Knowing our finitude, we cannot but admit our potential for failure and need for correction. David Hollenbach writes about the virtue of "intellectual solidarity,"[90] which should flow easily from Christian notions of virtue and from convictions about the nature of truth going back to Thomas Aquinas: The eternal law is known to God alone, and humans can only grasp the natural law; and even then we need proper formation, and we admit that the more specific we become, the more likely it is that we will need to allow for variation, the possibility of error, and the potential for future development.[91]

Kaveny, too, advocates working for gradual legal reform, emphasizing that people of faith must "proceed incrementally in their efforts to inculcate virtue," especially when a consensus is lacking.[92] Most of her energy goes to showing how laws cultivate virtue, though she is keen to show that this happens not only by criminal or civil sanctions but also through other means, such as incentives, tax laws, and custody courts.[93] The law is not a blunt instrument; it offers many tools for addressing social problems. Mainly, she wants people on both the left and the right to acknowledge the range of political options available to them and to understand what the law can and cannot accomplish.

However, if Christians ought not give up on politics or place all their hope in it, there must be other sorts of work to do. There is good reason to worry that faith-based activism may eat away at what makes churches distinctive. Moreover, Volf is right about the diffuse nature of power in postmodern societies (in which "nobody is in control" and social change is effected through many, diverse channels).[94] It is no longer clear that politics is always the best strategy. Of particular importance, Kaveny allows that when a consensus on legal change is lacking, it can be built through alternative strategies.[95]

Similarly, Pope Benedict XVI's radical message in *Caritas in Veritate* is that for Christians, there is one ethic for family, culture, and society, and it is an ethic of solidarity, participation, and, most important, gratuity—"all of which stand in contrast with *giving in order to acquire* (the logic of exchange) and *giving through duty* (the logic of public obligation, imposed by State law)" (emphasis in the original).[96] "Charity," Benedict says, "is at the heart of the Church's social doctrine," the key principle for both micro and macro relationships.[97] He calls for the adoption of new lifestyles, where the quest for "truth, beauty, goodness and communion with others" drives all kinds of life choices.[98] He also names movements, both local and international, that bring people into relationships of gratuity rather than keeping them locked in adversarial ties. Because this encyclical is less invested in politics than practices, it could point to a new way of putting Catholic Social Teaching into action. In Christian circles, most energy has gone to the personal or the political realms, while the space between has been all but ignored. Today, especially given the limits of politics, Christians need to think more seriously about what might be accomplished through local, community practices.

This approach is of a piece with Volf's call for recognition of the pluralism of the postmodern world as well as the love and forgiveness that stand at the heart of the Christian faith. It takes seriously Kaveny's call for humble and realistic participation in politics. It takes note of the reservations of Hauerwas and Cavanaugh without fully succumbing to their pessimism about pluralistic societies. Most notably, it attempts to take up the unfinished business of many of these thinkers by focusing on the alternative strategies that almost everyone seems to advocate but few explore in depth. Christians need not avoid the world or (foolishly) hope to totally change it. But they can find ways to powerfully work for a fuller vision of human flourishing at the level of culture rather than in the realm of politics. Perhaps it is difficult to imagine what this might look like, but enlarging our imaginations may be exactly what we need to do. Realism and humility about politics should lead to the exploration of other spaces for the work of social change.

"BE THE CHURCH"?

Thus far, I have argued that faithful citizenship involves approaching politics with a chastened optimism that is realistic, humble, and hopeful, but I have suggested that Christians ought to begin to explore alternative strategies. In the next chapter I develop the case for beginning at the local level, but first I want to distinguish my argument in another important way from that of Hauerwas and like-minded thinkers. I take very seriously the concerns of those who argue that Christians ought to first of all "be the church" rather than worry about changing the world. However, I cannot divide these two realms as neatly as they are often divided.

In the main, the radical thinkers whom the sociologist James Davidson Hunter calls the "neo-Anabaptists" worry that most Christians give in to the world too much and lack faith in God's work of salvation, which relies on the church rather than the state.[99] C. C. Pecknold, who could be placed in this camp, surveys the history of Christianity and politics and gives his highest praise to Saint Augustine's view of the city of God and the earthly city.[100] He ends the book with a chapter on the contemporary church, which he believes offers the only true community to which Christians can give allegiance.[101] Cavanaugh, too, ultimately concludes that nation-states are so compromised that Christians cannot possibly put faith in them, whereas the church is the appropriate locus of our hopes.[102] For these thinkers, Christians are people defined by the biblical story, and this story is not about democratic government but the Cross. The City of God is deserving of our ultimate allegiance, and the narrative of God's action in the world should be definitive for our own way of acting in the world.

However, it is not clear that we can divide these two cities so starkly. In a recent article Aaron Conley writes that Hauerwas's narrative pits the church against the liberal story of the Enlightenment and calls for obedience to church over culture.[103] But Conley argues that instead, Christians need to "loosen the grip of certainty" and listen not just to the church but also to "the other," especially those whose lives are not often narrated because they are oppressed.[104] Contemporary social ethics—even social ethics that focuses on local action—should have something to say about what role people of other faiths and none can play in healing the world. We need room to see that the culture is sometimes ahead of the church, pulling it along to more equality and compassion. The need for humility is clear. In Conley's terms, Christians like Hauerwas who call the church to "be the church" and not save the world need to be disrupted by marginalized people who are "living outside his community of character."[105]

It is important not to neglect the good that politics can do so as not to overstate the holiness of the church or the limits of the state. Cavanaugh takes pains to acknowledge the flaws of the church, and he identifies the penitential side of the church, or its practice of confessing sins, as essential to its strength.[106] Yet he sees mostly the worst in the state because of his focus on issues such as violence and homeland security. Nations do more than he gives them credit for, if less than some would claim.[107] In the face of pessimism about nation-states, it is good to remember achievements such as Social Security, the national parks, the protection of human rights, and fair elections. Cavanaugh's acknowledgment of the possibility of churches collaborating with other communities has potential, but further acknowledgment that all institutions—including the church—are but partial solutions is needed to enable people to face the future together.[108]

In the end, the Catholic tradition is not quite as pessimistic as the neo-Anabaptists. It remains hopeful about what people of many faiths and none might be able to do together in politics. Surely, we are capable of doing more than deliver mail and provide telephone service. We do not have to give up completely on the American experiment. As Murray saw, there is something right and good, if not perfect, in the American vision of limited government. As Stout shows, the democratic tradition offers strengths that have often been lacking in the church. Politics can bring about desirable social change. At times, the church has been a part of this, and at times it has dragged behind on the wrong side of history. Ongoing political dialogue and action are important not just for the world but also for the church.

However, acting in local communities is also a key part of both the Christian and American stories. As Hauerwas recently wrote, "We do not bear reality alone; rather we share the load by being called to participate in the body of Christ"; and he acknowledges that we do this work through "incorrigible institutions, . . . open meetings, forgiveness, economic sharing, and sacramental processes."[109] I would only add that this hard work sometimes happens in the churches he no doubt has in mind, but it also happens in homes, schools, neighborhoods, and community organizations, and is done by people of all different faith commitments and none. Part II of this book is devoted to exploring the possibilities of these institutions. But first, in the rest of part I, it is necessary to identify a common foundation for a broad commitment to social change, in chapter 2, and to firmly establish the possibilities for local action, in chapter 3.

NOTES

1. See USCCB Ad Hoc Committee for Religious Liberty, "Our First, Most Cherished Liberty," http://www.usccb.org/issues-and-action/religious-liberty/our-first-most-cherished-liberty.cfm; and Charles J. Chaput, OFM, "Repair My House: Renewing the Roots of Religious Liberty," http://www.usccb.org/issues-and-action/religious-liberty/fortnight-for-freedom/fortnight-for-freedom-speeches-and-statements.cfm.

2. See Network: Nuns on the Bus, http://www.networklobby.org/bus2015. Sister Simone Campbell of Network and Representative Paul Ryan testified on different sides at a US House of Representatives Budget Committee meeting; see "Catholics Differ at 'War on Poverty' Hearing," Religion News Service, July 31, 2013, http://www.religionnews.com/2013/07/31/catholics-differ-at-war-on-poverty-hearing/.

3. Cathleen Kaveny, "*Employment Division v. Smith*: The Eye of the Storm," April 13, 2012, https://www.commonwealmagazine.org/blog/?p=18465.

4. Ed Whelan, "The HHS Mandate vs. the Religious Freedom Restoration Act—Introduction," *National Review*, January 26, 2012, http://www.nationalreview.com/bench-memos/289341/hhs-contraception-mandate-vs-religious-freedom-restoration-act-introduction-ed.

5. For a breakdown of Catholic opinion, see Pew Forum, "Catholics Share Bishops' Concern about Religious Liberty but Catholic Voters Back Obama on Social Issues," http://www.pewforum.org/2012/08/01/2012-catholic-voters-religious-liberty-issue/.

6. Miroslav Volf, *A Public Faith: How Followers of Christ Should Serve the Common Good* (Grand Rapids: Brazos, 2011), 6–9.

7. Ibid., 71.

8. Cathleen Kaveny, *Law's Virtues: Fostering Autonomy and Solidarity in American Society* (Washington, DC: Georgetown University Press, 2012).

9. Ibid., 28.

10. Pope Benedict XVI, *Caritas in Veritate*, 2009, no. 7, http://w2.vatican.va/content/benedict-xvi/en/encyclicals/documents/hf_ben-xvi_enc_20090629_caritas-in-veritate.html.

11. Pope John Paul II, *Familiaris Consortio*, 1981, nos. 36–41, http://w2.vatican.va/content/john-paul-ii/en/apost_exhortations/documents/hf_jp-ii_exh_19811122_familiaris-consortio.html.

12. Pope Benedict XVI, *Caritas in Veritate*, no. 7.

13. Volf, *Public Faith*, 56–60.

14. See, esp., Pope Benedict XVI, *Caritas in Veritate*, nos. 34, 53.

15. Kaveny, *Law's Virtues*, 54.

16. Pope John Paul II, *Centesimus Annus*, 1991, no. 40, http://w2.vatican.va/content/john-paul-ii/en/encyclicals/documents/hf_jp-ii_enc_01051991_centesimus-annus.html.

17. Ibid., no. 48.

18. See, e.g., US Conference of Catholic Bishops, *Economic Justice for All* (Washington, DC: US Conference of Catholic Bishops, 1986), http://www.usccb .org/upload/economic_justice_for_all.pdf; and US Conference of Catholic Bishops, *The Challenge of Peace* (Washington, DC: US Conference of Catholic Bishops, 1983), http://www.usccb.org/upload/challenge-peace-gods-promise-our-response -1983.pdf.

19. See, e.g., US Conference of Catholic Bishops, *Economic Justice*, 134–35.

20. Kaveny, *Law's Virtues*, 48–49.

21. Ibid., 34–37.

22. Ibid., 59.

23. Ibid., 61.

24. Ibid., 65.

25. See, e.g., Volf, *Public Faith*, 125.

26. Ibid., 37–38.

27. Stephen L. Carter, *The Culture of Disbelief: How American Law and Politics Trivialize Religious Devotion* (New York: Random House, 1993), 219–20.

28. Ibid., 229.

29. Kaveny, *Law's Virtues*, 46.

30. Ibid., 47–48.

31. Kent Greenawalt argues that faith is a legitimate motivation, as long as arguments are expressed in universal terms; see Kent Greenawalt, *Religious Convictions and Political Choice* (New York: Oxford University Press, 1991). See also Richard Rorty, "Religion as Conversation-Stopper," in *Philosophy and Social Hope* (London: Penguin Books, 1999): 168–74.

32. Kaveny, *Law's Virtues*, 142–47.

33. Jeffrey Stout, *Democracy and Tradition* (Princeton, NJ: Princeton University Press, 2004), 89.

34. Ibid., 73.

35. Ibid., 77.

36. Ibid., 91. Stout speaks of finding common ground with Jews, Protestants, and Catholics during the civil rights movement. Carter argues similarly about the power of claims about the humanity of the fetus shared by many Americans who disagree on the basis for the claim; Carter, *Culture of Disbelief*, 231.

37. William Cavanaugh criticizes Martin Marty for holding this position; see William Cavanaugh, *Migrations of the Holy: God, State, and the Political Meaning of the Church* (Grand Rapids: William B. Eerdmans, 2011), 47–48.

38. Stout convincingly critiques John Rawls in *Democracy and Tradition*, 65–77, arguing that even Rawls's later qualification of the position that he originally advanced in *A Theory of Justice* (Cambridge, MA: Harvard University Press, 1971) remains inadequate.

39. Carter, *Culture of Disbelief*, 56, referencing Michael Perry, *Morality, Politics, and Law: A Bicentennial Essay* (New York: Oxford University Press, 1991).

40. Carter, *Culture of Disbelief*, 33–43.

41. Christopher Hitchens, *God Is Not Great: How Religion Poisons Everything* (New York: Warner, 2009).

42. Discrimination is necessary as believers navigate the complexities of public life. See William A. Galston's contribution to "The Bishops & Religious Liberty," *Commonweal*, June 15, 2012, 8–10.

43. Kaveny, *Law's Virtues*, 52.

44. Robert P. Putnam and David E. Campbell, *American Grace: How Religion Divides and Unites Us* (New York: Simon & Schuster, 2010), 120–32.

45. Ibid., 122–23.

46. Pew Research Center, "America's Changing Religious Landscape," May 12, 2015, http://www.pewforum.org/2015/05/12/americas-changing-religious-landscape/.

47. Ibid.

48. Putnam and Campbell, *American Grace*, 126.

49. Ibid., 121, 130.

50. Ibid., 131.

51. See Volf, *Public Faith*, 23–36, on idleness, and 37–54, on coercion. The emphasis on avoiding coercion in politics is consistent with Volf's significant work on nonviolence. See Mirslav Volf, *Exclusion and Embrace: A Theological Exploration of Identity, Otherness, and Reconciliation* (Nashville: Abingdon Press, 1996).

52. Volf, *Public Faith*, 40. He argues that the Christian doctrines of the Trinity, creation, redemption, and the new creation all point toward noncoercion (pp. 41–51).

53. John Courtney Murray, *We Hold These Truths: Catholic Reflections on the American Proposition* (Kansas City: Sheed & Ward, 1960).

54. Ibid., 28–30.

55. Ibid., 23.

56. Ibid., 155–74.

57. Ibid., 54, 69. Murray also praises "the American solution to the problem of religious pluralism" because it leaves the church "entirely free to define herself and to exercise to the full her spiritual jurisdiction" (pp. 69, 70).

58. See, e.g., Michael J. Baxter, "'Blowing the Dynamite of the Church': Catholic Radicalism from a Catholic Radicalist Perspective," http://cjd.org/1999/04/01/blowing-the-dynamite-of-the-church-catholic-radicalism-from-a-catholic-radicalist-perspective/.

59. Cavanaugh, *Migrations*, 49–55.

60. See, e.g., David Hollenbach, "Faith in Public," in *The Global Face of Public Faith: Politics, Human Rights, and Christian Ethics*, by David Hollenbach (Washington, DC: Georgetown University Press, 2003), 3–18, at 13.

61. Volf, *Public Faith*, 72–74.

62. John F. Kavanaugh, *Following Christ in a Consumer Society: The Spirituality of Cultural Resistance*, 25th anniversary ed. (Maryknoll, NY: Orbis, 2006), 122. See also Dean Brackley, *The Call to Discernment in Troubled Times: New Perspectives on the Transformative Wisdom of Ignatius of Loyola* (New York: Crossroad, 2004).

63. H. Richard Niebuhr, *Christ and Culture* (New York: Harper & Brothers, 1951).

64. Volf, *Public Faith*, 93.

65. Pope Paul VI, *Gaudium et Spes*, 1965, nos. 40–45, http://www.vatican.va/archive/hist_councils/ii_vatican_council/documents/vat-ii_cons_19651207_gaudium-et-spes_en.html.

66. Stanley Hauerwas, *A Community of Character: Toward a Constructive Christian Social Ethic* (Notre Dame, IN: University of Notre Dame Press, 1981), 92.

67. Stanley Hauerwas, *After Christendom: How the Church Is to Behave If Freedom, Justice, and a Christian Nation Are Bad Ideas* (Nashville: Abingdon Press, 1999), 43.

68. Stanley Hauerwas, *In Good Company: The Church as Polis* (Notre Dame, IN: University of Notre Dame Press, 1995), 155.

69. Cavanaugh, *Migrations*, 44.

70. Ibid., 42.

71. Ibid.

72. Ibid.

73. Ibid.

74. Ibid., 194.

75. Ibid., 189.

76. Volf, *Public Faith*, 132. The term "contrast society" is used by those holding this position to describe what the church ought to be.

77. Ibid., 82–83.

78. Ibid., 83.

79. Kaveny, *Law's Virtues*, 83–84.

80. Ibid., 85.

81. Volf, *Public Faith*, 78, 84–88.

82. Ibid., 89.

83. Ibid., 91–92.

84. Ibid., 93.

85. Ibid., 97.

86. Ibid., 108, 110, 113.

87. Ibid., 106–16.

88. Ibid., 126.

89. E. J. Dionne, *Souled Out: Reclaiming Faith and Politics after the Religious Right* (Princeton, NJ: Princeton University Press, 2008), 183–203.

90. Hollenbach, "Faith in Public," 13.

91. Thomas Aquinas, *Summa Theologica* I-II, qs. 93, 94, 97; *St. Thomas Aquinas, On Law, Morality and Politics*, trans. Richard J. Regan, ed. William P. Baumgarth and Richard J. Regan (Cambridge: Hackett, 1988).

92. Kaveny *Law's Virtues*, 89–90, 65.

93. Ibid., 46–47.

94. Volf, *Public Faith*, 83, 82.

95. Kaveny, *Law's Virtues*, 64–65.

96. Pope Benedict XVI, *Caritas in Veritate*, no. 39.

97. Ibid., no. 2.

98. Ibid., no. 51.

99. James Davidson Hunter, *To Change the World: The Irony, Tragedy, and Possibility of Christianity in the Late Modern World* (Oxford: Oxford University Press, 2010), 150–66.

100. C. C. Pecknold, *Christianity and Politics: A Brief Guide to the History* (Eugene, OR: Cascade, 2010), 148.

101. Ibid., 149–51.

102. Cavanaugh, *Migrations*, 187–90.

103. Aaron D. Conley, "Loosening the Grip of Certainty: A Case-Study Critique of Tertullian, Stanley Hauerwas, and Christian Identity," *Journal of the Society of Christian Ethics* 33, no. 1 (2013): 26–27.

104. Ibid., 39.

105. Ibid., 38.

106. Cavanaugh, *Migrations*, 165.

107. Cavanaugh admits that he has drawn the line between church and state too starkly and sometimes failed to acknowledge the strengths of nation-states. See William Cavanaugh, "On Being Thankful: A Rejoinder to Brad Littlejohn's Rejoinder," July 29, 2013, http://www.politicaltheology.com/blog/on-being-thankful-a-rejoinder-to-brad-littlejohns-rejoinder/.

108. Terrence W. Tilley, "Minuet with Caesar," *Commonweal*, September 26, 2011, https://www.commonwealmagazine.org/minuet-caesar.

109. Stanley Hauerwas, "Bearing Reality," *Journal of the Society of Christian Ethics* 33, no. 1 (2013): 16, 15.

CHAPTER 2

Cooperation with Evil

Personal Responsibility for Social Problems

Cooperation with evil, a classic concept in Catholic moral theology, has recently been invoked by some US bishops to discourage Catholics from voting for pro-choice politicians and supporting the Affordable Care Act.[1] Some theologians have criticized these bishops for failing to acknowledge the need for toleration of differences in a pluralistic society. However, at least implicitly, cooperation with evil is not only invoked by conservatives and criticized by liberals.[2] Liberal Christians sometimes seek to disentangle themselves from cooperation with what they call sinful social structures by refusing to pay that portion of their taxes that goes to war, to buy clothing from companies that utilize sweatshops, to eat conventionally produced foods, or to shop at "big box stores" that fail to pay their workers a living wage.[3] Some conservatives worry about Catholic charities working with nonprofits that advocate contraception, Catholic hospitals forming partnerships with health care systems that provide sterilization, or Catholic universities hosting speakers who publicly disagree with official Catholic teachings. Others counter that once the door is opened to thinking about the many ways we facilitate wrongdoing, one can hardly move without cooperating with evil.

Nonetheless, the idea that we are complicit when we lend support to those who do things we deplore has a certain resonance, no matter where one is on the liberal–conservative spectrum. As Thomas Kopfensteiner

rightly points out, when a voter supports a candidate who chooses to tolerate evil for the sake of public peace, the voter is several steps removed
from the actual evil act.[4] Yet voters sometimes feel so contaminated by
their potential association with a politician's opinion on a single issue
that they vote for an opposing candidate, or cannot bring themselves to
vote at all. Public campaigns effectively invoke the idea of cooperation to
emphasize individual responsibility for the maintenance of evil systems.
When someone points out that our jeans or T-shirts were most likely
made in sweatshop factories, it is difficult not to feel that we are benefiting from exploitation even if we did not will it. Vincent Miller argues that
it makes little sense to hold people in the United States responsible for the
death of sweatshop workers in East Asia. We do not desire that workers
slave away in unjust conditions so that we can buy cheap goods, and we
often do not know how to avoid giving our money to corporations that
engage in these practices.[5] Though Miller rightly insists that a lack of
full knowledge, an absence of bad intentions, distance, and the reality of
limited options make a difference in calculations of moral blame, he also
admits to feeling implicated because he knows what goes on in clothing
factories but does not know how to avoid benefiting from it. Supporters of the Supreme Court's decision in *Burwell v. Hobby Lobby* (2014)
similarly believe that employers should not be forced to in any way aid
their employees' decisions to purchase contraceptive methods that they
oppose.[6] Many people agree that, even if it is complicated to assess culpability, it seems inadequate to deny all responsibility for social sin aided
by votes and money.[7]

　　In this chapter I argue for building on this shared sense of responsibility for social sin by retrieving and developing the principle of cooperation
with evil. First, I explore how the principle was used in the manuals of
moral theology that dominated Catholic moral thought in the nineteenth
and early twentieth centuries. Then I describe its use in recent discussions of political behavior by those on both the left and the right. Next, I
turn to recent discussions of social sin in Catholic social ethics that correctly identify the problem of cooperation but often fail to provide a way
to think through the particular responsibilities of individuals. Finally, I
bring the manuals' concept of cooperation enhanced by sensitivity to
social sin to the case of sweatshop clothing. A contemporary rendering
of cooperation acknowledges the difficult choices that human beings
must make, while recognizing our obligations to avoid social evil and

to contribute to social good. Despite serious differences, people of many political affiliations all have a negative reaction to cooperation with evil at a gut level. I want to name this shared experience, to link it to the tradition of Catholic moral theology, and to reformulate it so that it can be used to analyze contemporary social problems. My hope is that finding a common way to think about cooperation with evil will enable people of different perspectives to act together in the space between the personal and political.

COOPERATION IN THE MANUALS OF MORAL THEOLOGY

In the classic manuals of moral theology, cooperation with evil is defined as "help afforded another . . . to carry out his purpose of sinning."[8] An accomplice shares in the sin and intention of the original actor; a cooperator assists but may not intend evil.[9] In acts of formal cooperation, the actor intends the evil act and always sins. However, the manuals that dominated US Catholic moral theology in the pre–Vatican II period held that when it was not someone's intention to do evil and when his or her own action was good or indifferent, then they were ordinarily engaged in material cooperation with evil, which could be justified.[10] The manuals employed a complex casuistry to apply the concept of material cooperation to cases of concern to US Catholics in the nineteenth and early twentieth centuries. For instance, may a nurse assist in an "illicit operation" (probably sterilization) in a public hospital? May a servant deliver a letter to his employer's lover? Might a taxi driver take a customer to a brothel? May a publisher print books opposed to the church's teachings on faith or morals? Might the owner of a hall rent it to the director of an illicit show?[11] According to the manualist Henry Davis, cooperation with evil can occur via command, counsel, consent, flattery, concealment, participation, silence, or nonresistance.[12] The potential to do evil is everywhere, in action or inaction. The manualists attempted to use a common set of questions to discern when cooperation could be licit, and they designed appropriate methods of restitution to redress any sin committed. They asked if the object of the action under consideration was good, evil, or indifferent; if the person's cooperation was immediate or mediate, proximate or remote, indispensable or not; and if the harm done was serious. They investigated whether there was sufficient cause to justify the action.[13]

For example, the manualist Heribert Jone considers the case of material cooperation in the publication of printed materials opposed to Christian faith or morals.[14] He assumes that cooperators do not share the sinful intentions of the writers, and that the object of their act is good or neutral. Those whose cooperation is mediate or closely connected to the evil act itself (i.e., the printer, publisher, or editor) are judged to be always in the wrong. However, many other workers (i.e., the proofreader, typesetter, ink mixer, or press operator), who would contribute in less significant ways, may do so for a truly grave reason, such as their need to make a living. Those farther away (i.e., the ink and paper sellers) are judged to be only remote cooperators, and their actions are lawful "for the sake of profit" alone, while advertisers may cooperate for a just cause, as their actions are not indispensable to the evil acts. Likewise, a writer may contribute to an immoral publication for sufficient cause (i.e., the greater good that he or she may accomplish), even though he or she is furthering the work of that publication. However, to be an associate editor of that same publication would be justifiable only for a truly grave reason, such as the need to support a family. Regular subscribers to illicit magazines also need a grave reason, such as giving great advantage to one's business. Jone works carefully and cautiously to discern where connections to evil are too close to be tolerated, while remaining sensitive to the primary moral obligations of the actor.

Many of the specific concerns that preoccupied the manualists are no longer relevant today, rooted as they were in the social and religious location of pre–Vatican II US Catholicism. Catholics today welcome opportunities to collaborate with fellow Christians. Most, though certainly not all, have greater economic security and choice in employment than did earlier generations of Catholics. Ethnic and religious parochialism and an understandable concern with economic security have been replaced by a socially engaged faith with a broad range of ethical concerns.[15]

The moral methodology of the manuals is far from perfect. They were based on and developed from the penitential manuals that were originally written to help priests in the confessional, and they are devoted to examining the problems of individuals and thus are blind to sinful social structures such as racism, poverty, and sexism. Their treatment of justice is limited to questions about contracts, and the authors draw on legal commentaries to help them determine appropriate restitution when a sin is committed.[16] What Charles Curran says about Aloysius Sabetti, author of *Compendium theologiae moralis* (1884), could rightly be said of most manualists: He "does not discuss the political order" or question the law, but rather accepts the status quo and "urges readers to obey it."[17] Rather than bringing Gospel values into dialogue with the culture, he "deals with the practical aspects of Catholic life in the US as if it existed in a vacuum."[18] Moreover, the manualists were much more likely to condone actions when the evil in question was not nearby, which led them to overlook a great deal. The Catholic moralist Joseph Boyle, among others, questions whether the manuals' focus on "proximity" needs to be reexamined.[19]

If the manuals were limited by their focus on individuals, they were even more limited in what they asked of those individuals. Instead of encouraging moral growth or excellence in light of the Christian vocation of discipleship, they saw moral theology as "what one is strictly bound to do" and viewed the job of the moral theologian as an attempt "to limit moral obligation."[20] For the most part, the higher ground of aspiration to holiness was left to other branches of theology. This limitation is critical, especially for those who seek to encourage a greater consciousness among Christians of the pitfalls of cooperation with social evils and a stronger sense of the duty to challenge systemic problems.

However, what the manuals get right is significant. Though often viewed as legalistic, they treat cooperation under the categories of charity or love of neighbor.[21] Though they could be obsessive (especially on sexual issues), their attention to daily life suggests that individual actions, even those that seem insignificant, matter. Actions say something about who we are and enhance or diminish the lives of those around us. We can further evil even when we do not intend it, and sometimes rightly understand ourselves as stained by association with it. We have a duty not to contribute to the harm of others that cannot be lightly excused. We need questions to help us discern how substantial our contribution to evil is in order to avoid being either too hard or too easy on ourselves. In the face of the common tendency to separate life from faith, the manuals can be seen as calling not for obsessiveness but for right judgment about even our most seemingly ordinary actions.[22]

Despite their many faults, the manuals managed to balance moral concern and tolerance for imperfect human beings. James Keenan illustrates the usefulness of cooperation with the tragic and shocking case of a wife who offers a belt to her husband, who intended to use a bat to beat their children. Arguing by analogy that the church can permit the distribution of condoms to prevent the spread of AIDS, he holds that "like the belt-offering wife, the bishops are able to distinguish their cooperation from the illicit intended activity of the persons with whom they cooperate."[23] Just as the wife does not intend for her husband to harm their children, the bishops do not intend the sexual acts that are going to take place with or without their assistance. According to Keenan, their material cooperation is justified in light of their intention to preserve life. Material cooperation is helpful as "a paradigm for the modern Christian who seeks to make the world a better place by neither compromising values nor detaching oneself from a world ridden with complexities."[24]

The manuals are especially helpful because they assume that individuals are limited by the circumstances of their lives, their professions, their need to support a family, and the realities of living in a society where their views are not widely shared. Though the manualists' lack of confidence in the abilities of lay people can rightly be questioned, their realism is not so far off the mark.[25] Some material cooperation with evil is unavoidable. The duty to avoid unintended evil is greater "the more the duties of our state of life or of our vocation command us to prevent such evil effects."[26] Although the manuals may have limited the scope of moral responsibility too much, their respect for human limitation should not be lost. We are "all responsible for all," as Pope John Paul II wisely claimed, but individual responsibilities are particular and limited by location.[27] We cannot avoid all connections with evil, and those who seek total nonparticipation face certain frustration as well as limited opportunities to do good amid imperfection. The manuals' approach to cooperation with evil thus should be maintained today as realistic, balanced, and responsible moral discernment. However, it must take account of the new situation in which today's Catholics, like most in the United States, find themselves.

COOPERATION AND THE CONTEMPORARY
POLITICAL SCENE

If the moral manuals were limited by a sensitivity to social sin that was less than fully developed, more recent discussions about how to avoid cooperation with evil in the political realm reflect the new place of

Catholics in American society. In the manuals, concern for justice was, for the most part, limited to the family, neighborhood, church, and workplace. Harm was understood in a very limited way. For instance, in the case of the cab driver, the question was cooperation with the sexual sin of the customer who wanted to meet a prostitute, not cooperation with the social structure of prostitution that disadvantages marginalized women. Today, many Catholics have moved into the middle class, and they have greater economic and political power—and, consequently, more is asked of them.

Since 2007 the US Conference of Catholics Bishops (USCCB) has issued *Forming Consciences for Faithful Citizenship*, a guide designed to help Catholics form their consciences and vote with integrity. Its very modern premise is that American Catholics have a responsibility to "consider the challenges in public life and contribute to greater justice and peace for all people."[28] The most controversial and widely quoted section (nos. 21–39), "Doing Good and Avoiding Evil," urges the faithful to embrace their duty to shape their society, saying that "responsible citizenship is a virtue," and that participation in political life is a moral obligation "rooted in our baptismal commitment to follow Jesus Christ."[29] The document upholds both the necessity to oppose intrinsically evil acts and the obligation to "contribute to the common good and act in solidarity with those in need."[30] While acknowledging the complexity of politics, the place of prudential judgment, and the reality that sometimes only limited progress is possible, the bishops say of politicians: "Those who knowingly, willingly, and directly support public policies or legislation that undermines fundamental moral principles *cooperate with evil*" (emphasis added).[31] Voters, too, are held accountable; "a Catholic cannot vote for a candidate who takes a position in favor of an intrinsic evil, such as abortion or racism, if the voter's intent is to support that position. In such cases a Catholic would be guilty of *formal cooperation in grave evil*" (emphasis added).[32] A Catholic who rejects the candidate's position may vote for such a candidate, but only "for truly grave moral reasons," and Catholics are reminded that the duty to "oppose intrinsically evil acts has a special claim on our consciences and actions."[33]

Some bishops, citing both *Faithful Citizenship* and the 2002 doctrinal note of the Congregation for the Doctrine of the Faith, made pastoral judgments that politicians who supported abortion, stem cell research, euthanasia, gay marriage, or cloning, all declared to be intrinsically evil acts—are engaged in "public cooperation with a gravely sinful act" and thus should not receive the Eucharist.[34]

The strength of this admittedly controversial discussion of political responsibility lies in the USCCB's understanding of the grave responsibility that Catholics bear for shaping public life. Acknowledging the reality of deep divisions on issues of concern to Catholics and the limitations of a pluralistic society, they insist that it is unacceptable for politicians or those who vote for them to give up or to deny that some actions advance particular evil acts. The bishops call for "prophetic witness" in the face of the denial of human dignity, claiming that Catholics must state their opposition to evil with vigor.[35] To do otherwise in an age when Catholics make up 25 percent of the population in the United States and have strong representation in the government is to deny the power that exists in the US Catholic Church and the connection between an individual's choice and the social evils to which those individuals might well be personally opposed. Harold E. Ernst, questioning the ease with which many Catholics vote for candidates who are not pro-life, asks: "Have we lost, to some degree, the revulsion we should feel at these 'most serious and deplorable' offenses against the inviolable dignity of human life? Do we shudder, as perhaps we should, to license even the smallest degree of cooperation in those great evils which the Second Vatican Council denounced as *'nefanda sunt crimina'* (*Gaudium et Spes*, no. 51)?"[36]

However, if the USCCB is right to point out the seriousness of linking ourselves to the evil of others through public acts, they do not identify the myriad ways in which politicians and voters cooperate with evil and perhaps oversimplify their moral dilemmas. As Cathleen Kaveny has pointed out, intrinsically evil acts are not the only kinds of evil acts that ought to concern voters and politicians.[37] For instance, war is not intrinsically evil, but a particular war may be egregiously unjust and may involve the deaths of both soldiers and noncombatants; this may lead a voter or candidate to prioritize efforts to end the conflict. Similarly, due to poverty-related causes, 2.6 million children die each year.[38] In the Confiteor at Mass, Catholics beg forgiveness "for what I have done, and for what I have failed to do." Acknowledging some responsibility for failing to do enough to combat evil could involve consideration of poverty. Though poverty is not identified as intrinsically evil, if some candidates are more capable than others of fighting it, voters may be justified in weighing this concern, along with concerns about lives to be lost through other means. Through our votes, we cooperate with both war and poverty and/or with solutions to end them. Politicians and voters must weigh all the evil for which they bear some responsibility.

Prudence, as the bishops note, is the virtue needed for this sort of discernment, especially when it comes to politics, which involves "the art of the possible."[39] Voters and politicians need to discern when prophetic witness is necessary versus when it would be more helpful to forgo witness in the hope of minimizing the evil that might otherwise be done. For example, the bishops engaged in prophetic witness with regard to the Affordable Care Act when they voiced concern about the federal financing of abortion and the failure to extend health care to immigrants. Some argue that it might have been more prudent to support a bill that would bring affordable health care to many, even if it would involve tax-paying citizens in remote material cooperation with the evil of abortion.[40] The moral manuals themselves allow that in some cases, one can try to "diminish the cycle of evil" by cooperating with lesser evils.[41] Attempts to avoid all material cooperation can result in marginalization and a diminished ability to do good. Some prudential weighing of the potential good likely to result from various courses of action seems necessary.

The call to prophetic witness should also be tempered by consciousness of the pluralistic nature of American society and the obligation to respect the consciences of others with whom we might disagree. In an early article on the dilemma of those Catholic doctors and/or hospitals that were being pressured to offer sterilization or abortions, Charles Curran held that doctors could participate in sterilization operations out of respect for the views of their patients; and Catholic hospitals could tolerate the provision of services they deemed immoral using the same reasoning.[42] As Germaine Grisez notes, Curran's particular examples seem to involve cooperation rather than toleration.[43] However, Curran correctly points out that toleration has traditionally been acknowledged as necessary in a fallen world. Consciousness of pluralism tempers the duty to engage in prophetic witness without diminishing it entirely.

Similarly, using the insights of the manualists, Kaveny urges caution in the application of cooperation with evil; we are not responsible for all the evil to which we are connected, in spite of our best intentions.[44] She argues that some of those accused of cooperating with evil in reality only foresee and "appropriate" or benefit from evil and are thus less culpable.[45] Actual cooperation must be intentional and substantial to be morally problematic; the tradition holds that "the most significant aspect of a human action is the way in which it shapes the character of the person who performs it."[46] Though Kaveny agrees that cooperating can "contaminate us by association," she sets the bar for such sullying high in order to leave room for the complexities of a pluralistic society.[47] Her argument effectively challenges official Catholic concerns about cooperation by allowing for a certain measure of appropriation of evil for the sake of a greater good. Her emphasis on complexity leads her to greater acceptance of at least some kinds of complicity with evil.

In sum, the US bishops rightfully remind us to think through the good and evil effects of our choices vis-à-vis others, particularly the most vulnerable.[48] We should feel "contaminated" when our votes are connected to human suffering. However, it is important to understand the many complex ways in which this happens and to admit, as did the manualists, that sometimes toleration, appropriation, and even material cooperation with evil will be the unavoidable or better choice. Still, it is important not to minimize the call to examine potential ways in which persons cooperate with evil. Though cooperation is sometimes prudent, other times it is not. Theologians who have considered social sin offer a necessary corrective to the caution of moral theologians like Curran, Keenan, and Kaveny. They point to more rather than less cooperation with evil in the social realm, and thus bring us closer to formulating a better way to use this concept to analyze contemporary issues.

A DEEPENING AWARENESS OF SOCIAL SIN

If theologians responding to discussions of cooperation in political life have argued that cooperation, appropriation, and toleration of evil are sometimes licit, theologians who consider social sin have attempted to encourage a certain intolerance of evil and broaden our sense of moral responsibility. Although the desire to "free people from an exaggerated sense of duty and guilt" is understandable and helpful in some instances, most people are probably less aware than they ought to be about their cooperation in sinful social structures, making the efforts of theologians who ponder social sin all the more necessary.[49] Most of us are so used to contributing to social evil that we fail to see our own complicity.

Unintentionally, we harm others in significant ways. We need to ask hard questions about culpability in order to clarify moral obligations.

Social sin can be broadly defined as social forms of opposition to the Kingdom of God, and our participation in this opposition can involve personal sin.[50] All that opposes the peace and justice that God intends for the world can be understood as social sin. Any way in which we advance the opposition is "a way in which we participate in the sinfulness of society."[51] Sinful social structures can be formal (e.g., legal, institutional, political, or economic policies) or informal (e.g., language, customs, and social roles).[52] Our cooperation with those structures can be active or passive. Though this definition may appear overly broad, if we only hold ourselves accountable for sins in our personal lives, then no one is responsible for hunger, war, and so on. Furthermore, "if we absolve ourselves of responsibility for these great evils, we are condemning the world to destruction by its unredeemed powers. And that world in turn deforms us."[53]

This sense of social sin is present in Catholic Social Teaching. In *Ecclesia in America*, John Paul II calls attention to "social sins which cry to heaven."[54] In place of Gospel values, he mourns, "an unbridled greed for wealth and power takes over, obscuring any Gospel-based vision of social reality." He condemns neoliberalism, which is "based on a purely economic conception of man," "considers profit and the law of the market as its only parameters," and results in offenses against human dignity. In view of this reality, the pope claims that we have a positive duty to work for the good of others; we must look beyond our own families and "hear the cry of those most in need."[55] Not to do so would be to participate in social sin.

One can affirm the existence of structures of social sin while also acknowledging that all sin is first of all personal.[56] Some may worry that this acknowledgment will diminish concern for social sin. However, it can be a way to drive home the reality that sinful social structures are sustained by individuals. The contemporary discussion of social sin acknowledges human freedom but emphasizes that "the world we build is broader than just that of our individual identity. . . . Because of the inextricable involvement of the world in our lives and vice versa, our moral responsibility extends beyond our personal lives."[57] Although intentions matter, "because our involvement in the world extends far beyond our intentional acts, our responsibility cannot be limited to those actions that are knowingly and willingly done."[58]

Although, in the past, guilt was sometimes overemphasized, we may need to revive it today. Limiting sin to our private lives "endangers our freedom by blinding us to our participation in, and thus our responsibility for, the social dimensions of life; . . . [and then the church's] great efforts at raising people's consciousness about the terrible injustices existing around the world are undermined."[59] Without personal guilt for cooperation in social sin, there is little chance that Catholic Social Teaching will be internalized and acted upon.

Nonetheless, increasing guilt is not the ultimate goal; the question is not what was done but what we will do.[60] For instance, in their pastoral letter on racism, *Brothers and Sisters to Us*, the National Conference of Catholic Bishops insists that "we must seek to resist and undo injustices we have not caused, lest we become bystanders who tacitly endorse evil and so share in guilt for it."[61] The point is not to wallow in guilt but to acknowledge responsibility and act on it. We are enmeshed and involved—"we are more than just bystanders. We are participants."[62] The real challenge is to become involved in the work for social change.

To be sure, it is appropriate to make distinctions and to discuss degrees of responsibility for social sin—measuring, for instance, "the depth to which racism has seeped into our soul, . . . the extent to which our state of being affects the sinful condition of society, and . . . the ability we have to redress this destructive situation."[63] We are not equally implicated or responsible. Here the warnings of contemporary moral theologians are helpful. It may be necessary to cooperate with an unjust situation (or to choose the lesser evil) in order to avoid greater evil because right now this particular evil cannot be overcome.[64] We can acknowledge that sinfulness in the world may prevent us from avoiding certain evils in any situation. We can recognize that "because of human sin, persons in concrete situations may only gradually be able to realize the full demands of the relevant norms. While always striving to attain the ideal, persons need to accept the limitations present in the situation and within themselves."[65] Traditional Roman Catholic thought rightly affirms that "it is impossible in a complex and sinful world to avoid all involvement with evil."[66] This insistence offers solace to those likely to be overcome with guilt for acts of cooperation with social evil that can never be fully eradicated.

However, the tradition's good sense of complexity can be pushed too far. Excusing sins because of "we just didn't know" can mask social sin.[67]

Ignorance can be culpable. We are responsible for knowing about injustice in the world, if not for knowing everything. The theologians who consider social sin also question the traditional impulse to assign moral responsibility only to those with voluntary and direct connections to suffering. This tendency "to place greater emphasis on mitigating factors in determining individual responsibility to overcome social sin . . . [may] encourage complacency."[68] Few among us will the suffering of others. Most have no direct responsibility for social oppression. But this understanding of sin is simply too narrow and individualistic. If none of us bears full responsibility, surely we all bear some responsibility. We can acknowledge real limitations in any one person's knowledge, ability to change structures, or ability to devote energy to a few issues.[69] Yet it is also necessary to cultivate "a constant inner tension" that can propel us to lessen our cooperation with sinful structures and begin to live in alternative ways.[70]

WHITE PRIVILEGE

Recent theological analyses of white privilege have illuminated the specific ways in which cooperating with sinful social structures harms others and affects those who sin. These theologians analyze social sin and call for conversion but narrow their focus to particular actors and actions. In so doing, they provide a good model for bringing cooperation into contemporary social ethics.

Seeing racism as a social sin about which many are ignorant but from which we must extricate ourselves is not new. Martin Luther King Jr. held that blindness rather than malice allows good people to stand by in the face of suffering. According to King, Jesus identified blindness as the primary manifestation of evil in the world. For "when Jesus says from the cross, 'Forgive them, Father. They know not what they do,'" it is an expression of Jesus's awareness of man's intellectual and spiritual blindness. "'They know not what they do,' said Jesus. Blindness was their trouble; enlightenment was their need."[71] Enlightenment, King said, remains our need, as we remain unmoved and uncommitted, cooperating with evil instead of good. King called on people to disobey unjust laws "because noncooperation with evil is as much a moral obligation as is cooperation with good."[72]

Recent discussions of white privilege have illuminated how structures of racism, of which most white people are insufficiently aware, function not only to harm people of color but also to advantage and harm whites. Laurie Cassidy identifies racism as a "spiritual wound that afflicts all who dwell in the house built on race."[73] It is not only an external social structure but also something that "imprints itself on the human imagination."[74] Most are unaware of their connection to racist structures, which they would oppose in theory because "being white is having the privilege of functioning in a society blind to the system into which one is born and from which one benefits."[75] The challenge is to understand how, as Margaret Pfeil puts it, we "have been crippled by [our] formation and complicity in white privilege. . . . Left unexamined and unchallenged, my whiteness continues to function as a form of social violence and therefore renders me incapable of truly opting for the poor."[76] If we do not attend to the blindness, we cannot claim to be free from complicity.

But what sort of complicity is blind? Can anyone be blamed for benefits for which they did not ask, for advantages they did not seek, for kinds of harm they do not understand? Pfeil and others contend that we can and must be blamed, because "white beneficiaries of race-based advantages contribute to the destruction of our own humanity precisely by silently accepting such privilege, and that is a choice we make as moral agents."[77] She uses the example of a judge who decided a case within the limits of definitions of race current in his time. Using the more formal language of traditional moral theology, she writes, "With some degree of freedom as a moral agent, he chose to cooperate with an objectively sinful system."[78] She agrees with Thomas Wyatt Turner, founder of the Federation of Colored Catholics, who "rightly noted the sinful complicity of white priests and laity in maintaining ecclesial structures of white supremacy."[79] Pfeil and Turner call attention to the complicity of individuals and institutions that cooperate with evil in specific ways that are properly called sinful, even if the persons involved would not be conscious of, let alone be intentional about, their complicity.

Becoming conscious allows us to see that even when we do not intend to be, we are "gripped by the structures of white privilege to which we have given at least tacit assent by virtue of our uncontested and bloody accrual of advantage from them."[80] With this evocative language, Pfeil recalls the traditional idea that one can be stained by sins to which our action or inaction contributes, along with Kaveny's judgment that persons who appropriate evil can be contaminated by their actions. White privilege can be understood as material cooperation with evil and appropriation of evil. Though unseen, it "grips" whites in its pervasiveness and pernicious-ness. Its evil shackles seem nearly impossible to escape.[81]

How is any one white person to reduce his or her cooperation with this evil? The manuals of moral theology directed the confessor to counsel a penitent who has cooperated with evil to make restitution in order to be forgiven. Theologians writing about white privilege offer several options. Pfeil argues that salvation lies in "subverting societal structures of white privilege" by "exchanging the power of racial domination for the power of solidarity on the periphery."[82] She suggests that whites embrace the asceticism of living simply on the margins without many of the privileges they currently enjoy. Cassidy recommends beginning with prayer that imagines God as black.[83] Barbara Hilkert Andolsen emphasizes the need for ongoing engagement with public policy debates in order to understand how racism continues to function and to discern what sorts of political actions are necessary.[84] Curran acknowledges that conversion is necessary to rightly see the enormity of the problem.[85]

The broader suggestions for extrication and restitution are prophetic but limited. On one hand, as Curran recognizes, white privilege is not an action but "a structural sin that has to be made visible and removed. . . . There is a need for conversion and especially continuing conversion."[86] Immediate restitution is not possible; nor is complete extrication from the sinful structures. Ongoing growth is the only option. Yet on the other hand, this sort of conversion seems too much for any one person to bear. This gravity, of course, is partially the point. Social sin is committed by many and can only be eradicated by many working together.[87] As Roger Haight points out, there is a certain problematic lack of preciseness in the conversation; as useful as it is to point out the many ways in which whites benefit from white privilege, whites are not equally blameworthy for all privileges that accrue to them and are not all equally able to make the same kind of restitution.[88] However, unlike Curran—who writes, "I finally realized to some extent that I was the problem"—Haight fails to acknowledge the need for particular responses to the specific forms of cooperation functioning in destructive ways.[89] This early work on white privilege shows how unintentional cooperation or complicity with evil is pervasive, identifies particular forms of cooperation that wound the sin-ner, and calls for disentanglement and restitution.

More recent work on white privilege questions the usefulness of the cat-egory of cooperation with evil. While acknowledging that the principle, as retrieved by contemporary theologians, is helpful in its ability to help people consider their unintentional participation in social sin, Mikulich and Cassidy worry that it assumes "we are innocent; the evil is 'out there' in the social system," whereas in truth, "systems of oppression are a matrix within which we live—they are in us and we are in them."[90] Instead of beginning with the innocent subject, whites need to begin to understand whiteness itself as unintentional, unconscious complicity with evil and ask not "What can I do?" but "How can I listen to and form alliances with people of color?"[91]

It is true that the traditional framework of cooperation does not consider systemic social evil. However, the manualists did not necessarily envision an innocent subject. As noted above, they are more often identified with the heavy focus on sin in pre–Vatican II moral theology. Sometimes, out of compassion for the penitent, they excused too much. If an action was not definitely sinful, they left room for prudential judgment. Some rightly accuse them of being too lax in this regard, though they were stricter in some areas than others. Yet the questions of the manualists were limited to whether an action was licit or not. It is only by dialogue with theologians of social sin that the principle can be usefully applied to the many dilemmas modern Christians face. These theologians rightly paint a broad picture of sin so that all understand the pervasiveness of evil and the far reach of our participation in it even when we are blind to it. Cassidy, Mikulich, and Pfeil are undoubtedly right to insist that white people need to de-center themselves and listen to people of color.

However, I contend that the principle of cooperation with evil is still helpful. For many, the starting point of complicity is too broad, too overwhelming. Catholic Social Teaching has often "lacked teeth" because it does not identify particular sins or leave people feeling individually responsible. Using cooperation as a lens, we can begin to see how each of us is implicated in social sin in specific ways by the seemingly innocent things we do every day (e.g., buying factory-farmed meat, indulging in excess luxury, failing to give enough to the poor, or enjoying the privileges of public schools in elite neighborhoods). Identifying particular connections need not be the end point. Rather, once I begin to see how I am involved, I can slowly make my way into broader understandings not of my innocence but of my complicity. With this admittedly complex example of white privilege in mind, we are now better able to consider other areas where we may be particularly implicated. This is where the manuals' analysis of cooperation with evil can be useful, if it is brought up to date.[92]

THE CASE OF SWEATSHOP CLOTHING

To show how an analysis of cooperation with evil might proceed, I offer a brief analysis of the case of retail clothing. I begin with consumption, because everyone makes consumption choices and because many people would agree that both buying and boycotting can be moral actions. I take as my starting point the claim that it is nearly impossible to avoid sweatshop connections when buying clothing in mainstream retail venues. Unless we make our own clothing or buy only used or fair trade clothes, we are buying clothes made by people who are treated unjustly. I also assume that readers are convinced that workers should not be subjected to unsafe working conditions and wages insufficient for basic sustenance. More thorough examinations of cooperation with social evils, such as those I undertake in subsequent chapters, will need to address the nature of the evil with which we might or might not be cooperating, but my intention here is solely to show that if social evil is occurring, we can be held morally accountable for contributing to it.[93]

This evil is dismissed by many, though not by radicals who want no connection to the factories that produce regular clothing. Though not academics, these thinkers offer valuable insights into the moral dilemma of buying clothing. A Saint Louis Catholic Worker community member, Jenny Truax, holds that if Catholics want to truly honor the dignity of the worker, it is important "to try to acquire things like clothes and shoes through dumpstering or the thrift stores to avoid supporting industries that use sweatshop labor."[94] Others in her Saint Louis Catholic Worker community explain that all of their life choices flow out of a commitment to love. To them, "the most pure and effective resistance is in the creation and attempted execution of a viable alternative" to the status quo. Though the critiquing of unjust structures is important, they suggest that "actual change can only come from our nonparticipation in them." So, they say, we "attempt to extract ourselves from the systems and choices that destroy, and try to embrace instead a lifestyle that, if everyone were to join us, would reverse the destructive spiral of the dominant culture and land us instead on the path toward justice, peace, sustainability, holistic health, and, ultimately, love."[95]

Though they do not employ the language of cooperation with evil, reliance on the concept is still clear. These Catholic Workers see a connection between their money and the unjust working conditions necessary to produce the cheap clothing they could buy. They seek to "extract" themselves from evil systems and to resist them by "beginning to live in a different way."[96] Finding clothes elsewhere can be a form of cooperating with good, in that buying from thrift stores is an environmentally friendly and often charitable choice.

Is this use of the concept of cooperation with evil consistent with the tradition of the manuals? Keenan's shorthand list of six questions constituting the core of cooperation can illustrate that buying clothes made by laborers who are treated unjustly might be viewed as morally culpable material cooperation with evil.[97]

Keenan's first question is, Is the object gravely evil? The action of buying clothing for one's family is neutral or good, provided that one is not buying more than one can afford or so much that it is compatible with what John Paul II calls a life centered on "having rather than being."[98] However, the money we pay goes in part to corporations that exploit workers by refusing to recognize their fundamental rights to a living wage and just working conditions. Tom Beaudoin, who spent six months trying to determine how his favorite clothing items were made, determined that none of the companies was transparent about its labor practices and that most employed young adults who worked 50–60 hours a week or more making less than a living wage.[99] Moreover, investigative reporters have found egregious abuses, including "cramped living conditions, dangerous treks to and from work, bans on pregnancy, [and] reprisals against those who organize unions."[100] According to Beaudoin, "the specifics of the excesses may change from country to country, but the fact of the excesses is numbingly clear. There are now more than enough research reports, videos, and testimony from workers to convince any fair-minded consumer that most of us are implicated in an economy whose violence is our business."[101] Furthermore, though a lack of full knowledge can excuse cooperation, most of us know what Beaudoin is saying to be the case in general, even if corporations make it all but impossible to know the truth about particular cases.[102]

Second, is the cooperation formal or material? No fair-minded person intends to exploit workers when he or she buys clothes, so their cooperation is material. Their assistance makes possible the corporation's existence and enables its exploitation, even if, like the nurse who gives instruments to the doctor performing an illicit operation, they do not approve of what is being done. Thus the manualists would hold that it could be justified for a proportionate reason, but the bar of justification would be high because harm to others is involved.

Third, is the cooperation mediate or substantial? Certainly, any one purchase cannot be considered as substantial as driving one's employer to the house of his lover. Even a lifetime of purchasing a favorite brand of shoes can be considered inconsequential in the context of the workings of a large corporation. Because the manuals considered individuals' sins, they were blind to how individual choices added together can be substantial. This understanding of substantial also seems to be missing in some types of contemporary analysis that excuse cooperation. By employing the concept of social sin and considering the potential impact of a boycott, we can name purchasing clothing as a substantial form of material cooperation with evil. Clearly, if a significant number of people stopped cooperating by no longer buying the clothing in question, the sinful working conditions would need to come to an end. But if they continue to buy, their combined cooperation is substantial, and they can be understood as having "aggregated agency."[103]

Fourth, is the cooperation proximate or remote? In terms of distance, my cooperation with any corporation is likely to be remote. I am not a manager, supplier, or renter of a factory. If the manuals could excuse remote cooperation in the publishing of immoral books for those who had no other way to make a living, surely they would excuse the single working mother who finds her best bargains at Walmart.[104] But the concept of social sin allows us to see that we are responsible for more than actions involving those who are nearest to us. Due to globalization, the world today is much smaller than the world of the manuals. We can no longer limit our discussion of justice to direct relationships with shopkeepers, neighbors, and employers. Almost everything we use or buy connects us with people around the globe. Our responsibility for the evil done to produce these things surely differs from that of the corporate executives or factory owners, but it cannot be dismissed as remote simply because it comes from a distance.[105]

Fifth, is the cooperation necessary or indispensable for the evil to be done? Using the lens of social sin, we can say that it both is and is not. Someone has to buy the clothing for the factory to remain open; but my particular purchase is not necessary to its solvency at any given moment in time. However, organized boycotts can be effective tools for forcing corporations to change, and if more people bought fair trade clothing, more workers would be paid living wages. I could remove my cooperation with evil and instead cooperate with good. My cooperation—along with that of others—is necessary for evil or good to occur. Thus buying clothing is not simply an appropriation of evil, that is, predicting and making use of the fruits of evil acts without intending evil when one has no causal power over another's actions.[106] The wife who, in desperation, hands the abusive husband a belt to prevent his use of a bat has no power to stop the abuse altogether and does not cause the evil action. Likewise, approving of condoms does not cause people to use them. However, in the case of consumption, our collective actions do have power, albeit limited, over the continuance of the evil action.

Surely we are less responsible for unintended but foreseen evil with which we are associated than we are for evil that we intend.[107] Otherwise, our responsibilities would be infinite. The moral manuals rightfully uphold the central importance of intention for the "ratification of evil," which constitutes culpable cooperation, while reminding us that an "intimacy with evildoing" can still corrupt character by "contamination" or "seepage."[108] This tension between ratifying evil and being contaminated by it is worth retaining. However, consciousness of social sin should compel us to ask not only if our character is contaminated by buying clothes made in sweatshops (certainly, many Catholic Workers would say it is) but also if our actions contribute to the maintenance of evil when they could be contributing to good. When bishops, theologians, and activists call for public witness against abortion, torture, capital punishment, or the mistreatment of animals, they are calling people to think about how their actions, added to those of others, shape reality, even if they intend to harm no one, and even if their one vote, phone call, or purchase will not change the system.

Sixth and finally, is there a proportionate reason for the material cooperation with evil? Do I buy my clothes at a particular chain because I sincerely believe that its factories in developing countries are the best possible option for the present and will result in economic growth in the future? Could I claim that buying clothing at my local big box store is for the good of my family, given limits of time, money, and energy? Am I unaware of other options? Is fair trade clothing too expensive and limited? Is thrift shop shopping too time consuming or incompatible with my station in life? If so, one might decide that committing to an alternative buying practice, as the Catholic Workers do, would constitute an undue burden. However, if the manuals held that "the graver the sin that will be permitted, the graver the reason required for the cooperation," the sins committed in sweatshops demand graver reasons than inconvenience.[109] Surely, for many, "duress" is not an undue burden because alternatives are available, though they may cost more time and money.

However, even if one can make a reasonable case that buying retail clothing can be considered material cooperation with evil, the manuals recognized that for most people, the primary areas of moral responsibility are family, community, and work. If so, some duress is reasonably recognized as a legitimate mitigating factor. Modern moral sensibilities might move us to correct this vision without losing its central insight. Because I am only one finite human being, I cannot be responsible for everything all at once. Though a Catholic Worker once told me that "I want to be in right relationship with all the people I'm in relationship with," even she realizes that she cannot do this perfectly every day. She strives to buy as little and as locally as possible, shares her home with homeless migrants, and produces most things she cannot get from a dumpster or come by second hand.[110] But occasionally, she needs to give in. Every day, she can think of many more positive things that she could be doing. The days are only so long. The manuals' modest sense that some material moral cooperation with evil is unavoidable, extended through our contemporary vision of the complexity of social sin, allows us to claim duress as a reasonable limit on moral duty without allowing it to obscure a calling to continual conversion toward less cooperation with evil and more cooperation with good.

CONCLUSION

In this chapter I have argued that it is possible to apply the classic concept of cooperation with evil to contemporary moral problems by drawing on and extending the Catholic moral tradition. The moral manuals used cooperation to deal with the complexity of moral life and relieve undue guilt while making individuals aware of their responsibilities. Recently, the US Catholic bishops have called on Catholics to oppose social sin by engaging in public witness of opposition to the Affordable Care Act and the contraception mandate of the US Department of Health and Human Services. The good impulse behind this campaign guards against too much acceptance of evil. Yet some moral theologians have raised questions about the bishops' claims. They have described the actions in question as remote rather than proximate cooperation with evil. They have recalled the tradition's emphasis on intention as essential to determining the morality of an action. These theologians have rightfully retrieved from the manuals an emphasis on prudence, complexity, and the limits of individual responsibility for the social order. However, this emphasis may lead us to underappreciate the reality of unconscious contributions to social evil and to be insufficiently conscious of the duty to shape the social order in light of a firm belief in human dignity. Theologians writing on social sin give us a broader understanding of sin by analyzing how social structures implicate individuals and by emphasizing the power of individuals acting together to oppose current structures. This analysis leads to new responsibilities. Contemporary theologians writing about white privilege show how social sin implicates and corrupts even when it is unintentional and unseen. Their early work calls for beginning with an analysis of our particular situations and for extricating ourselves from as much evil as we can while joining in work for good. They give us a model worth imitating, and we can apply it using the good questions given to us by the manualists. A preliminary analysis of the process of buying clothes made in sweatshops shows the potential of the framework for cooperation with evil to help people assess their moral responsibilities in the face of social evil.

A blending of the moral manuals with the theology of social sin calls us to pay attention to specific forms of cooperation with evil and to develop alternative practices of noncooperation with evil and cooperation with good. Cooperation with social sin is a matter of moral concern, not only for politically concerned bishops and radical Catholic Workers but also for many Christians on both the right and the left today. Every time someone wonders about the unintended moral consequences of voting, shopping, or other ordinary actions that—along with the actions of others—shape society, he or she is thinking about cooperation with evil. This shared sense of responsibility for the world's problems, when paired with the tradition's healthy respect for the complexity of assessing culpability, is a sound foundation for linking the personal choices we all face to the common good for which we all profess concern.

NOTES

1. See Raymond L. Burke, "Prophecy for Justice," *America*, June 14, 2004, http://americamagazine.org/issue/488/article/prophecy-justice; and Archbishop Joseph F. Naumann and Bishop Robert Finn, "Kansas Bishops Issue Health Care Reform Statement," *The Catholic Key*, September 2, 2009, http://www.catholic.org/news/politics/story.php?id=34354.

2. *Catechism of the Catholic Church*, no. 1868, http://www.vatican.va/archive/ccc_css/archive/catechism/p3s1c1a8.htm; Pope John Paul II, *Evangelium Vitae*, 1995, no. 74, http://w2.vatican.va/content/john-paul-ii/en/encyclicals/documents/hf_jp-ii_enc_25031995_evangelium-vitae.html.

3. In 1953 Dorothy Day wrote, "Whatever you buy is taxed, so that you are, in effect, helping to support the state's preparations for war exactly to the extent of your attachment to worldly things of whatever kind." Dorothy Day, "Little by Little," reprinted in *Dorothy Day: Selected Writings*, ed. Robert Ellsberg (Maryknoll, NY: Orbis, 1998), 111. Modern Catholic Workers follow her reasoning with greater sensitivity to environmental concerns, as I show below.

4. Thomas R. Kopfensteiner, "The Man with a Ladder," *America*, November 1, 2004, 9–11.

5. Vincent J. Miller, *Consuming Religion: Christian Faith and Practice in a Consumer Culture* (New York: Continuum, 2005), 16–18.

6. Robert P. George, "What *Hobby Lobby* Means," *First Things*, June 2014, http://www.firstthings.com/web-exclusives/2014/06/what-hobby-lobby-means.

7. Social sin is acknowledged as a reality in contemporary Catholic teaching, though it is understood as "the expression and effect of personal sin." *Catechism of the Catholic Church*, no. 1869, http://www.vatican.va/archive/ccc_css/archive/catechism/p3s1c1a8.htm.

8. John A. McCugh, OP, and Charles J. Callan, OP, *Moral Theology: A Complete Course*, rev. ed. (New York: Joseph F. Wagner, 1929), vol. 1, 616.

9. Ibid.

10. Charles E. Curran, *A History of Catholic Moral Theology in the United States* (Washington, DC: Georgetown University Press, 2008), 56. An intermediate category used by some moralists is "immediate formal cooperation," or "implicit formal cooperation," in which someone does not consciously intend the evil but is judged by another to not be able to distinguish his act from the evil act in

question. See Benedict M. Ashley and Kevin D. O'Rourke, *Healthcare Ethics: A Catholic Theological Analysis*, 5th ed. (Washington, DC: Georgetown University Press, 2006), 56–57. I follow Curran and others in distinguishing intentional formal vs. foreseen but unintentional material cooperation. Further exploration of disagreement on this point is necessary but beyond the scope of this chapter.

11. Many of these cases are discussed by Heribert Jone, *Moral Theology* (Westminster, MD: Newman, 1945), trans. Urban Adelman, 247–49. The case of the cab driver was first presented by John A. McHugh, *The Casuist*, vol. 5 (New York: Joseph F. Wagner, 1925), reprinted in *The Historical Development of Fundamental Moral Theology in the United States*, ed. Charles E. Curran and Richard A. McCormick (New York: Paulist Press, 1999), 115–19. The case of the nurse is recounted by Gerald Kelly, SJ, *Medico-Moral Problems* (Saint Louis: Catholic Hospital Association, 1958).

12. Henry Davis, SJ, *Moral and Pastoral Theology*, rev. ed. (New York: Sheed & Ward, 1936), vol. 2, 10–14.

13. James Keenan summarizes this tradition with six questions: Is the object good, evil, or indifferent? Is the cooperation formal or material, immediate or mediate, proximate or remote? Is there sufficient cause? Is the cooperation indispensable? Keenan, "Prophylactics, Toleration, and Cooperation: Contemporary Problems and Traditional Principles," *International Philosophical Quarterly* 29, no. 2 (June 1989): 209.

14. Jone, *Moral Theology*, 94–96.

15. E.g., according to McHugh and Callan, *Moral Theology*, 621, it is always evil to assist in the manufacture or distribution of obscene literature, drugs, or objects used for immoral purposes, but it is licit to assist with weapons or poisons. For a brief overview of Catholic mobility in the United States, see Julie Hanlon Rubio, "A Familial Vocation beyond the Home," *CTSA Proceedings* 63 (2008): 75–79.

16. Charles E. Curran, *The Origins of Moral Theology in the United States: Three Different Approaches* (Washington, DC: Georgetown University Press, 1997), 159.

17. Ibid.

18. Ibid.

19. Joseph Boyle, "Principles for Cooperating with Evil," unpublished manuscript.

20. Curran, *Origins*, 278. Curran is discussing John Hogan, the author of *Clerical Studies* (1898) and *Daily Thoughts for Priests* (1899). James Keenan documents the deficiencies of the manuals. See James Keenan, *A History of Catholic Moral Theology in the Twentieth Century* (New York: Continuum, 2010), 9–34. See also Charles Curran, *The Development of Moral Theology: Five Strands* (Washington, DC: Georgetown University Press, 2013), 20–27.

21. See Jone, *Moral Theology*, 92–98; Thomas Slater, SJ, *Manual of Moral Theology*, vol. 1, rev. ed. (London: Burns Oates & Washbourne, 1928), 132–34; and Davis, *Moral and Pastoral Theology*, 341–52.

22. Jone, for instance, writes in the preface to *Moral Theology* that he hopes his book will benefit "the educated laity, interested in religious matters, whom it may help in solving such questions of conscience as occur in their daily lives." Servais Pinckaers defends the manualists while criticizing a "morality of obligation"; see Servais Pinckaers, OP, *Morality: The Catholic View* (South Bend: St. Augustine's Press, 2003), 37–41.

23. Keenan, "Prophylactics." 215.

24. Ibid., 218.

25. Keenan, *History of Catholic Moral Theology*, 30, is more critical than I am here.

26. Bernard Häring, *The Law of Christ*, vol. 1 (Westminster, MD: Newman, 1961), 293. It is notable that this admission comes from Häring, a revisionist whose work is often distinguished from that of the manualists; see Keenan, *History of Catholic Moral Theology*, 88–95.

27. Pope John Paul II, *Sollicitudo Rei Socialis* (Washington, DC: USCCB, 1987), no. 38. The pope makes the first point, but not the second.

28. USCCB, *Forming Consciences for Faithful Citizenship: A Call for Political Responsibility from the Catholic Bishops of the United States* (Washington, DC: USCCB, 2007), no. 3. The USCCB has issued documents on related issues since 1976.

29. Ibid., no. 13.

30. Ibid., no. 24.

31. Ibid., no. 31.

32. Ibid., no. 34.

33. Ibid., nos. 35 and 37, respectively.

34. See Congregation for the Doctrine of the Faith, "Doctrinal Note on Some Questions regarding the Participation of Catholics in Political Life," no. 4, www.vatican.va/roman_curia/congregations/cfaith/documents/rc_con_cfaith _doc_20021124_politica_en.html; Burke, "Prophecy for Justice"; and Bishop Thomas J. Tobin, "Dear Congressman Kennedy," *Rhode Island Catholic*, November 12, 2009, www.thericatholic.com/opinion/detail.html?sub_id=2632. I cannot address the propriety of denial of the Eucharist here. I only wish to note the use of the language of cooperation with evil that is employed by bishops advocating denial.

35. Cathleen Kaveny notes the turn toward the language of prophetic witness to describe the Christian in arguments over cooperation with evil and argues for a more modest "pilgrim on the way"; Cathleen Kaveny, "Tax Lawyers, Prophets and Pilgrims: A Response to Anthony Fisher," in *Cooperation, Complicity and*

Conscience: Problems in Healthcare, Science, Law, and Public Policy, ed. Helen Watt (London: Linacre, 2005), 65–88.

36. Harold E. Ernst, "Catholic Politicians, Voters, and Cooperation in Evil: A Response to Rev. Thomas Kopfensteiner," *Chicago Studies* 44, no. 2 (2005): 217, referencing "abominable crimes."

37. Cathleen Kaveny, "Intrinsic Evil and Political Responsibility," *America*, October 27, 2008, 15–19.

38. Simon Tisdall, "Poor Diet Kills 2.6 Million Infants a Year, Says Survey by Save the Children," *The Guardian*, February 14, 2012, http://www.theguardian .com/global-development/2012/feb/15/life-free-from-hunger-save-the-children.

39. USCCB, *Forming Consciences*, no. 32.

40. The bishops' support for health care as a right of all persons is long-standing. See USCCB, *A Framework for Comprehensive Health Care Reform* (Washington, DC: USCCB, 1993), http://www.usccb.org/issues-and-action/human-life-and -dignity/health-care/upload/health-care-comprehensive-care.pdf.

41. Keenan, "Prophylactics," 21.

42. Charles E. Curran, "Cooperation in a Pluralistic Society," in *Ongoing Revision: Studies in Moral Theology*, by Charles E. Curran (Notre Dame, IN: Fides, 1975), 210–28.

43. Germain Grisez, *The Way of the Lord Jesus, Volume III: Difficult Moral Questions* (Quincy, IL: Franciscan, 1997), 892.

44. Cathleen Kaveny, "Appropriation of Evil: Cooperation's Mirror Image," *Theological Studies* 61 (2000): 280–313.

45. Ibid., 300–301.

46. Ibid., 303.

47. Ibid., 305–6. Contamination involves "seepage," whereby the evil becomes part of a person's identity, and "self-deception" whereby a person deludes himself or herself about what he or she is doing.

48. Ernst rightly criticizes Kopfensteiner for advocating otherwise and thereby diminishing the traditional duty to vote for the common good; Ernst, "Catholic Politicians," 212–13.

49. Thomas F. Schindler, *Ethics: The Social Dimension* (Wilmington: Michael Glazier, 1989), 136–37.

50. Ibid., 140.

51. Ibid., 143.

52. Ibid., 141.

53. Ibid., 144.

54. John Paul II, *Ecclesia in America*, no. 56, http://w2.vatican.va/content /john-paul-ii/en/apost_exhortations/documents/hf_jp-ii_exh_22011999_ecclesia -in-america.html.

55. Ibid., no. 58.

56. Pope John Paul II, *Evangelium Vitae*, no. 74. See also *Catechism of the Catholic Church*, 1868.

57. Schindler, *Ethics*, 138.

58. Ibid., 139.

59. Ibid., 140.

60. Ibid., 143.

61. USCCB, *Brothers and Sisters to Us* (Washington, DC: USCCB, 1979), http://www.usccb.org/issues-and-action/cultural-diversity/african-american /brothers-and-sisters-to-us.cfm.

62. Schindler, *Ethics*, 145.

63. Ibid., 146.

64. Mark O'Keefe, *What Are They Saying about Social Sin?* (New York: Paulist Press, 1990), 67.

65. Ibid., 68.

66. Ibid., 68–69.

67. Ibid., 70.

68. Ibid.,74.

69. Ibid., 74–75.

70. Ibid., 75.

71. Martin Luther King, "Love in Action," in *Strength to Love* (Philadelphia: Fortress Press, 1981), 43.

72. Martin Luther King, "Loving Your Enemies," in *Strength to Love*, 56.

73. Laurie M. Cassidy, "'Becoming Black with God': Toward an Understanding of the White Catholic Theologian in the US," in *Interrupting White Privilege: Catholic Theologians Break the Silence*, ed. Laurie M. Cassidy and Alex Mikulich (Maryknoll, NY: Orbis, 2007), 147.

74. Ibid., 152.

75. Ibid., 147. E.g., "White privilege has made white theologians unable to notice the theological significance of the suffering of black human beings" and has blinded them to "patterns that connect white existence and black suffering" (p. 152).

76. Margaret R. Pfeil, "The Transformative Power of the Periphery," in *Interrupting White Privilege*, ed. Cassidy and Mikulich, 129.

77. Ibid., 131.

78. Ibid., 133.

79. Ibid., 134.

80. Ibid., 137

81. Ibid.

82. Ibid., 137, 141.

83. Cassidy, "Becoming Black," 153.

84. Barbara Hilkert Adolsen, "Social Justice, the Common Good, and New Signs of Racism," in *Interrupting White Privilege*, ed. Cassidy and Mikulich, 56–74.

85. Charles E. Curran, "White Privilege: My Theological Journey, " in *Interrupting White Privilege*, ed. Cassidy and Mikulich, 181, 183.

86. Ibid., 181.

87. See Garth Kasimu Baker-Fletcher, *Dirty Hands: Christian Ethics in a Morally Ambiguous World* (Minneapolis: Fortress Press, 2000), 125. He writes that small acts "are part of a large chorus of choices others are also making."

88. Roger Haight "The Dysfunctional Rhetoric of 'White Privilege' and the Need for 'Racial Solidarity,'" in *Interrupting White Privilege*, ed. Cassidy and Mikulich, 89.

89. Curran, "White Privilege," 181.

90. Laurie Cassidy and Alex Mikulich, "Introduction," in *The Scandal of White Complicity in US Hyper-Incarceration: A Nonviolent Spirituality of White Resistance*, ed. Laurie Cassidy, Alex Mikulich, and Margaret Pheil (New York: Palgrave Macmillan, 2013), 8, 9.

91. Ibid., 10.

92. John Berkman attempts a similar appropriation of the tradition; see John Berkman, "Are We Addicted to the Suffering of Animals? Animal Cruelty and the Catholic Moral Tradition," in *A Faith Embracing All Creatures: Addressing Commonly Asked Questions about Christian Care for Animals*, ed. Tripp York and Andy Alexis-Baker (Eugene, OR: Wipf & Stock, 2012), 124–37.

93. Curran notes that most Catholic discussions of cooperation assume the evil in question; Curran, *Ongoing Revision*, 218. We must do better, but here I replicate this traditional limitation.

94. Jenny Truax, "Laboring to Resist," *The Roundtable: Beginning to Live in a Different Way*, Spring 2004, 17, available at http://newsite.karenhousecw.org/.

95. Julie Jakimczyk and Tony Hilkin, "The Greening of Anarchism," *The Roundtable: Beginning to Live in a Different Way*, Spring 2004, 7.

96. *Roundtable*, Spring 2004.

97. Keenan, "Prophylactics," 209.

98. John Paul II, *Sollicitudo Rei Socialis*, no. 28.

99. Tom Beaudoin, *Consuming Faith: Integrating Who We Are with What We Buy* (Lanham, MD: Sheed & Ward, 2003), 10.

100. Ibid., 66.

101. Ibid. Recent fires in sweatshops in Bangladesh brought additional scrutiny to clothing manufacturing and showed again how very vulnerable most workers are to unsafe conditions, low wages, and lack of oversight; see Stephanie Clifford, "Some Retailers Say More about Their Clothing's Origins," *New York Times*, May 8,

2013, http://www.nytimes.com/2013/05/09/business/global/fair-trade-movement-extends-to-clothing.html?pagewanted=1&_r=1&hpClothing.

102. See Jason Burke, "Bangladesh Factory Fires: Fashion Industry's Latest Crisis," *The Guardian*, December 8, 2013, http://www.theguardian.com/world/2013/dec/08/bangladesh-factory-fires-fashion-latest-crisis.

103. Cathleen Kaveny, *Law's Virtues: Fostering Autonomy and Solidarity in American Society* (Washington, DC: Georgetown University Press, 2012), 262–63.

104. Jone, *Moral Theology*, 94–95.

105. Germaine Grisez calls for reexamining the manualists' reliance on the category of remoteness in *Way of the Lord Jesus*, 890. I agree, but hold that when we begin to name remote material cooperation with evil, because of the nearly limitless ways in which we cooperate, the principle should function only as a tool for discernment and growth in virtue.

106. Kaveny, "Appropriation of Evil," 300–301.

107. Ibid., 303.

108. Ibid., 305–6.

109. McHugh, *Moral Theology*, 623–24. Grave reasons include loss of a day's wages, loss of one's job or a large portion of goods, a severe illness, death, or disgrace.

110. Second-hand clothes are not completely free of the taint of the sweatshops from which they emerge. Though one is not cooperating with evil, one is still appropriating it. As one Catholic Worker friend puts it, "I'm not buying evil, but I'm wearing it!" It is, one hopes, a temporary measure as we move toward a world of just wages for all workers and fewer and somewhat more expensive clothes for most.

CHAPTER 3

Why Bother to Act Locally?

The Potential of the "Space Between"

In the last chapter, I argued that the Catholic concept of cooperation with evil is helpful in connecting individuals to social problems, at both the local and global levels. In a complex world, connections to others are more numerous, and figuring out how to honor the Christian admonition to love one's neighbor becomes much more difficult. How am I best to love those who grow my coffee, harvest my oatmeal, sew my clothes, repair things in my home, ring up my groceries, attend my kids' schools, live in the shelter on the other side of town, or offer hospitality when I visit their country? In so many aspects of our lives, we rely on others and/ or affect their lives. We cooperate with evil or good.

Because we are so closely connected, questions about how to avoid evil and shape a better world through our actions inevitably arise. When they do, there is often a divide between those who advocate working "from above" for a reformation of social and political structures and those who believe in working "from below" for personal transformation that may lead to social change. In chapter 1 I upheld the humble optimism of faithful citizenship while beginning to raise questions about how much hope Christians place in politics. In this chapter I argue for a prioritization of the local, defined as "the space between" the personal (i.e., individual) and the political (i.e., governmental), including families, neighborhoods, and community organizations. Simply acknowledging the need for personal and political approaches might be seen as congruent with the "both-and" of the Catholic tradition. It is much-needed wisdom for a public mired in unhelpful, divisive binaries (e.g., big government vs. small government, social justice vs. moral reform, and structural vs. personal change). However, I go a step further in claiming that although an effective and truly compassionate approach to social problems demands a serious look at strategies for both political and personal change, we also must begin to pay more attention to the local level—that is, to associations such as neighborhoods, schools, community organizing groups, health care centers, businesses, charitable organizations, civic groups, unions, and churches.

Some worry that focusing on the local entails ignoring more significant political issues.[1] They ask, "Does what we do locally really matter? Is all the energy devoted to local issues misplaced? Given the influence of social structures, should we pay more attention to politics rather than less?" This chapter takes these questions as its starting point, arguing through five propositions that local strategies deserve greater attention in Christian social ethics. First, I claim that most people do not have the privilege of working for systemic change. Second, faithfulness and effectiveness are not necessarily opposed. Third, political reforms are necessary but insufficient. Fourth, personal conversion cannot be dismissed because of its potential to transform people and their practices. And fifth, local efforts can be even more effective means of social transformation if we pay more attention to them.

From a theological perspective, all thinking about how to approach social ethics is also ecclesiological thinking, because for Christians the church is the primary local community.[2] However, I argue that believers do not live out their faith solely through the church. Christians also live out their faith as they attempt to uphold the values of their tradition in their families, neighborhoods, and communities; and as they work alongside people of many faiths and no faith. Although churches are key sites where Christian social ethics is enacted, for most Christians, the local church is but one of many overlapping groups in which to move. Some churches provide ample opportunity for community, service, and advocacy. Others are much less socially concerned. For some Christians, both formation in solidarity and its practical application will be far easier in "the secular city."[3] By defining the "local" inclusively, as community, I hope to provide a broader base for locally focused Christian social ethics. Furthermore, I contend that it is in the local sphere where Christians of differing perspectives—along with those of other faiths and "nones," such as atheists and agnostics—can find common ground and collaborate in new ways for the common good.

A SOCIAL ETHIC FOR ORDINARY CHRISTIANS

It is crucial to begin by acknowledging the profound good that government can do. The Civil Rights Acts of 1964 and 1968 prohibit racial discrimination in schools, workplaces, polls, public facilities, and housing. The Americans with Disabilities Act of 1990 recognizes and protects the dignity of vulnerable persons. Programs such as the Special Supplemental Nutrition Program for Women, Infants, and Children (known as WIC), Section 8 Housing, and Medicaid provide food, shelter, and health care for millions of low-income people. Social Security and Medicare have severely decreased the poverty rate among the elderly. The public education system provides a strong foundation for many students, but changes in how schools are funded could extend these benefits to those who live in poor neighborhoods and struggle in failing schools. Current immigration laws allow many undocumented workers to suffer under brutal conditions, but comprehensive legal reform could give them a chance for a better life.

In comparison with achievements like these, the efforts of ordinary people may seem paltry. Cooking at a soup kitchen, tutoring a child, helping to provide shelter for homeless men and women on winter nights in a church basement, offering legal aid to immigrants at a community center, visiting a friend who is in the last months of life, counseling a pregnant woman in crisis—all these actions are good, but they are small. They do not seem to address the larger social problems that lead people to ask for help in the first place.

Yet, though all Christians have an obligation to aid the oppressed, not all Christians have the capacity to address serious social problems at the macro level. According to Pope Benedict XVI, in *Caritas in Veritate*, love of neighbor means working for the common good so that each person can effectively pursue what is good on his or her own terms. "To love someone," the pope argues, "is not simply to have good will toward another but rather to desire that person's good and to take effective steps to secure it."[4] Still, the ways in which people take up this responsibility will vary.

Some have vocations for the work of political or social reform, but most will work at the neighborhood or community level.[5] Some have more power, money, or influence than others. Nonetheless, the duty to engage in some kind of work for social justice as a manifestation of love of neighbor applies to everyone.

The call to conversion of *Caritas in Veritate* stands as a challenge to US Catholics. Ninety percent agree that concern for the poor is essential to Christian life, and a slightly smaller percentage claim to believe that an option for the poor is essential. However, 40 percent also believe that one can be a good Christian without actually doing anything for people who are poor.[6] Even if a majority agrees that making an option for the poor means doing something concrete, active concern for the poor is not central to their daily lives. Though most Catholic parishes collect food, presents, and/or clothes for the poor at various times of the year, very few have strong social ministry organizations that involve parishioners in ongoing service to their poor neighbors.[7] Though most Christians give some money to charity, the average family gives only 2 percent of its total income.[8] A recent study found that the wealthy give less as a percentage of their income than do those who are poor.[9] The words of Benedict XVI call this separation between feeling and action into question. Similarly, Pope Francis has consistently spoken of the obligation to act on behalf of the poor. In *Evangelii Gaudium*, he says that in the context of great inequality, "we can understand Jesus' command to his disciples: 'You yourselves give them something to eat!' (Mk 6:37): It means working to eliminate the structural causes of poverty and to promote the integral development of the poor, as well as small daily acts of solidarity in meeting the real needs which we encounter."[10]

Yet only a small percentage of Christians are lawyers, politicians, lobbyists, business leaders, or employees of nonprofit institutions with the capacity to reform society from the top down. One can certainly hope that more Catholic universities will encourage students to study in developing countries and major in political science, public health, or environmental studies; that more business schools at Catholic institutions will ensure that their many majors in business practices are informed by Catholic social teaching; and that Catholic law schools will turn out more graduates willing to use their skills to help the most vulnerable.[11] But the vast majority of Christians will encourage social change less from above than from below. For most, the sphere of influence is rather small: family, neighborhood, workplace, church, and community. The best opportunities for influencing how society is structured will come from their ordinary, day-to-day choices about where to live and work, what to buy and what not to buy, how much to give away, how to raise children, how to care for aging parents, and how to spend time in their communities.

This is why Benedict XVI's call in *Caritas in Veritate* for new lifestyles—in which the quest for "truth, beauty, goodness, and communion with others" drives economic choices of consumption, investment, and savings—is so significant.[12] For most people, apart from the few times a year they vote, write a letter, or give money to national or international organizations, the gap between personal and social ethics is not overly wide. Being a good person and making the world a better place both primarily entail engaging in action at the local level.

However, in large part, Christian discussions of social issues ignore the majority. Most of the focus is on solving systemic problems rather than working through everyday dilemmas.[13] In the first part of the twentieth century, however, some theologians did insist on the importance of personal action. William J. Engelen, SJ, wrote in the Saint Louis–based *Social Justice Review* that "reform cannot take place merely through legislation, for only a change of heart will bring back the observance of the natural law and social peace and prosperity."[14] Engelen's ideal was the organic, medieval society organized around families and small cooperatives with a limited role for government. In his view, that kind of change could only come through the power of grace and the medium of conversion.[15]

In his history of American Catholic social ethics, Charles Curran criticizes Engelen for the vagueness of his plan of action, and also for the insufficiency of relying on a change of heart.[16] In Curran's view, the more radical Catholic theologians of the twentieth century naively believed that social change could come about through a "change of heart" rather than through government intervention. From his vantage point, these thinkers seemed unaware of the complexity of modern social problems and of the need for reform at the macro level. In response, theologians of the later twentieth and early twenty-first centuries rightly focused on top-down structural change, and thus they put their energies into evaluating legislation and other political courses of action.[17]

However, many contemporary Catholics are coming to see that though work for structural change is important, a myopic focus on politics is just as insufficient as total reliance on personal conversion. Turning to politics is not always the best way to change structures. Change of heart is not the only alternative to politics. A range of strategic options should be considered. In a critique of Curran's history of the social mission of the American Catholic Church, William Cavanaugh claims that his narrative of progress from a focus on the parish to a focus on politics "oversimplifies the relationship of the Church to the world by reading it through the church/sect dualism, and in doing so too easily dismisses the relevance of pre–Vatican II efforts to conform the world to the Gospel."[18] US Catholics were not always as aware as they should have been of their political responsibilities, but Cavanaugh shows that they were still involved in important social change projects in their neighborhoods and parishes.

Catholic Social Teaching (CST) before and after the Second Vatican Council includes reflection on a diversity of ways of working for social reform. The principle of subsidiarity is central throughout the tradition, though the emphasis shifts toward politics as the tradition progresses. Thus in *Quadragesimo Anno*, Pope Pius XI taught:

> Just as it is gravely wrong to take from individuals what they can accomplish by their own initiative and industry and give it to the community, so also it is an injustice and at the same time a grave evil and disturbance of right order to assign to a greater and higher association what lesser and subordinate organizations can do. For every social activity ought of its very nature to furnish help to the members of the body social, and never destroy and absorb them.[19]

This principle, which has recently been summarized as "the lowest level possible and the highest level necessary,"[20] suggests the importance of family, neighborhood, church, and community action—all of which should precede a turn to politics.[21] References in all the documents of CST to prayer, family, virtue, and "intermediary groups" can serve as a foundation for an approach to social problems that is accessible to a broad range of people with varying degrees of power and influence. The theologian John Coleman asserts, "No one theme has so consistently been remarked on by commentators on the papal encyclicals as their insistence on a pluralism of societal authority and the right—derivative from the very sociality of human nature—of individuals to form associations intermediate between the state and individuals."[22] Owning the principle of subsidiarity means not just emphasizing the importance of personal conversion and lifestyles but also of intermediary associations or groups between persons and the government.

CST documents in the earlier part of the twentieth century, such as *Rerum Novarum* and *Quadragesimo Anno*, offered a vision of family, craft guilds, and smaller communities as an alternative to modern urban life. Later popes like John XXIII and John Paul II embraced the market, business and industry, and national and international governments. They exhorted Christians to enter and transform the world instead of withdrawing from it. Still, though the earlier visions of a simpler society are now seen by most readers of CST as nostalgic and unrealistic, they remain powerful reminders of a way of life that seems more human and suggest a need to envision new ways of humanizing the social order.[23]

Subsidiarity is not simply a principle celebrating the efficiency of smaller organizations. Rather, as Russell Hittinger points out, subsidiarity is "an account of the pluralism in society" or a principle emphasizing the reality of a "social diversity of functions."[24] In CST, the rightful place of associations is an essential component of a just society, and thus they are as important as the recognition of fundamental human rights and a system of checks and balances.[25] The role of associations flows from a recognition of human dignity and of the inherent goodness of the personal interaction that is only possible in smaller groups.

The very public debate during the 2012 election campaign about vice presidential candidate Paul Ryan's economic plan is but the most recent example of how Catholics and others have debated how this might work in practice.[26] However, Catholics on both the right and the left most often agree about the ideal of a rich associative life in civil society. In principle, everyone is for subsidiarity. Many mourn the loss of local spaces in which to make a contribution to the common good. In a recent essay, Cavanaugh describes the changes affecting the town of Westphalia's local Catholic parish, which in the 1950s sponsored a store, credit union, beauty parlor, garage, school, recreation hall, clubhouse, and baseball field.[27] Although, from our vantage point, we might be tempted to view this parish as monolithic and authoritarian, Cavanaugh cautions against dismissing it too quickly as constituting a "ghetto" or "sect" that took care of its own but ignored "the world." In fact, he argues, for the citizens of Westphalia, economics was not something one voted on, but rather "a community project of cooperative ventures that required the active participation of all the members of the body of Christ, . . . [and] their active involvement in each other's lives. . . . The people of Westphalia were profoundly engaged with the world. . . . For better and for worse, people were in each other's business, in all senses of that word."[28] Cavanaugh cautions that "the church should not abandon the hope that the followers of Christ can contribute distinctive visions of how to engage the temporal order, how to create new spaces of engagement with earthly life that do not simply bow to the inevitability of 'the world.'"[29]

In the associations to which CST so often refers, ordinary people are able to make their mark on society. As the social critic Wendell Berry puts it, "We need better government, no doubt about it. But we also need better minds, better friendships, better marriages, better communities. We need persons and households that do not have to wait upon organization, but can make necessary changes in themselves, on their own."[30] A Christian vision of social change should enable better reflection on just what each person is called to do in the spaces where most of us move most of the time. Cavanaugh's narrative of the pre–Vatican II parish underscores the point that local action is not simply the privilege of the wealthy. Often, those in less-privileged communities are more likely to support each other. Still, it is important to ask whether these kinds of actions are actually effective.

FAITHFUL AND EFFECTIVE

Although "the world" prizes effectiveness, as the ethicist Stanley Hauerwas rightly insists, faithfulness is the most fundamental ethical obligation of Christians. Our first responsibility is "to be faithful to the way that manifests the conviction that we belong to another."[31] Personal growth in faith takes place within a particular narrative and a particular community, where people's characters are formed as they attend to the stories of their tradition. Even when it comes to social ethics, we begin not "with attempts to develop strategies designed to make the world more 'just,' but with the formation of a society shaped and informed by the truthful character of the God we find revealed in the stories of Israel and Jesus."[32] Especially considering that most Christians have little political power and influence, it is certainly plausible that their primary responsibility, even their primary social responsibility, is not to change the world but to be good and faithful family members, neighbors, and members of local communities, especially churches.

Hauerwas further argues that small ways of acting in the world are justifiable precisely because Christians will be judged not by the effectiveness of their actions but by their faithfulness to Christ. Effectiveness, Hauerwas claims, is not a primary concern because "Christians are not simply called to do the 'right thing,' but rather we are expected to be holy."[33]

Similarly, Dorothy Day promoted "the little way" as a good choice, even though it does not always yield big results. She encouraged service to the poor without the expectation of positive outcomes, for at times, "there is nothing to do but love; . . . there is no chance of rehabilitation, no chance, so far as we can see, of changing them; certainly no chance of adjusting them to this abominable world about them—and who wants them adjusted anyway?"[34] She and fellow members of the Catholic Workers did hope "to change the world—make it a little simpler for people to feed, clothe, and shelter themselves as God intended them to do. . . . We can to a certain extent change the world. . . . We can throw our pebble in the pond and be confident that its ever-widening circle will reach around the world."[35] But theirs was a realistic hope, born of the belief that "we are sowing the seed of love, and we are not living in the harvest time. We must love to point of folly, and we are indeed fools, as Our Lord Himself was who died for such a one as this."[36] Living faithfully is the most important thing: "It is by the Works of Mercy that we shall be judged."[37]

Advocates of faithfulness as the essential mark of Christian ethics are onto something crucial. It does not make sense to judge persons solely by the outcomes of their actions. Consequences are not always under our control. Sometimes well-intentioned actions turn out badly. Social programs or policies that were once thought to be sound are later found to be lacking or even damaging. Thus, in the Last Judgment story (Matt 25:31–46), so often referred to by Dorothy Day, what separates the sheep and the goats is not whether they solved the problems of hunger and oppression, but whether they faithfully cared for those who were suffering through the works of mercy.[38]

However, valuing faithfulness does not necessarily mean forgoing, let alone being unconcerned about, effectiveness. To love one's neighbor well, one must aim to figure out what is truly needed, what is effective, and what is not. Concern about the poor is admirable, but evaluating the effectiveness of various strategies for ending poverty should be seen as an essential part of this concern. True compassion, as Maureen O'Connell has recently argued, means going beyond sympathy to asking hard questions about how to solve seemingly intractable problems. O'Connell urges reflection on the sort of compassion practiced by US Christians. She contends that the individualism and privatism of American Christianity "perpetuate a bourgeois complacency with the injustices inherent in the national status quo. . . . As a result, . . . we are more willing to believe in peace than live peacefully, to believe in equality than to treat others equally, to believe in the promises of abundance more than to work to create abundance for all. . . . Ultimately, we believe in compassion more than we act compassionately."[39]

Using the case of Hurricane Katrina, O'Connell shows how compassion inspired many to feel sorry for the victims or send money from afar, but not to question the "practical ineffectiveness of our suffering with fellow Americans."[40] To be truly compassionate, O'Connell claims, would mean moving beyond the comfort of charity to "wrestle with the social causes of Katrina's suffering."[41] Christians might need to become students of poverty reduction, as I argue in chapter 5, so that their efforts stand a chance of bearing fruit.

Though O'Connell encourages Christians to replace distant charity and vague feelings of compassion with social analysis and political action, she does not count on the government to solve structural problems. Rather, she puts her faith in nonprofit agencies working with local communities for social change. Having compassion does not mean abandoning local solutions. Rather, it means understanding social systems and then supporting local action that is effective not just in caring for victims but also in changing the very structures that victimize them. In the twenty-first century, new generations of Christians want to be truly helpful, but they are far less confident in the possibility and promise of political change. In this context, working "from below" with more modest hopes is not simply holy, nor is it utopian; it is both faithful and practical.

Those who work on the front lines often resist the insistence that, to be justified, their work must be successful. Gregory Boyle, SJ, the founder and executive director of Homeboy Industries in Los Angeles, makes just this point in his well-known book *Tattoos on the Heart*. He quotes Mother Theresa—"We are not called to be successful, but faithful"—and writes:

For once you choose to hang out with folks who carry more burden than they can bear, all bets seem to be off. Salivating for success keeps you from being faithful, keeps you from truly seeing whoever's sitting in front of you. Embracing a strategy and an approach you can believe in is sometimes the best you can do on any given day. If you surrender your need for results and outcomes, success becomes God's business. I find it hard enough just to be faithful.[42]

Boyle connects his own aversion to outcome-driven assessments to Jesus, who "just stood with the faithful until they were welcomed or until he was crucified—whichever came first."[43] He claims that Jesus could have chosen "a strategy that worked better (evidence-based outcomes)—that didn't end in the Cross—but he couldn't find a strategy more soaked with fidelity."[44] He even criticizes Dorothy Day (someone I would place more on his side of this argument) for asking, "Where were the saints to try and change the social order? Not just minister to the slaves, but to do away with slavery."[45] Contemporary Catholic Workers sometimes echo Boyle in their questioning of those who ask for results when the most important thing is to walk with people who are suffering.

Boyle and others who do the hard work that most of us avoid are right to speak of the unevenness of most social progress and to point out that seeking superficial success can lead people to choose less faithful and relational ways of helping. However, I would argue that they do want change for the people with whom they walk, and they choose those means that they believe are *both* faithful and effective, even if they would resist this language. No one wants suffering to continue unnecessarily, even if they believe we can never entirely escape it, and that we can grow from accompanying people who are in the midst of it. Jesus may have chosen a strategy that was foolish in the eyes of the world, but Christians believe that, ultimately, it is the only strategy that will actually save the world. Perhaps Boyle is right—we simply need to "stand with the vulnerable," "allowing our hearts to be broken," and trust that "God, through us, creates a community of resistance without our even realizing it."[46] But if we are trusting in the "slow work of God," does it not make sense to avoid work that we know to be harmful and do the work that will, as best as we can tell, bring healing and hope? Is there not an obligation to use our intelligence to figure out what this work is, and to do it? Surely "boundless compassion" must extend to wanting better lives for the people we care about?

In fact, Boyle claims success for his methods. He tells his audience that his organization "seek(s) to tell each person this truth: They are exactly what God had in mind when God made them—and then we watch, from this privileged place, as people inhabit this truth."[47] He says again and again that what broken people need is unconditional love, and when they receive it, they begin to see themselves differently and become different people. Not everyone. Not always. Not quickly. But no other strategy is ultimately more effective than love. For Christians, faithfulness involves finding more effective ways to love.

POLITICS: NECESSARY BUT INSUFFICIENT

The principle of subsidiarity discussed above requires an emphasis on the local but does not rule out investment in large-scale solutions. Pope Benedict argues that love of those neighbors who live outside one's home entails involving oneself in "the life of society, juridically, civilly, politically and culturally, making it the polis or city."[48] No one who claims to love others can avoid the social or political responsibility for creating and sustaining a society wherein people can pursue the good life as they understand it.

Pope Benedict challenges Christians to take the concept of gratuity beyond personal relationships into economic and political systems. Rather than allowing competition to rule the public sphere while calling for love in private, the pope puts forward the idealistic view that "social relationships of friendship, solidarity, and reciprocity can also be conducted within economic activity, and not only outside it or 'after' it."[49] Because the economic sphere is human, it must be ethical.[50] The "logic of the gift" must have a *place within normal economic activity*" (emphasis in the original).[51] We need to think about how larger economic systems and policies serve the true needs of human beings and make space for alternative economic initiatives that go beyond the ordinary moral demands of the public sphere in order to prioritize the needs of vulnerable populations.[52] In an age of great cynicism about business and government, Benedict nonetheless asserts that "both the market and politics need individuals who are open to the reciprocal gift."[53] His emphasis on development makes either isolationism at the national level or parochialism at the local level untenable.[54] He calls Christians to think more deeply about how the economic structures and institutions they support in their daily lives contribute to the common good, and in particular to the good of the neediest.

Yet many are justly suspicious or even cynical about the potential of politics. For instance, Alasdair MacIntrye claims that in contemporary society, because we lack shared conceptions of the good, advocate and vote based on our particular interests, and agree to a very limited kind of debate, "no place is left any longer for a politics of the common good."[55] It is only in smaller communities where practical reason and virtue can develop, and thus it is far better to place one's hopes in farming, crafts, and households than in political parties of any kind.[56]

Moreover, as more research is done on the effectiveness of social programs and political advocacy, more questions arise about their effectiveness. Often, Wendell Berry suggests, attempts to work on problems "from above" ends up not achieving the promised results. He sees enthusiastic advocacy for abstract causes without long-term, personal investment as ultimately futile. Local action must accompany political action, in his view, because this is the only way to effect lasting change:

> If we are to hope to correct our abuses of each other, of other races, and of our land, and if our effort to correct theses abuses is to be more than a political fad that will in the long run be only another form of abuse, then we are going to need to go far beyond public protest and political action. We are going to need to rebuild the substance and the integrity of private life in this country. We are going to need to gather up the fragments of knowledge and responsibility that we have parceled out to the bureaus, the corporations, and the specialists. And we are going to need to put all these fragments back together again in our own minds, and in our families, households, and neighborhoods.[57]

Similarly, in *Caritas in Veritate*, Pope Benedict XVI names love and relationships as central aspects of Christian social ethics. "Charity," he says, "is at the heart of the Church's social doctrine," the key principle for both micro and macro relationships.[58] Benedict knows how countercultural this will sound. He is aware of the growing pervasiveness of the market and technology, and he is asking what that does to us. What happens when so many of our interactions are founded on utility and not mutuality? He calls alienation "one of the deepest forms of poverty," and he challenges us to live more of our lives in a relational mode that is truer to our essence, saying that the more authentically persons live in relationships, the more human we become.[59] Because this is the truth of who we are as human beings, "the earthly city is promoted not merely by relationships of rights and duties, but to an even greater and more fundamental extent by relationships of gratuitiousness, mercy, and communion."[60]

Politics, nonprofit organizations, and other top-down solutions are necessary, but they alone cannot address social problems. Although some worry that small-scale solutions do not get to the root of problems, large-scale efforts also often miss the mark. The logic of gratuity must penetrate society from the bottom up. Because large programs that lack knowledge from below are bound to be less effective, they can only go partway toward solving problems. Families and communities must also work at the root level from below. As Paul Furfey wrote in the early twentieth century, though there is a real obligation to engage in political action, "our legislative program is, after all, only a minor part of our whole program. It forms only that part which concerns the state. Catholics have never believed that it was the function of the state wholly to reform society. . . . Such reform is the work of divine grace. The state can at most reform the external acts of man. The state cannot renew the whole man as a member of the Mystical Body."[61] Politics can force external actions (e.g., taxation, school integration, regulation of monopolies), but it cannot instill love for the poor, acceptance of others, or beneficence. "Yet," Furfey wrote, ""it is precisely this internal reform with which the Kingdom of God is ultimately concerned."[62] Therefore, if our political goals are not met, all is not lost: "There still remains our program of personalist action, and this is the real heart and soul of all Catholic social and political action."[63]

Furfey is right to stress not just personal conversion but also "the personal practice of social virtue."[64] Faith demands something of each Christian, not just socially important people, and personal transformation is an essential part of social change. However, Furfey's willingness to accept ongoing social sin and eschew effectiveness is troubling. If work "from below" alone is not effective, practicing social virtue must also mean developing better local, national, and international programs of action.

Charles Curran points out that early Catholic social thought, including Furfey's, can be justly criticized for being "conservative, cautious, and individually oriented. There was no talk about changing structures," at least in part because of a parochialism that kept Catholics from working alongside radicals, Protestants, and nonbelievers.[65] Curran upholds as a better model John Ryan, who advocated structural socioeconomic advances in the early twentieth century, including the minimum wage law, the eight-hour workday, child labor laws, unemployment relief, and Social Security.[66]

Today, however, it may be that structural change will come not primarily from the government but from local efforts that build on yet differ from traditional Christian practices. In his groundbreaking book *To Change the World*, the sociologist of religion James Davison Hunter criticizes Christian efforts at bringing about the kind of world they want to see. Hunter provocatively asks if the vast majority of Americans are already Christian, why has not more been accomplished?[67] He points out that other groups have been able to accomplish far more with far fewer people in much less time.[68] According to his analysis, effective groups contribute to lasting social change primarily by working through powerful social networks and institutions (i.e., the media, education, and the arts) to advance their agenda and move it so far inside the culture that opposing views become nearly unthinkable.[69] Rather than seeking "true believers" on the ground, they work in multifaceted ways with powerful people and networks that are capable of convincing not just one or two more souls to be "fools for Christ" but also an entire generation to embrace a radically different viewpoint.[70]

Following Hunter, Christians who seek "to change the world" must become more knowledgeable about how social change happens. If they want to be not only faithful but also effective, they should not only rely on the traditional strategies of politics, conversion, and charity but should also learn to use alternative powerful social and cultural tools, as other successful groups have done. Hunter shows how both the religious left and religious right have been corrupted by political parties and left without the change they so desire.[71] His call to diversity in social strategies is in keeping with a Catholic sensibility about the nature of society, which includes not only the state but also, and even more important, a "public sphere of social forms and norms."[72] Enacting political programs may seem radical, but it does not always get to the roots of the problem.[73] At least some radical work for social change must be done at the local level.

PERSONAL TRANSFORMATION THROUGH
LOCAL ACTION

Through their actions, especially their intentional practices, people are formed and transformed. This wisdom from the tradition of virtue ethics is as relevant to social ethics as it is to personal ethics. We become more just, compassionate, and merciful people through participation in socially just daily practices within the context of particular communities and traditions.[74] Thus, Christians should be concerned with forming people who embody the social virtues through involving them in local practices.

Though some theologians claim too much for the local, their defense of particular, relational experiences is an important corrective to the contemporary tendency to minimize the theological and ethical importance of ordinary daily life. These theologians mourn the dehumanizing effects of the postmodern, global world and urge Christians to imagine a different sort of life. Many emphasize the importance of "place" for human identity:

> To be human is to be placed: to be born in this house, hospital, stable. . . . It is to live in this council house, semidetached, tower block, farmhouse, mansion. It is to go to school through these streets or lanes, to play in this alley, park, garden; to shop in this market, that mall; to work in this factory, mine, office, farm. These facts are banal, but they form the fabric of our everyday lives, structuring our memories, determining our attitudes.[75]

Because "place" is crucial to identity, acting "in place" is acting in a fully human way, much more so than making an online donation to a nongovernmental organization. Local theology seeks to reclaim humanity from a mechanized system of powers. It is critical of universalizing tendencies and emphasizes that human beings are organisms, not machines, who, by acting in their local environments, become their very particular selves.

According to some, it is primarily in local environments that human beings encounter reality and are transformed. At the local level, claims Timothy Gorringe, God dwells and sustains us for "as triune, God possesses space. God in turn gifts space and time to us. Space is the form of creation in virtue of which, as a reality distinct from God, it can be the object of God's love."[76] Jesus himself, argues Clemens Sedmak, becomes human in a particular culture and offers human beings the chance to encounter the divine in the concrete and be converted.[77] The church, then, must be "first and foremost a *local community*, globally networked" (emphasis in original).[78] Here, Christians will come to understand what is real, because, according to Jürgen Moltmann,

> To be alive means existing in relationship with other people and things. Life is communication in communion. And, conversely, isolation and lack of relationship means death for all living things, and dissolution even for elementary particles. So if we want to understand what is real *as* real, and what is living *as* living, we have to know it in its own primal and individual community, in its relationships, interconnections, and surroundings.[79]

In coming to know reality in the concrete, Moltmann claims, people will come to know God in creation, begin to see the interconnections among all living things, and become motivated to change things, not through domination but through relationships with God, other human beings, and the Earth.[80]

Perhaps most notably, Stanley Hauerwas insists that the primary way in which Christians respond to the mess the world is in is not by trying to make the world more just but by participating in "the formation of a society shaped and informed by the truthful character of the God we find revealed in the stories of Israel and Jesus."[81] Christians strive "to be faithful to the way that manifests the conviction that we belong to one another."[82] Practices shaped by the narrative of tradition and a particular local community allow for personal transformation, communal transformation, and a powerful witness to the world of the way God intends human beings to live. Like Gorringe, Sedmak, and Moltmann, Hauerwas calls for a refocusing of attention on the local.

However, the Catholic tradition recognizes the importance of local action without absolutizing it; without claiming that it is the only way to know oneself, reality, or God; and without losing sight of the potential of a globalized world.[83] For instance, Benedict XVI makes a firm critique of globalization as we know it, while admitting its potential to unite people and calling Christians to transform it, saying: "The earthly city is promoted not merely by relationships of rights and duties, but to an even greater and more fundamental extent by relationships of gratuitiousness, mercy, and communion."[84] Still, the most important and transformative relationships for most people will be local.

Poverty is a prime example. In *Ecclesia in America*, Pope John Paul II argues that encountering Christ in the poor will reveal the truth of our interdependence and lead to genuine solidarity with the needy.[85] Convinced that only encounter leads to true conversion, he returns again and again to the theme of finding Christ in the poor, whose suffering recalls Christ's suffering.[86] He directs his listeners to spend time with people in need, assuring them that the practice of accompaniment is essential to the Christian faith. Similarly, Shane Claiborne, perhaps the best-known of the New Monastics, often says that "the great tragedy in the church is not that rich Christians do not care about the poor but that rich Christians do not know the poor. When the worlds of poverty and wealth collide, the resulting powerful fusion can change the world. But that collision rarely happens. . . . When the poor meet the rich, riches will have no meaning. And when the rich meet the poor, we will see poverty come to an end."[87]

The philosopher John Kavanaugh, too, challenges ordinary Christians by insisting on the value of "continuing and regular contact with the very poor, the dying, the lonely, the handicapped."[88] Without this contact, he is pessimistic about the chances of a Christian worldview taking root in people's hearts.

Working directly with the poor and vulnerable brings both privilege and poverty into sharp relief. Those who are wounded, Kavanaugh says, "have an unequalled power to educate us to our pretenses, our fears, and the rejection of our humanity. . . . They bear the wounds of humanity, visible before all, reminding us of our most dependent, fragile beginnings, of our diminishment and our dying, of our ultimate inability to manage and control either our bodies or our world."[89] In coming to know their poverty, we recognize our needs. This recognition of human incompleteness that comes in walking with the marginalized makes possible growth in love.[90] Direct contact can enable us to approach relationships with family and friends with a greater humility and willingness to sacrifice. This sort of service is practice in love, a school of virtue with the potential to transform the lives of both givers and receivers.

Many who engage in local efforts of this kind find themselves becoming connected to issues previously outside their sphere of concern. In response to growing personal connections with immigrants, homeless women, and needy children, they are compelled to reevaluate their habits of consumption, their charitable giving, and even their voting patterns. Attending political fundraisers or collecting canned food or running a clothing drive are much less likely to lead to those kinds of questions because they do not involve a personal connection with those on the margins.

This emphasis on the local does not lessen the urgent need for more people in Christian communities to invest in national politics, international aid organizations, and so on. It does not assume that the world can change only through personal conversions or changes of heart. Nor does it assume that we can only work locally because it is all we know. Local action is simply identified as the primary way Christians will engage the world. Yet, Christians must become more sophisticated about where and how they practice compassion and solidarity if they are to have any real hope of "changing the world."

POSSIBILITIES OF SOCIAL CHANGE FROM BELOW

It is important not to overstate the case for beginning with the local. Some theologians argue that the focus of all Christians should be on working within local Christian communities. Stanley Hauerwas started a revolution in theology by shifting the task of social ethics from policy to church polity. "Our task," he said, "is not to make these nations the church, but rather to remind them that they are but nations."[91] Many of his readers took him at his word; but because their local churches seemed incapable of carrying the weight that he claimed they ought to bear, they started intentional communities in which they could live differently from those around them. For instance, today's New Monastic movement looks back to Saint Benedict, Saint Francis, and Saint Clare, to the Radical Reformation, and to the slave church—responding to "the monastic impulse [that is] always calling the church back to its roots underground."[92] The movement's adherents see the church as God's instrument of salvation in the world, and they claim that the only way to participate in this saving action is to be part of the church: "If the Bible is a story about God's plan to save the world through a people, then my salvation and sanctification depend on finding my true home with God's people. Apart from the story of this people, I can't have a relationship with God. Without the church, there's no chance of becoming holy."[93] Holiness, not effectiveness, is the priority, for the church's mission is faithful living, not transforming the culture.[94] Saving the world is ultimately God's work, not ours.

New Monasticism's Shane Claiborne allows for more interest in effectiveness and social structures. His community, the Simple Way, "is about ending poverty, not simply managing it. We give people fish. We teach them to fish. We tear down the walls that have been built up around the fish pond. And we figure out who polluted it."[95] The church is still the main agent of social change, but the idea of the "irresistible revolution" is that, like the Kingdom of God, it spreads from below "like disease— through touch, through breath, through life. It spreads through people, infected by love."[96] Instead of mounting "a frontal attack on the empires of this world," Christians are called to live "a way of life that exists organically and relationally and is marked by such a brilliant love and grace that no one could resist it."[97]

Perhaps if more Christians really did live like Claiborne, the Christian way of life he champions would spread just as he says it would. Undeniably, individual choices can make a difference.[98] For instance, when I choose to buy fair trade coffee, I may set in motion a chain of events that ripples outward. Others may ask about my choice and reconsider their choices, I may ask that fair trade coffee be served at my workplace, more people in my social networks may begin buying and requesting fair trade coffee, and we may ask our churches to serve and sell it. If the same thing happens in many other communities, growers may see a spike in demand and produce more of it, and more farmers may be paid a just wage. This project may lead me to further reflect on what workers at my grocery store are paid and even to support living wage campaigns in my city. Through personal cooperation with good, we may be able to effect social change.

Cavanaugh argues that the church needs to "break its imagination out of captivity to the nation-state; it must constitute itself as an alternative social space."[99] He notes that though Murray praised the US experiment with a limited state that left plenty of room for intermediary associations to pursue higher goods, in fact the rise of the nation-state has been accompanied by the decline of associations.[100] In the place of the traditional Catholic distinction between state and society, we now have a fusion of the two, with the state claiming primary loyalty.[101] Instead, Cavanaugh claims, we need to look again to the parish-based model and think about what can be done by Christians working together to cooperate economically and help the needy who are close in proximity.

The potential of actions like these is worth exploring, but it is important to assess and improve their effectiveness. They are not praiseworthy simply due to our good intentions. We need to ask hard questions—for example, How much have fair trade coffee sales grown in the last decade? And what effect has that had on rural communities in Latin America and Africa? How many people have church-based programs helped move into jobs? Does microfinance really change communities, and if so, could churches adapt this model for local impoverished communities? Do marriage promotion and education programs have a track record of strengthening marriage? How transformative are service immersion trips? How effective are crisis pregnancy centers and abstinence education in preventing abortion and unwanted pregnancies? What would it take to ensure respectful care and good treatment decisions for more people as they approach the end of their lives?

The possibilities of effecting social change from below are there. Both what Furfey called "personal acts of social virtue," as well as what I would call "communal acts of social virtue," are worth considering and studying. The local realm includes families, neighborhoods, schools, workplaces, community organizing groups, churches, nonprofit agencies, and many other institutions that shape society. Hunter points out that Christians have placed too much hope in politics and that this has "delimited the imaginative horizon through which the church and Christian believers think about engaging the world and the range of possibilities within which they actually act."[102] He advocates a "disentangling" of the church from politics and an opening up of other possibilities for influencing culture via the arts, education, relief work, care for the sick, and the market.[103] Though not completely denying the need for political action, he calls for "a theology of faithful presence," suggesting that the more important work will occur in "families, neighborhoods, voluntary activities, and places of work, . . . [where we] do what we can to create conditions in the structures of social life we inhabit that are conducive to the flourishing of all."[104] I would only add that, to be truly faithful, this presence ought to be as effective as possible.

Christians cannot and should not completely disentangle themselves from politics. We do not need to choose between being faithful or effective, between a change of heart and social change. The Catholic tradition offers a more complex approach, in which personal, political, and local actions are all valued. However, because most Christians have more power and competence in the local realm and because relationships are so crucial to lasting social change, it is primarily in local places—in churches, families, and other groups of concerned people—where they can practice social justice and try to "change the world."

NOTES

1. In theology, most ethicists today focus on structural issues (e.g., war, racism, economic inequality, environmental destruction, hyperincarceration) rather than personal or local issues. Questioning of local solutions is also widespread outside theology. See, e.g., James E. McWilliams, *Just Food: Where Locavores Get It Wrong and How We Can Truly Eat Responsibly* (New York: Little, Brown, 2009).

2. Stanley Hauerwas challenged the field of Christian social ethics by making social ethics more ecclesial and more local. Many of his students follow his lead. See Hauerwas, *The Peaceable Kingdom: A Primer in Christian Ethics* (Notre Dame, IN: University of Notre Dame Press, 1991). See also Charles Pinches, "Hauerwas and Political Theology: The Next Generation," *Journal of Religious Ethics* 36 (2008): 511–42. Movements such as the Ekklesia Project, the New Monasticism, and the Catholic Workers can also be seen as localist in orientation.

3. Harvey Gallagher Cox, *The Secular City: Secularization and Urbanization in Theological Perspective*, 25th anniversary ed. (New York: Collier Books, 1990).

4. Pope Benedict XVI, *Caritas in Veritate* (Washington, DC: US Catholic Conference, 2009), no. 7.

5. Ibid.

6. For data on Catholics and the poor, see William V. D'Antonio, James D. Davidson, and Dean R. Hoge, *American Catholics Today: New Realities of Their Faith and Church* (Lanham, MD: Rowman & Littlefield, 2007), 37.

7. Mary Beth Celio, *Celebrating Catholic Parishes: A Study Done in Conjunction with the Cooperative Congregational Studies Project, Faith Communities Today (FACT)—A Preliminary Report on Roman Catholic Parishes* (Seattle: Archdiocese of Seattle, 2001), 10–11.

8. Dean R. Hoge, Charles Zech, Patrick McNamara, and Michael J. Donahue, *Money Matters: Personal Giving in American Churches* (Louisville: Westminster, 1996), 49. Other studies are similar, finding that Americans give 1.6 to 2.2 percent of their income away to all charities, with Christians averaging 2.4 percent, as cited by Craig L. Blomberg, *Neither Poverty Nor Riches: A Biblical Theology of Material Possessions* (Grand Rapids: William B. Eerdmans, 1999), 20. Charles Zeich notes that the finding of 1 to 2 percent is well established; see Charles E. Zeich, "Population Shifts Pose Problems, Opportunities for Church Finance," *National Catholic Reporter*, August 12, 2005, 6a.

9. Ken Stern, "Why the Rich Don't Give to Charity," *The Atlantic*, April 2013, http://www.theatlantic.com/magazine/archive/2013/04/why-the-rich-dont

-give/309254/. See also Paul K. Piff, Michael W. Kraus, Stéphane Côté, Bonnie Hayden Cheng, and Dacher Keltner, "Having Less, Giving More: The Influence of Social Class on Prosocial Behavior," *Journal of Personality and Social Psychology*, July 12, 2010, http://www.krauslab.com/SESprosocialJPSP.2010.pdf.

10. Pope Francis, *Evangelii Gaudium*, 2013, no. 118, http://w2.vatican.va /content/francesco/en/apost_exhortations/documents/papa-francesco_esortazione -ap_20131124_evangelii-gaudium.html.

11. Gregory R. Beabout with Bonnie Wilson, "Sustainability and the Proper Role of Business Leaders: Economics, Moral Philosophy, and Jesuit Education," *Journal of Jesuit Business Education* 5, no. 1 (Summer 2014): 51–69.

12. Pope Benedict XVI, *Caritas in Veritate*, no. 51.

13. For a more sustained discussion of this problem, see Julie Hanlon Rubio, *Family Ethics: Practices for Christians* (Washington, DC: Georgetown University Press, 2010).

14. Quoted by Charles E. Curran, *American Catholic Social Ethics: Twentieth-Century Approaches* (Notre Dame, IN: University of Notre Dame Press, 1982), 103.

15. Ibid., 126.

16. Ibid., 129.

17. Ibid., 287.

18. William T. Cavanaugh, "Westphalia and Back: Complexifying the Church–World Duality in Catholic Thought," *Journal of Catholic Moral Theology* 2, no. 2 (2013): 10–11.

19. Pope Pius XI, *Quadragesimo Anno*, http://w2.vatican.va/content/pius-xi /en/encyclicals/documents/hf_p-xi_enc_19310515_quadragesimo-anno.html.

20. Meghan Clark, "Subsidiarity Is a Two-Sided Coin," http://catholicmoral theology.com/subsidiarity-is-a-two-sided-coin/.

21. Subsidiarity is a particularly strong focus in the early documents of Catholic Social Teaching, In *Rerum Novarum* and *Quadragesimo Anno*, Pope John XXIII and Pope Paul VI turned their gaze to international issues, emphasizing solidarity. Pope John Paul II reclaimed the dual focus and spoke much more about the social responsibilities of individual families, and Pope Benedict XVI turned even more to the local. See Rubio, *Family Ethics*, 37–65.

22. John A. Coleman, *100 Years of Catholic Social Thought: Celebration and Challenge* (Maryknoll, NY: Orbis, 1991), 37–38.

23. See Christine Firer Hinze, "Commentary on *Quadragesimo anno*," in *Modern Catholic Social Teaching: Commentaries & Interpretations*, ed. Kenneth R. Himes, OFM (Washington, DC: Georgetown University Press, 2005), 168–72.

24. Russell Hittinger, "Introduction to Modern Catholicism," in *The Teachings of Modern Roman Catholicism on Law, Politics, and Human Nature*, ed. Johan Witte Jr. and Frank Alexander (New York: Columbia University Press,

2007), 22–23. See also Russell Hittinger, "The Coherence of the Four Basic Principles of Catholic Social Doctrine: An Interpretation," *Nova et Vetera* 7, no. 4 (2009): 791–838.

25. Ibid.

26. See, e.g., Julie Hanlon Rubio, "A Wide Space for Prudence" (and the debate that follows in the comments section), http://catholicmoraltheology .com/a-wide-space-for-prudence/.

27. Cavanaugh, "Westphalia," 3.

28. Ibid., 18.

29. Ibid., 19–20.

30. Wendell Berry, "Think Little," in *A Continuous Harmony* (New York: Harcourt Brace, 1972), 71–86.

31. Stanley Hauerwas, *A Community of Character: Toward a Constructive Christian Social Ethic* (Notre Dame, IN: University of Notre Dame Press, 1981), 130.

32. Ibid., 92.

33. Stanley Hauerwas, *In Good Company: The Church as Polis* (Notre Dame, IN: University of Notre Dame Press, 1995), 155.

34. Dorothy Day, "Love Is the Measure," reprinted by Robert Ellsberg, ed., *Dorothy Day: Selected Writing* (Maryknoll, NY: Orbis, 1998), 98.

35. Ibid.

36. Dorothy Day, "The Scandal of the Works of Mercy," reprinted in *Dorothy Day*, ed. Ellsberg, 99.

37. Ibid., 100.

38. Day quotes an unnamed work of Henri de Lubac on the duty of Christianity to form saints, not leaders: "The saint does not have to bring about the great temporal achievements; he is the one who succeeds in giving us at least a glimpse of eternity despite the thick opacity of time"; quoted by Dorothy Day, "Here and Now," reprinted in *Dorothy Day*, ed. Ellsberg, 102.

39. Maureen O'Connell, *Compassion: Loving Our Neighbor in an Age of Globalization* (Maryknoll, NY: Orbis, 2009), 28.

40. Ibid., 9.

41. Ibid., 157.

42. Gregory Boyle, *Tattoos on the Heart: The Power of Boundless Compassion* (New York: Simon & Schuster, 2010), 167, 168.

43. Ibid., 172.

44. Ibid., 173.

45. Quoted in ibid., 173.

46. Ibid., 177.

47. Ibid., 192.

48. Pope Benedict XVI, *Caritas in Veritate*, no. 7.

49. Ibid., no. 36.

50. Ibid.

51. Ibid.

52. Ibid., nos. 37, 38.

53. Ibid., no. 39.

54. Ibid., no. 8.

55. Alasdair MacIntyre, "Politics, Philosophy, and the Common Good," in *The MacIntyre Reader*, ed. Kelvin Knight (Notre Dame, IN: University of Notre Dame Press, 1998), 238.

56. Ibid., 243.

57. Berry, "Think Little," 86.

58. Pope Benedict XVI, *Caritas in Veritate*, no. 2.

59. Ibid., no. 53.

60. Ibid., no. 6.

61. Paul Furfey, *Fire on the Earth* (New York: Macmillan, 1936), 90–91.

62. Ibid., 92.

63. Ibid.

64. Ibid., 94.

65. Curran, *American Catholic Social Ethics*, 22–23.

66. Ibid., 51–52.

67. James Davidson Hunter, *To Change the World: The Irony, Tragedy, and Possibility of Christianity in the Late Modern World* (New York: Oxford University Press, 2010), 19.

68. Ibid., 20–21.

69. Ibid., 32–47.

70. Robert Putnam and David Campbell point out that liberal views on homosexuality have risen extraordinarily rapidly and are currently the single most important factor influencing the movement of young adults away from organized religion. See Robert D. Putnam and David E. Campbell, *American Grace: How Religion Divides and Unites Us* (New York: Simon & Schuster, 2010), 129.

71. Hunter, *To Change the World*, 111–49.

72. Russell Hittinger, "Social Roles and Ruling Virtues in Catholic Social Doctrine," *Annales theologici* 16 (2002): 317.

73. Jon Sobrino, SJ, *Where Is God? Earthquake, Terrorism, Barbarity, and Hope* (Maryknoll, NY: Orbis, 2004), 84. Many people suggest that local efforts do not get to the root but that political solutions do. For Sobrino, the roots are not only structural but also cultural and spiritual.

74. Here I am drawing upon MacIntyre's chapter titled "The Nature of the Virtues," in *After Virtue: A Study of Moral Theory*, 2nd ed., by Alasdair MacIntyre (Notre Dame, IN: University of Notre Dame Press, 1984), 181–203.

75. Timothy Gorringe, *A Theology of the Built Environment: Justice, Empowerment, Redemption* (Cambridge: Cambridge University Press, 2002), 1.

76. Ibid., 43.

77. Clemens Sedmak, *Doing Local Theology: A Guide for Artisans of a New Humanity* (Maryknoll, NY: Orbis, 2002), 16.

78. Gorringe, *Theology*, 185.

79. Jürgen Moltmann, *God in Creation* (Minneapolis: Fortress Press, 1985), 3.

80. Ibid.

81. Hauerwas, *Community of Character*, 92. See also Stanley Hauerwas and Samuel Wells, "Christian Ethics as Informed Prayer," in *The Blackwell Companion to Christian Ethics*, ed. Stanley Hauerwas and Samuel Wells (Oxford: Blackwell, 2004), 3–12. Hauerwas drew upon the work of John Howard Yoder, *The Original Revolution: Essays on Christian Pacifism* (Scottsdale, AZ: Herald Press, 1971). Wells, among others, followed Hauerwas's lead. See Samuel Wells, *Improvisation: The Drama of Christian Ethics* (Grand Rapids: Brazos, 2004).

82. Hauerwas, *Community of Character*, 130.

83. See, e.g., Charles Curran's defense of the Catholic tradition and critique of Hauerwas: Charles Curran, *Catholic Moral Theology in the United States: A History* (Washington, DC: Georgetown University Press, 2008), 158–60. See also William T. Cavanaugh, *Being Consumed: Economics and Christian Desire* (Grand Rapids: William B. Eerdmans, 2008), 59–88.

84. Pope Benedict XVI, *Caritas in Veritate*, no. 6.

85. Pope John Paul II, *Ecclesia in America* (Washington, DC: US Catholic Conference, 1999), no. 52.

86. Ibid., no. 12.

87. Shane Claiborne, *The Irresistible Revolution: Living as an Ordinary Radical* (Grand Rapids: Zondervan, 2006), 113–14.

88. John F. Kavanaugh, *Following Christ in a Consumer Society*, 25th anniversary ed. (Maryknoll, NY: Orbis, 2006), 189.

89. Ibid.

90. Ibid., 204.

91. Hauerwas, *Community of Character*, 100.

92. Jonathan Wilson-Hartgrove, *The New Monasticism: What It Has to Say to Today's Church* (Grand Rapids: Brazos, 2008), 53.

93. Ibid., 58.

94. Jonathan R. Wilson, *Living Faithfully in a Fragmented World: Lessons for the Church from MacIntyre's After Virtue* (London: T&T Clark, 1998), 60.

95. Claiborne, *Irresistible Revolution*, 123.

96. Ibid., 159.

97. Ibid., 348.
98. Michael Pollan, "Why Bother?" http://michaelpollan.com/articles-archive /why-bother.
99. Cavanaugh, "Westphalia," 43.
100. Ibid., 25–29.
101. Ibid., 33–35.
102. Hunter, *To Change the World*, 185.
103. Ibid., 186.
104. Ibid., 247.

PART II

———

Cases

CHAPTER 4

Family

What Does It Mean to Be Promarriage?

What does it mean to defend marriage and the family? The left and right see the problems differently, and understandably they have adopted different strategies. For those on the right, same-sex marriage is the key focus. Conservative Christians hold that unless marriage is publicly defined as between one man and one woman, the deinstitutionalization of marriage will continue.[1] People will increasingly choose to delay marriage, redefine it, or avoid it altogether; and society will cease to privilege one family form over others. In the public rhetoric of the US Conference of Catholic Bishops (USCCB), exemplified on its website, the defense of marriage is primarily associated with fighting against same-sex marriage and promoting traditional gender roles.[2] However, the USCCB's recent pastoral letter on marriage has a somewhat wider focus.[3] The letter is organized around four threats to marriage: divorce, cohabitation, contraception, and same-sex marriage. The website includes links to pastoral initiatives that address the serious issues faced by all married couples, but the energy placed here is minor compared with the huge resources devoted to the defense of marriage at the policy level.[4] Especially notable is the limited attention given to the problems of commitment, domestic violence, infidelity, and conflict that destroy so many marriages.[5] Also nearly absent is sustained attention to everyday problems, such as money, sex, housework, time, parenting, and the work/life balance that couples themselves typically identify as serious threats to marriage.[6] Advocacy groups and think tanks—such as the Knights of Columbus, the National Organization for Marriage, Focus on the Family, the Heritage Foundation, the Family Research Council, and ProtectMarriage.com—are similarly invested in defending marriage by blocking same-sex marriage initiatives in the courts and legislatures, while rarely addressing the problems of ordinary married couples.[7]

On the left, support for same-sex marriage continues to grow, and the tide of change seems almost impossible to reverse.[8] Supporters see the expansion of same-sex marriage as just rather than as threatening, given that one of their main concerns is supporting diverse family arrangements. Many liberal organizations, rather than seeing marriage and the family as policy concerns, identify their concerns as lesbian, gay, bisexual, and transgender issues; women's issues; and poverty.[9] For organizations such as the Center for American Progress, the Brookings Institute, CLASP, Voice of the Faithful, DignityUSA, Call to Action, and Catholics in Alliance for the Common Good, defending marriage and the family means expanding access to marriage for those who desire it, decreasing the stigmas associated with divorce and cohabitation, and advocating government support for families in need. Here, too, the everyday problems of ordinary families are only rarely addressed because the focus is primarily on policy change.

In the middle, a "New Conversation on Marriage" is emerging. The formerly right-wing Institute for American Values recently moved to the center with its call for dialogue involving liberals and conservatives who could put aside some important questions in order to focus on others, including high divorce rates, rising cohabitation rates, and increased childbearing outside marriage.[10] An interesting coalition of people is finding agreement on the enduring relevance of marriage and worrying about the consequences of current family instability.

When it comes to the issue of family instability, the conservative Heritage Foundation and the liberal Brookings Institution sound remarkably alike. Ron Haskins, codirector of the Brookings Center on Children and Families and Budgeting for National Priorities Project, argues that "there is no issue of greater importance to the future of the nation than the decline of marriage and the ascendency of nonmarital births." He claims that "the most important promarriage argument is that children grow and develop best when they live with their married parents."[11] The Heritage Foundation's Marshall Plan for Marriage responds to family breakdown with recommendations to eliminate marriage penalties in social welfare, health care, and tax laws, as well as with advocacy for education designed to help parents develop skills for healthy relationships.[12] A same-sex marriage advocate, Jon Corvino, acknowledges continuing divisions yet asks, "But, meanwhile, there are important questions that deserve more attention than they're getting: What is the social and personal significance of marriage? How can we promote a healthy marriage culture, for both adults and children?"[13] Isabel V. Sawhill, a senior fellow at the Brookings Institution, sees concern for "the wholesale retreat from stable two-parent families" as part of her commitment to vulnerable children.[14]

Thus far, Catholics have not been major participants in the New Conversation, but they could be. Certainly, conservative Catholics articulate concerns about divorce and cohabitation, though strategies to strengthen marriage and reduce divorce are far less visible than efforts to oppose same-sex marriage. Liberal Catholics are often embarrassed by their church's public message on marriage and thus are reluctant to talk about single parenting, cohabitation, or divorce for fear of being seen as judgmental or as neglecting what they see as the more serious problems of poverty, racism, and sexism.

In this chapter, however, I contend that common ground between left and right can be found in a shared belief in the enduring relevance of marriage, in acknowledgment of the need to prepare men and women for the challenges of married life and parenting, in recognition of the duty to help more families find financial security, and in an obligation to help couples avoid divorce if possible or find support if they do part. If those with differing identities can set aside the more contentious marriage debates for a season, they can spend time considering how to better respond to the most serious threats to marriage. In this chapter I argue that by offering the best of our contemporary theology—and by focusing on marriage and relationship education, family-friendly economic initiatives, and support for those who are considering or are affected by divorce—Catholics can find common ground and strengthen the families they all care so much about.

A THEOLOGICAL VISION OF MARRIAGE

Given the difficult concrete problems of cohabitation, divorce, domestic violence, difficult relationships, and economic instability, why begin with vision? If those involved in the New Conversation on Marriage are right, trends in family life are seriously compromising the health of individuals, families, and society. It may seem more practical to begin rolling up our sleeves to work together on the problems we all can see, rather than asking esoteric questions such as "What is marriage?" If common ground and tangible progress are the goals, some might think that beginning with foundational issues is exactly the wrong strategy. If we try to talk about vision, perhaps those on the left will privilege romance and diversity of form, while resisting the traditional condemnations of "pelvic theology," whereas those on the right will continue to speak of marriage as procreative, exclusive, permanent, and complementary, and thus place a high priority on holding to traditional boundaries. Perhaps it would be more prudent to simply agree to disagree on big picture issues.

In fact, it does make sense to leave some unresolvable disagreements aside for the sake of conversation and tangible progress. However, we still need a language that can allow speech across common fault lines and orient people for common work. Moreover, we may find that common language is not impossible because we agree on more than we think we do. One only needs to look at social media to see that liberals and conservatives alike use the language of "best friends," "partners," and "love of my life" to celebrate engagements, weddings, and anniversaries. In popular culture, agreement is also very much in evidence, as evidenced by the popularity of the movies *Before Sunrise*, *Before Sunset*, and *Before Midnight*, which mark moments in the relationship of a couple, played by the same actors over two decades. These movies' appeal transcends culture war boundaries. Viewers have connected with the realistic portrayal of two people drawn to each other, despite distance and circumstance, and have relished the opportunity to see the couple growing and changing in their twenties, thirties, and forties. Valuing the beauty and difficulty of long-term relationships transcends cultural divides. Thus the New Conversation on Marriage must involve building on this large piece of common ground. Many people can come together around a vision of marriage that centers on lifelong companionship, an equal partnership, and shared contributions to the common good.

Sociologists confirm that the desire for intimacy is increasing and that "companionate marriage" is fast becoming a worldwide norm. Whereas previously, families and communities played important roles in the selection of lifelong partners and delight in one's spouse was a pleasant but unexpected bonus, today many more see romantic love at the center of the choice to marry; they understand its lack as a serious deficiency. Couples themselves, rather than extended family or community, form the core of marriage and the family. Although most seek the blessing of family and value participation in an extended family, neither is required. Children continue to be a fundamentally important part of marriage and are often the impetus for marriage following cohabitation, but they are no longer the primary reason for getting married.[15] Most couples still marry with the expectation that they will bring children into the world, adopt, or coparent the children they already have, but home or marriage often precede children, and most will share long years together after their children are grown. Their loving relationship is the heart of their marriage.

In the United States, which is perhaps the epicenter of the movement toward companionate marriage, young adults overwhelmingly say that they would like to marry their "soul mate."[16] Only a small minority thinks that marriage is primarily about having and raising children.[17] To "settle" for someone who has the potential to be a good provider and partner would be, for most Americans, to deny something fundamental to marriage. Instead, they seek what the sociologist Andrew Cherlin calls "a Super relationship," an intensely private spiritualized union, combining sexual fidelity, romantic love, emotional intimacy, and togetherness."[18]

Christians ought to rejoice in this development. Contemporary Christian theology, too, has increasingly come to appreciate the value of intimate companionship. Married theologians have been particularly good at describing how marriage can be "an intimate partnership of life and love," though few use the formal language that is sometimes favored in traditional theology.[19] Instead, they speak of spouses as best friends who belong to each other, of lovers who delight in each other's touch, of partners who share a willingness to stretch and be changed for each other. Through the graced and the heartbreaking moments of marriage, theologians have written, we become who we are meant to be: people who can love with our whole beings.[20]

The contemporary, positive view of marriage also has its problematic underside, because higher expectations for personal relationship are accompanied by greater instability, which is evident in high rates of divorce and single parenthood. Furthermore, according to recent surveys, nearly 40 percent of Americans say that marriage is obsolete, and only half are currently married, though the overwhelming majority wants to marry and eventually does.[21] However, in the United States, without the institutional structures, social norms, and family pressures that kept couples together in the past, family breakdown has become pervasive. If one includes breakups of marriages and cohabiting relationships, "family life in the United States has more transitions than anywhere else."[22] This instability has troubling consequences for children that are well documented.[23] Interestingly enough, liberal views on marriage and the family predominate in the more educated classes, where family stability still reigns. Stephanie Coontz points out that "highly educated people are much more likely than any other group to think that remaining single or having a child out of wedlock is an acceptable choice. Yet they are also more likely to marry than their less educated counterparts and are much less likely to have children out of wedlock."[24] Those with less education hold more conservative views of marriage; but because they, like the well-off, want "to be economically set" before marrying, they end up marrying later or not at all.[25] Marriage "is now a discretionary item that must be weighed against other options for self-protection or economic mobility."[26]

It seems nearly impossible to separate intimate companionship and relational instability. At the end of her study of the evolution of marriage, Coontz concludes, "Over the past century, marriage has steadily become more fair, more fulfilling, and more effective in fostering the well-being of both adults and children than ever before in history. It has also become more optional and more fragile. The historical record suggests that these two seemingly contradictory changes are inextricably intertwined."[27] Most social scientists who study marriage concur.

However, though Christians can agree that marriage has become more fragile as it has become more focused on the couple, they may reject the claim that those who want intimacy will need to sacrifice stability. The contemporary Catholic tradition draws from the dominant companionate marriage model but insists that lifelong vows provide the framework that allows for vulnerability and depth.[28] Covenant and commitment in marriage provide the context for intimacy. Fallible human beings need the discipline of covenant to hold them fast so that they can grow. Marriage is embraced not as a necessary institution to be endured for the sake of children, or as a crown to add to one's achievements, or as a natural state of bliss, but as one of the best possibilities that life offers for experiencing and practicing love, as a path to holiness involving both pain and joy. The grace that Christians find in marriage does not assume that wedded life will be free of trouble, but it does hold that God can be found in moments of great joy, experiences of painful growth, and the everyday gift of life in community. Most also allow that when staying together is too painful, it is better for spouses to part. But Christians hold out the hope that broken unions will be rare exceptions. This is a theology of intimacy grounded in covenant, a celebration of and challenge to the secular companionate marriage paradigm.

Similarly, the Christian vision both embraces and challenges the contemporary emphasis on egalitarianism. The belief that men and women should have equal opportunities and the freedom to choose a life in keeping with their talents and preferences rather than proscribed roles is growing.[29] Though a mismatch between men's and women's attitudes persists, both men and women are increasingly egalitarian in their views.[30] Egalitarianism is associated with greater satisfaction and stability, although some kinds of conflict will occur more often as men and women transition to different kinds of relationships.[31] Equality is sometimes blamed for rising divorce rates, because men and women with overlapping roles may no longer have as great a need for the other sex as they did in earlier eras. Yet decreasing functional dependence does not necessarily mean that marriage is unnecessary, as the stability associated with two-parent families shows. Rather, men and women are discovering a mutual interdependence based on individual strengths and weaknesses.[32]

Christian theology, too, has become more egalitarian, recognizing the rights of women to work outside the home and the gifts they bring to society. Although debate about gender differences continues, the vast majority of official Catholic teaching on marriage is addressed to both men and women, and asks of them the very same commitments to love, life, society, and the church.[33]

However, Christian theology affirms the growing acceptance of egalitarianism while emphasizing the necessity of mutual self-gift. Although the language of self-gift can be dangerous without a foundation of equality, when this foundation is intact, it is crucial.[34] Theological renderings of egalitarianism tempered by the language of self-gift cut against some secular accounts that can overlook the need for sacrifice and imbalances that are often (but not always) worked out over the life of a marriage. Equality need not be exact to be real. Because individualism and consumerism are connected with the rise of equality, it can be skewed in a self-asserting-over-the-other direction. Likewise, a theology of self-gift that is unaware of sexism can err by unintentionally providing support for a gendered appropriation of self-sacrifice and self-promotion.[35] However, an egalitarian theology of mutual self-gift rooted in a healthy self-love and a desire to give of the self can provide a solid foundation for all states of life, including marriage.

Finally, the contemporary Christian theology of marriage is marked by a call to couples to deepen their relationship and take their love outward to share with the world. Marriage is not simply about love, but also moves toward wider circles of community and solidarity, often beginning with the rearing of children. David Matzko McCarthy claims that marriage within the church "is a witness of faith. This great joy is ours because we are not alone; we are part of a people, a body, and a countersociety that sets itself to the task of living in light of God's self-giving love. . . . The promises of self-giving love are not our private possessions, but shared in the worship and works of the Church."[36] In his book *Sex and Love in the Home,* McCarthy writes about the ordinary practices of everyday life that sustain both families and communities. He contrasts the independent, upper-middle-class "closed" suburban home, where goods and services are purchased rather than exchanged, with the open home, where "ordinary practices of local interdependence are the substance of a complex system of interchange and a rich community life."[37] He explains that when people offer hospitality to other families' children, labor on home improvement projects, extra baked goods, or produce from a garden, they are engaging in an informal, asymmetrical network of gift exchange that, unlike the money economy, creates interdependent relationships.[38] Keeping up these practices is essential, in his view, for building community and maintaining a Christian home that is more than a private haven.

If, in the current cultural context, marriage is highly valued and yet often insular, a Christian vision insists that couples who will be together over the course of long lifetimes can be sustained by their commitment to community and draw strength from the people around them. This focus is absolutely essential to broadening the cultural understanding of love. The beautiful love story that begins in the movie *Before Sunrise* and develops in the sequel *Before Sunset* finally deteriorates in *Before Midnight.* The lovers, Celine and Jesse, are too familiar for the romance of first meetings or reunions, and too bitter to hold back anger over what being together has cost each of them. Though they still experience moments of passion, the two seem incapable of compassion or mutual support. Despite the fact that in *Before Midnight*, Jess and Celine are vacationing with friends and family, in the end they are alone in a hotel room with their anger. They have no larger narrative within which to place the suffering they are experiencing, no way to understand what contribution their witness of fidelity might make, no strong enough sense that their children deserve better from them, no community to which to turn for wisdom. Watching them fight is almost unbearable.

Although there is great beauty in the romance between the two, the dimension of solidarity is missing, and this makes their union more difficult to sustain. Romance alone is simply insufficient for grounding a lifelong relationship. But Christian theology can speak into this context with affirmation and a challenge, calling couples—young, middle-aged and old—to a communion of love grounded in community and compassion for others.

A vision of marriage marked by intimacy, equality, mutual self-giving, and solidarity can unite Catholics on both the right and the left who may normally find themselves disagreeing on concrete issues.[39] It is possible to build on shared desires for deep, long-term relationships, widespread valuing of equality over hierarchy, and an acknowledgment of responsibility for and support from others as essential to family life. The Christian vision is compelling and hopeful, and yet also realistic. A contemporary theology of marriage can bring together people from different sides of the culture war divide, challenge them to deeper love and fidelity, and call them into the good work of strengthening marriage, not just for themselves but also for all those who are touched by their union and for the wider society that needs the witness of their enduring love.

MARRIAGE AND RELATIONSHIP EDUCATION

How can Christians work to strengthen marriage so that more couples have the depth and joy that good marriage can bring? Both the conservative family values movement and the moderate "critical familism" promoted by the late Don Browning were controversial because they named the household as a crucial site where things were going wrong.[40] Many worry about public movements designed to encourage marriage or discourage divorce. The New Conversation on Marriage has the potential to be equally alienating. Especially when divorce, single parenthood, and cohabitation are upheld as problematic and marriage is promoted as a solution to economic and social problems, it can seem that those with less privilege are being blamed for not being virtuous while the social and economic structures that make marriage easier for those with more privilege to sustain are being ignored.[41] In the next section, I take up economic issues that need to be a part of a common ground approach to marriage and the family. In this section I ask, "If social scientists can point to significant differences between children born and reared in households with two married parents versus children reared in other family types, how should Christians respond?" Should we try to ensure that the government protects all families, especially those who are most vulnerable? Should the government, communities, or churches promote marriage? Could marriage promotion be disrespectful to those who make other choices? Are there other ways to strengthen marriage? I argue that because marriage fragility is disadvantaging vulnerable people but marriage promotion is tricky, we should strive to improve existing relationships by preparing engaged couples for marriage and by educating parents (married or not) about relationships and parenting. In all types of marriage and relationship education, Christians should highlight their foundational claim that marriage is a covenant made not for soul mates but for imperfect human beings who commit to work at loving each other and others well over a lifetime. We do need the New Conversation on Marriage, as long it respects people in all kinds of relationships and sees marriage as one part of a very complicated picture. This kind of conversation can lead to better marriage-strengthening practices and draw liberals and conservatives together.

Some who worry about the effects of nonmarital childbearing believe that marriage promotion should be a fundamental aspect of government and community responses to social problems. They argue that existing marriage penalties in tax and welfare laws should be eliminated and that funding should be given to states for marriage promotion.[42] Some would like to see promarriage messaging from the government and community organizations.[43] They argue that information on the disadvantages faced by children raised outside marriage and the benefits of marriage might be important, given that in low-income communities, marriage rates are lower and rates of children born outside marriage are far higher. For instance, the proportion of nonmarital births for white, college-educated women is

6 percent, whereas the proportion for white women who drop out of high school is 60 percent, and the rates are nearly as high for Hispanics who do not graduate from high school (58 percent) and even higher for blacks (86 percent).[44] Conservatives—arguing that low marriage rates disadvantage children and showing that marriage has much more potential to pull families out of poverty than increases in the minimum wage, high school completion, or other strategies commonly embraced by liberals—make a strong case for encouraging marriage.[45]

However, liberals tend to believe that poverty is really the problem. Young women with fewer resources make rational choices to wait on marriage because they are unsure about the stability of potential partners. They want someone who can and will support their children. Because good jobs for men with less education are lacking, women with less education have a small pool of "marriageable men" from whom to choose.[46] Support for marriage is actually higher among those who are less privileged than in more educated cohorts; there is no need to sell young women on the marriage ideal.[47] Marriage (especially marriage followed by divorce), however, is not necessarily the answer to these women's problems because poverty will disadvantage them no matter what relationship status they choose.[48] The gap between those who see poverty as the problem and those who see marriage as the solution seems unbridgeable.

But what if couples are already interested in marriage? Marriage preparation for couples seeking marriage in the church is an example of a good local marriage-strengthening initiative that addresses the problem of fragile families without stepping into controversy, but it can be improved. Programs vary by diocese and parish, but common elements include the "5Cs": communication, commitment, conflict resolution, children, and church.[49] Program length can range from one day to one night per week over several months. Though a priest is always involved in some stages of the program, most of the educating is done by married couples. Studies evaluating the effectiveness of marriage preparation typically find that a majority of couples rate the program they attend as at least "somewhat helpful," though only about a quarter rate their program as "very helpful."[50] A total of 5 to 15 percent of couples who complete a program decide not to marry, which is a valuable, if not intended, outcome.[51]

How can existing marriage preparation programs be improved? In surveys, couples who have attended programs say they would like to hear more about parenting, conflict resolution, and commitment but are less interested in discussions about housework, sex, or spiritual development.[52] However, research on the first five years of marriage suggests that the key problems for young couples are money, work/family balance, sex, and housework.[53] Couples that share a religious affiliation are more likely to stay together.[54] Given the changing sexual landscape of young adults, it is a serious obligation to discuss the potential challenges of how to maintain a good sexual relationship in marriage.[55] In addition, evidence suggests that unrealistic expectations set couples up for disappointment when commitment proves hard to sustain.[56] Discussion about money, time, housework, sex, spirituality, and realistic expectations should be important components of marriage preparation, and because these areas are likely to be areas of conflict, helping couples learn how to manage conflict is also crucial.

Current marriage preparation programs are less useful than they might be. They often fail to address work/family balance issues that accompany dual-career marriages.[57] Sex is also difficult to address. More than half of the couples participating in marriage preparation are cohabiting, and the overwhelming majority of participants disagree with official church teachings on premarital sex and contraception.[58] Only basic conflict resolution skills can be briefly introduced in such a short period. And only a minority of Catholics is even "somewhat interested" in learning more about Catholic teaching on marriage, and few view marriage as a vocation or calling.[59] The challenges are serious. Still, programs can be updated in light of contemporary realities, and the rich Catholic vision of marriage can be better communicated.[60]

Given the difficulty of preparing couples for marriage in one weekend, let alone in a day, mentoring couples in local parishes may seem to be an important contribution to the preparation phase. Catholics themselves say they prefer to learn more through printed materials rather than face-to-face contact, and those who have had experiences with mentor couples are no more likely to rate their experiences highly than are couples that have participated in traditional marriage preparation programs.[61] It may be that it is difficult to construct mentor relationships between couples that have no other connection, and it may also be difficult for couples to truly open up about problems when the cultural expectation is that marital problems are to be solved in private. Still, mentoring should be explored as a potential way for married couples to share their life wisdom with couples just beginning their life together.

The effectiveness of church-sponsored preparation programs is difficult to gauge. In a study completed by the Center for Applied Research in the Apostolate (CARA), the percentage of divorced or remarried Catholics who participated in various programs is not significantly different than the percentage of married Catholics who did the same.[62] Though the USCCB counts the programs as a success because a majority of couples find them at least somewhat helpful, the bar for success seems fairly low. Moreover, the longer couples have been married, the lower they rate the value of marriage preparation programs, indicating that this preparation did not give them the tools they need to improve marriage over time.[63] Larger studies of these programs find that participants report some benefit from them but do not show a correlation between participation and lower divorce rates; nor do they have sufficient data on more vulnerable lower-income populations.[64] Still, weddings offer an opportunity for church communities to reach out to couples that come to them and give them the perspectives, tools, and contacts they may need to sustain their marriages.[65]

Marriage and relationship education (MRE) targeted to low- and middle-income communities could be another key common ground marriage-strengthening program. Sometimes liberals worry that these kinds of programs substitute for antipoverty measures and impose values. However, it is possible to approach MRE as a complement to traditional antipoverty work, to make programs available to young adults regardless of marital status, and to focus on relationship skills rather than explicitly promoting marriage. Recent research suggests that, though much more testing needs to be done, there are good reasons to continue to pursue MRE. Knowing how to sustain marital relationships over time is much more important than finding "the one." Theodora Ooms concludes a study on marital stability by saying, "The overarching implication of the research to date is that, contrary to much popular opinion, the keys to marital success are not whether you choose a compatible mate, though this is important, nor how many differences you have, nor whether you can manage to stay 'in love.' Rather, success largely depends on the kind of relationship you build together and how you handle your differences."[66]

This conclusion is of a piece with the best of contemporary Christian theology of marriage. Stanley Hauerwas famously asserts that "we always marry the wrong person. We never know the person we marry; we just think we do. Or even if we do marry the right person, just give it a while, and he or she will change. For marriage, being what it is, means we are not the same person after we have entered it. The primary problem morally is learning how to love and care for this stranger to whom you find yourself married."[67] Or, he says in another place, the ethical challenge is learning how to care for those we are "stuck with."[68] Rejecting romanticism, he claims that "both Christianity and marriage teach us that life is not chiefly about 'happiness.' Rather, the Hebrew-Christian tradition helps sustain the virtue of hope in a world which rarely provides evidence that such hope is justified."[69] Though he might suggest that finding common ground on this understanding may be difficult, in fact, those who study marriage are similarly convinced that if people are to sustain marriages, they need help learning to love those with whom they are "stuck."

For parents who are expecting a child or already have a child, MRE can offer information on parenting and maintaining stable relationships. At the time of a child's birth, "a large majority of unwed parents have close and loving relationships."[70] Because "unwed parents have a host of demographic and human capital characteristics that complicate getting good jobs, forming stable families, and performing successfully as parents," they can potentially benefit from MRE.[71] Though research on outcomes is still emerging, voices from both the left and right argue that we should "refuse to give up on healthy marriage programs that have shown at least some promise in achieving the stability and positive parent relationships that could prove helpful for these couples, their children, and the nation."[72]

In Christian contexts, the emphasis of MRE should be more on character and community than skills. Thus David Gushee wisely points out that though many MRE programs assume that skills can be taught to anyone, "it takes a certain kind of person to actually practice the techniques being proposed."[73] Good communication

> requires an unselfish spirit of servanthood that many people do not have— and that no technique will magically produce.... Conflict resolution is actually, in biblical terms, peacemaking, ... [which] requires the willingness to initiate a reconciling conversation to repent and be forgiven, and to accept repentance and offer forgiveness. Thus, from a Christian perspective, this "technique" is a matter of moral commitment rooted in a disposition of the will developed with effort over time—and ultimately in devotion to Jesus Christ. Such character is nurtured in Christian community.[74]

This richer context gives churches offering MRE to Christians an advantage, but it does not mean that other community organizations cannot do effective MRE. The teaching of skills can be connected to the teaching of character in secular contexts. Educators can use the language of virtue ethics to talk about someone becoming a better person by engaging in practices and forming habits. Communities that offer classes are giving evidence of their support for relationships, especially potentially vulnerable relationships. Most churches will need to work just as hard as secular communities to inculcate in participants the idea that they offer not just benefits for individuals but also the accountability and support of a body of people committed to journeying together through life's joys and challenges.

Marriage strengthening is a cause that can be embraced by both liberals and conservatives, if programs are open to all couples and are skill based. Though there is still much to learn about how to adapt programs for low-income couples, researchers are finding out what works. People in communities of all kinds know that relationships are hard to sustain and see the value of getting information and training. MRE need not be punitive or preachy; it is not the old "family values" agenda in disguise. It is a new movement, responding to the challenges of the present, with practical concern for adults in intimate relationships and the children they bring into the world.

JOBS AND JUST WAGES

In the controversy surrounding fragile families, the key question remains, "Is marriage or poverty the problem?" The Center for Policy Analysis argues that attention to marriage is misguided. The real culprit is poverty, which makes women wary of marriage and men less marriageable due to unemployment or underemployment:

> It is indeed worthwhile to monitor and provide meaningful aid for this extraordinarily important symptom—the weakening and dividing of families—but to ultimately cure poverty, the nation must meaningfully address the problem of economic insecurity. Good job opportunities and high-quality wages will enable young adults to become ready for marriage, ready for life, and ready to increase their chances of success in the long haul.[75]

Some conservatives reject the claim that jobs are at the root of the problem, arguing that the majority of men have jobs that pay more than the jobs held by single mothers and are thus potentially good mates.[76] Scholars at the Heritage Foundation believe that because single parenting is strongly associated with poverty (e.g., single parents are almost six times more likely to be poor than married couples), and that because marriage, even between low-income spouses, is associated with greater wealth, the government should encourage marriage, much as it encourages high school graduation.[77]

Moderates concede that changes in cultural values are responsible for driving changes in family life, but they also agree that the virtual disappearance of good blue-collar jobs has played a role in the choices of low- and middle-income Americans to avoid or delay marriage.[78] A recent systematic study found that the lack of jobs with living wages is the most important factor in the persistence of poverty.[79]

Even the liberal Center for American Progress admits that poverty and family fragility are linked, though they do not back marriage promotion: "Despite these factors, marriage remains critically important and worthy of attention—not as a remedy but as a symptom of a much larger problem: the economic insecurity of those at the bottom of the economic ladder. Declines in well-paying jobs, unemployment, growing income inequality, and persistent poverty influence couples not to marry while generating pressures and conflict on those who are married, leading to separations and divorce."[80]

Poverty in the United States has been convincingly linked by liberal scholars to social and institutional racism. It is crucial to understand how neighborhoods develop, how schools are funded, how economic opportunities offered to whites are denied to blacks, and how severely continuing disparities in arrests and sentencing affect black communities.[81] In the case of my hometown of Saint Louis, for instance, Colin Gordon has documented the role of racism in the growth of the city, leaving no doubt that poor, predominantly black neighborhoods were shaped by the racist actions of politicians, real estate agents, and home buyers.[82] From the perspective of liberals, there is a great deal of work to be done in order to rectify the damage done to African American communities.

Agreement between liberals and conservatives as to whether the cultural values related to sex and marriage or the social structures of racism and poverty lie at the root of the growing class divide may be a long time in coming. In the meantime, both sides can find common ground by affirming that employment is a significant part of the problem. They can agree that good jobs make it easier for many Americans to sustain the marriages that most still say they desire. However, agreement on the best route for job creation from above remains elusive, because conservatives want to shrink government in order to free the private sector to create jobs but liberals believe that government programs and social benefits are needed to create true equality of opportunity.

At the local level, in contrast, it may be possible for Christians to engage in local actions as employers, cooperators with employers, and teachers of employment skills. To build a society in which people are able to form and sustain families, we need to be willing to pay living wages to the adults we employ. We may have a responsibility to buy, whenever possible, from businesses that pay living wages.[83] Catholic Social Teaching insists on the ethical imperative of the living wage. Because work is personal and necessary, any individual who contributes a day of labor deserves to be paid enough money "to support a frugal and well-behaved wage earner."[84] Although acknowledging the complexity of determining a living wage in particular contexts and in balancing the need of a business for profitability with the moral demand to pay living wages, Catholic Social Teaching does not back away from the bottom line: If people work, they must be paid enough to live. The moral implications for employers are clear.[85] Households have received far less attention. However, middle-class households may employ many different kinds of people—child care providers, house cleaners, yard workers, home renovators, home health care providers, repair people, and the like. One key question that needs to be asked when comparing bids is the question of a just wage.

The moral implications of the teaching on just wages for consumers have only recently been explored, but the modern popes have begun speaking of the consumer's responsibilities, suggesting that, to quote Benedict XVI, "purchasing is always a moral—and not simply economic—act. Hence *the consumer has a specific social responsibility*, which goes hand in hand with the social responsibility of the enterprise. Consumers should be continually educated regarding their daily role, which can be exercised with respect for moral principles without diminishing the intrinsic economic rationality of the act of purchasing" (emphasis in the original).[86] Ethical consideration of living wages in relation to consumption choices should be encouraged by churches and other community networks.

Although work to increase the minimum wage should continue, support for living wages can also be built from the ground up. The recent "Fight for 15" protests, advocating a national $15-an-hour minimum wage, have not yet led the federal government make major adjustments in the minimum wage, but they have made considerable progress. We are beginning to see states and large employers making changes in response to pressure from workers and consumers.[87] Christians can contribute to this movement from below.

In addition to taking advantage of the opportunities we have as employers and consumers to support just wages, Christians can also help disadvantaged people with job readiness. They can volunteer in and encourage their churches to support programs that provide job skills development and promote savings.[88] When most ordinary Christians engage in charitable work, they are helping people survive despite poverty rather than helping to move people out of poverty. By donating money, food, clothes, and presents, they hope to make the holidays a bit brighter or provide families with resources that will help them through the month. The more difficult work of ending poverty seems to belong to politicians and social workers. However, some churches are finding that they can fill a real need by helping people prepare for and find work.

A large number of unemployed people need more than a job.[89] Many lack the "soft skills" that make the difference in getting, retaining, and succeeding in a job. Some have never held a job, some have a history of starting and leaving jobs, some have been laid off, and some need to transition into a new kind of work.[90] Job readiness programs can be taught by volunteers who draw on the existing literature as well as their own experience in the workforce. For instance, the People First program developed by Midtown Catholic Charities in Saint Louis is designed to provide a comprehensive approach to unemployment.[91] From decades of experience working in a poor neighborhood, the program organizers understand that the obstacles to employment include drug and alcohol abuse, domestic violence, a lack of child care, a lack of transportation, spotty employment histories, and educational deficiencies. The four-week program addresses these issues through its staff and offers assistance to those who need it. It includes information about how to present oneself in an interview, write a résumé, and have conversations with an employer or fellow employees. There are opportunities to learn about networking, receive free second-hand business clothes, obtain bus vouchers, and get advice about banking and budgeting. Because the program meets four mornings a week for four weeks and allows only a limited number of absences, it gives participants a chance to practice the skills important to holding a job: showing up on time every day, conversing, reading, writing, and making plans with backups for child care and transportation. Staff members from the many other support programs at Catholic Charities visit the class to make participants aware of their services, including a Jobs Club that meets weekly to offer assistance throughout the job-seeking process. Over and over, participants are assured that the Midtown community is there to support them throughout the job-seeking process.

Churches are ideally placed to address both the complexity of unemployment and its spiritual underside. Bryant Meyers, a professor of transformational development, writes about the "marred identity" of the poor: "A lifetime of suffering, deception, and exclusion is internalized by the poor in a way that results in the poor no longer knowing who they truly are or the purpose for which they were created. This is the deepest and most profound expression of poverty."[92] The "internalization of poverty" makes it difficult for many of those who are poor to see their true worth.[93]

In one People First class at Midtown Catholic Charities, participants were practicing "30-second commercials" in which they describe themselves to a potential employer. One middle-aged woman had written down a description that included her strengths, but as she began to recite it, she stopped midsentence and sat down in distress, saying: "I can't do this. I haven't ever stayed at a job for more than a couple months." Because she felt that her commercial was a lie, she could not get through it. She did not think she had 30 seconds worth of good things to say about herself. When she first came to the class, it was even worse; she had been so isolated that just talking to new people was a strain. This time, others in the class were able to talk to her, advising her to leave the negativity behind and focus on the new person she was becoming. By the end of the class, she was not only able to articulate her own strengths; she actively affirmed the gifts of other participants and encouraged them to persist in working toward their goals. She knew that believing in herself was half the battle. The willingness of staff and volunteers at Catholic Charities to put so much time and energy into helping her succeed allowed her to recover a sense of herself, and she is now working her way toward finding long-term employment. We can acknowledge the profound social injustice that no doubt contributed to this woman's situation and yet agree that she, like many other unemployed people, needed personal and spiritual support as well as assistance with skills development before she could compete for a job.

Though advocacy groups should continue to push for the government reforms they favor, neither side needs to wait for Congress to act. Instead, they can work at the community level to address the jobs problem that all can acknowledge is related to family breakdown. Very few of the participants in the jobs readiness class at Midtown Catholic Charities have intact, two-parent families. One might argue that marriage promotion is the place to begin. However, to respond well to the problem of family breakdown, it is necessary to do more than strengthen families directly. Christians should also strive to strengthen the economic context that shapes personal choices. They should also seek ways to help people improve their lives within imperfect contexts. Despite disagreement about how to improve the economy, it is possible to find common ground and make common cause by supporting the sort of work that makes marriage easier to initiate and sustain.

HELPING MARRIED COUPLES AVOID DIVORCE AND PROVIDING SUPPORT AFTER DIVORCE

In the United States, divorce has affected more than 1 million children each year since 1973, and now one-quarter of young adults come from divorced families.[94] Although divorce rates have declined slightly since peaking in the 1980s, they have doubled since the 1950s and remain among the highest in the world.[95] In addition, 41 percent of all children are now born to unmarried mothers.[96] About half of these are single mothers, and half are cohabiting with a partner. So although these children are not usually counted in studies of children of divorce (CoD), they, too, experience disruption in their family lives and are at greater risk for problems in adolescence and young adulthood.[97] Though most adult CoD rebound, divorce is nearly always destabilizing in the short term, and a significant number of children struggle for years after a marital breakup. Two decades of substantial, qualitative research on the adult CoD have chronicled the suffering that marital conflict brings.[98]

In a recent study of CoD, Elizabeth Marquardt found that the home lives of children whose parents split up were much more unstable than those whose parents stayed together. Two-thirds of CoD versus one-fourth

of those from intact families agreed that "it was stressful in my family."[99]
Fifty-eight percent of CoD said they often felt like an adult during their
childhood.[100] Many CoD attest to the difficulty of trying to live in two very
different households after their parents split up. In addition to instability,
CoD have had more experience with suffering than most children. A total
of 57 percent of CoD, versus 40 percent of other young adults, confirmed
that they had "experienced many losses."[101] Two-thirds of young adults
from intact families strongly agreed that "children were at the center of
my family," while only one-third of CoD did.[102] Children from broken
families are three times as likely to say they were "alone a lot" as children.[103] Overall, the data show that in troubled families, children's needs
sometimes go unmet. Although the majority develop into well-adjusted
adults, they still look back on unhappy childhoods, and are much more
likely than their peers to share profound stories of confusion, isolation,
and loss.[104]

Even those social scientists who emphasize children's resilience tend to
agree with the essence of Marquardt's analysis. For instance, John Harvey and Mark Fine, the authors of *Children of Divorce*, stress children's
"unwillingness to submit to hopelessness and helplessness," yet attest that
"overall, divorce is painful even for young people [who viewed it as nec-
essary]."[105] They understand divorce as a kind of trauma that must be
coped with over time, and though they encourage acceptance of it, they
do not deny its profound effects.[106] Studies like these get underneath the
connection between family disruption and poverty discussed earlier in this
chapter. They seem to suggest an urgent need for divorce prevention and
support.

Some argue that there is no going back. The historian of marriage
Stephanie Coontz, for instance, believes that it is not possible to return
to earlier marriage ideals. We have chosen freedom over constraint, have
accepted divorce as the price we are willing to pay, and have claimed
the right to live as we wish—with or without marriage. Thus, we simply
need to accept the reality that though "many people will be able to carve
out satisfying and stable marriages on a new basis; . . . many others will
live their lives and construct their personal commitments outside marriage."[107] Even if studies show that, on average, marriage is beneficial for
men, women, and children, "using averages to give personal advice to
individuals or to construct social policy for all is not wise."[108] The days
of social and economic pressure to marry and stay married are gone, and

because we do not wish to return to a situation in which women especially had to simply resign themselves to lives of unhappiness if their marriages did not work out, we have no choice but to "adjust our personal expectations and social support systems to this new reality."[109]

However, others are less convinced that nothing can be done. The fact that divorce peaked in the 1980s and has since fallen suggests that trends are not unmalleable. From the 1960s to the 1980s, many adults believed that happier adults would be accompanied by happier children. Longitudinal research emerged in the 1990s to show that in fact most children do better when their parents stay together, except in very high-conflict situations.[110] We now know that adults are not always made happier by divorce; second and third marriages have higher failure rates than first ones.[111] The question of how to save troubled marriages for the sake of children *and* adults has just begun to be explored.

Conservative think tanks argue that the government's experiment with no-fault, easy-to-obtain divorce has been a failure. Because we can see the direct costs of divorce for the government, they believe that the government is justified in making divorce more difficult to obtain. However, initiatives such as covenant marriage laws and attempts to bring back fault divorce have not been successful.[112] The US bishops were not major players in either of these campaigns. Some have even accused them of inconsistency in tolerating divorce while much more strenuously fighting abortion, stem cell research, and same-sex marriage. But public support for returning to more rigid divorce laws is low, probably because most disapprove of divorce for unserious reasons but believe it is justifiable when conflict becomes serious; they do not want the government limiting options.[113] Though divorce rates were clearly lower when laws were tougher, it is not clear that we can go back. The current esteem for good companionate marriage is closely linked with lower tolerance for unhappy marriages, and most know cases in which suffering seems to make divorce the only logical choice. Forcing people to stay in miserable marriages makes little sense. However, it may be possible to give couples a better chance at avoiding breakups of marriages that are salvageable. Newer policy initiatives that look somewhat promising include waiting periods before a divorce becomes final, mandatory counseling for troubled couples, and the provision of better resources for what to do when your marriage is in trouble.[114] These legal initiatives can both provide practical help and reinforce the virtue of fidelity.

However, because law alone is not an effective instrument to stop divorce, how else might Christians help more families that suffer in unhappy marriages and care for more families after divorce? In fact, churches are in a difficult spot. There are emerging data that divorced adults and their children often leave Christianity, especially if they belong to churches with strict teachings on divorce.[115] Feeling judged and excluded, these families walk away without the support they need. Young adults from broken families tend to engage in less formal religious practice and have more tenuous institutional connections than other young adults.[116] Moreover, substantially fewer CoD remember their parents encouraging religious practice.[117] Religious institutions have a harder time drawing and keeping broken families and the young adults that emerge from them. Theologians are beginning to underline the gravity of the problem and advocate better pastoral care. They continue to call for reconsideration of rules that prohibit divorced and remarried people from receiving Communion, but there is much more work to be done.[118]

There are some helpful existing models. The Retrovaille program is an excellent resource for couples whose marriage is in trouble.[119] It is offered across North America as well as Europe, South America, Asia, and Africa. The initial weekend experience is followed by six to twelve sessions spread out over three months. Most of the presentations are given by couples that have been through very difficult times and emerged on the other side. Donations are requested, but no couples are turned away because of inability to pay. The idea of four stages of marriage—romance, disillusionment, misery, and awakening—offers a realistic perspective that grounds the hoped-for rediscovery. Program leaders claim that "today's unchallenged acceptance of divorce suggests that many friends, families, [and] church communities are providing only limited support for marriages," whereas they offer "a program that is solely dedicated to providing the necessary support to help save marriages."[120] Still, the program reaches only a small minority of troubled couples.

Following divorce, there are even fewer resources. No specific Catholic ministry reaches out to vulnerable CoD, whether or not their parents remarry. Often, couples who receive an annulment in order to remarry are treated no differently than other couples preparing for marriage. Their children receive no special counseling, despite the fact that their experience of brokenness and fragility may be similar to the experience of children whose parents did not seek an annulment. Resources are available in some dioceses, such as support groups based on the Catholic's Divorce Survival Guide DVD series and the Catholic Divorce Ministry.[121] However, "nationwide, support programs for the separated and divorced are few and far between. For example, . . . in the Archdiocese of Atlanta less than 15 percent of the archdiocese's 100 parishes offer any sort of programming for Catholics who are going through or have been through divorce. And those numbers . . . are fairly typical of (or better than) what you'll find in most dioceses."[122]

From the perspective of families that have experienced divorce, it can seem as though parish liturgies, religious education classes, and programs are designed for people whose home lives are "perfect." If churches want to minister to those suffering through divorce, they need to speak more of human weakness and imperfection, while not neglecting to teach the value of ideals. They need to make it possible for parents and children from all kinds of families to feel welcome, so that they may come to understand their brokenness as a source of wisdom for themselves and for the community. The needs of broken families cannot be ignored.

For those who come and stay, churches should offer support for the ideal and care for those who are wounded when the ideal is no longer possible to live out. Recently, *Commonweal* magazine offered a series of reflections from parents and adult children on raising children in the faith.[123] What might happen if parishes made space for married couples, single parents, remarried couples, and adult CoD to speak honestly of their own experiences about what it means to raise children alone, what it takes to stay together through hard times, what happens when a marriage falls apart, and what it is like to begin again in a new family? Christians should approach divorce with realism. Although it is true that covenant fidelity often makes possible a depth of relationship and fulfillment, there are profound connections between freedom and happiness and between human finitude and the inability to sustain all commitments. Postdivorce support is a crucial way to help both the children and adults affected by divorce see the church as a place of welcome rather than a source of shame.

However, accepting the reality of divorce and attending to the needs of those affected by it need not entail giving up on marriage. Christians have a prophetic theology that understands marriage's one-flesh unity as a fundamentally important answer to the deepest human longings for connection but also grasps the difficulty of the struggle to honor a covenant with one person over a lifetime. It should be possible to offer more help to those struggling to live out these covenants. Parishes are ideally placed to provide communities of support for couples that are struggling in their marriages with the hope of reducing divorce. The government and individuals can only do so much. To turn back the tide of divorce, we will need communities that are willing to uphold the ideal and to lovingly help more people realize it, while never abandoning those who are not be able sustain it.

COMMON GROUND AND PROGRESS

Thus far, I have argued that a divided Christian community ought to join together in initiatives rooted in a theology of companionate, covenantal, common good–focused marriage. These initiatives include better marriage preparation and education, job preparation, the promotion of just-wage jobs, and providing support for troubled married couples and postdivorce families. My claim is that these initiatives both have a foundation in and extend existing common ground inside and outside the church.

Some critics might argue that it is foolish to seek common ground in light of the obvious disconnects between US family practice and the Christian vision of the family. Hauerwas holds that unlike Americans, Christians are not romantic or realistic but hopeful because they place their trust in God and in practices of fidelity designed to help them become the kind of people who can participate in the mission of the church.[124] He is characteristically pessimistic about the potential for people outside the Christian community to share this vision.

However, the Christian belief in fidelity in marriage is not completely unintelligible. Despite the hopes of polyamorists, the overwhelming majority of Americans desire monogamy and expect fidelity.[125] And despite their ongoing experience with marriage failure, most continue to promise to stay with one other person until death, and most of those who do not marry would if they could. Movies about courtship leading to marriage abound, and proposal stories and pictures continue to show up on social media websites. Cultural narratives of long-term marriage suggest that there is something valuable about the witness of two lives intertwined. This is what most people continue to want for themselves, their children, and their grandchildren. Those on both the right and the left are really not far apart on this issue. The real divide is about how to respond when people do not manage to attain the ideal.

Some on the right will worry that focusing on divorce, cohabitation, and poverty distracts attention from the more basic issue of the redefinition of marriage. Girgis, Anderson, and George emphasize the serious harm that will come from legalizing same-sex marriage. First, a redefinition will lead to confusion about marriage and encourage further deinstitutionalization.[126] Second, changing the definition of marriage will be particularly harmful to children. They question the usefulness of oft-cited studies showing that children in same-sex households fare just as well as others, arguing that we have large numbers of good studies showing the benefits of two-parent households, and no comparatively rigorous study involving same-sex couples.[127] Thus, we should "expect that same-sex parenting is generally less effective" because reliable studies show all alternatives to married parents to be less effective.[128] According to these thinkers, redefining marriage will mean "pretending" that two people who are not married, are, and "shielding people from the truth about marriage."[129]

However, is it possible that those advocating same-sex marriage are actually helping to elevate the ideal of lifelong marriage at a time when some (particularly in the educated, privileged classes) have begun to question it? The claim that children will be harmed in same-sex families is difficult to maintain. If studies do not yet prove the goodness of same-sex parenting, they cannot prove its harm. It seems too early to conclude that two married parents of the same gender cannot offer the same love and stability as do two heterosexuals. More fundamentally, we are engaged in a societal debate on the nature and value of marriage. Stories of couples that want not just equal benefits but also the chance to declare their love for each other before friends and family and call each other "husband" or "wife" are arguably advocates of cementing the marriage ideal in place. Because these couples must fight for the right to marry, they remind everyone else of the beauty and value of their marriage promises. To be sure, theirs is a more inclusive vision. Some Christians continue to find it imperfect or deeply flawed, but the essential qualities of intimacy, covenant, and commitment to community at the center of the Christian vision are being reinforced. This may be a good time for those on the right to bracket their concern over legal same-sex marriage and focus on strengthening marriage relationships from below.

Some on the left may dispute the local promarriage agenda because they worry that focusing on marriage is disrespectful to those who are poor. Thus the womanist theologian Traci West criticizes the focus of white elites on the immorality of welfare mothers and calls for a "moratorium on any further open debate about poor black women's sexual reproduction."[130] Throughout American history, she notes, black women have been blamed for sexual immorality.[131] During slavery, they were praised for childbearing, for more children meant more wealth for the master, but today when poor children cost taxpayers money, women's desires to bear children are viewed with moral repugnance. Instead of trying to control black women's sexuality, she proposes paying attention to poverty, and also turning a critical eye to the sexual immorality of the elites.[132] We should recognize "the social and spiritual value of poor motherhood," and affirm black women's right to sexual expression and childbearing, a source of hope and participation in the recreation of the world.[133]

According to the womanist ethicist Keri Day, if churches go along with the government's efforts to control women's sexuality and childbearing by encouraging marriage and discouraging divorce, they implicitly affirm the narrative of the "immoral poor" who need only embrace personal responsibility to escape poverty.[134] Although the infusion of cash into church programs aiding the poor can help black families survive, unless churches pair these programs with efforts to change unjust social structures (e.g., a low minimum wage and the lack of affordable child care, health care, and housing), they do not recognize "the dynamic history of black people's work ethic from slavery to the present," they participate in the "cultural production of evil," and they fail to get to the root causes of poverty.[135]

The dangers to which womanist ethicists point are real. Christians cannot blame poor families for poverty. Efforts to address the structural problems alluded to by both West and Day must continue. The strength, love, and hope of poor mothers who continue to bear and raise children in imperfect circumstances must be recognized. Yet, as I noted in chapter 3, there are good reasons for combining structural work with empowerment work at the local level. When we consider what is the best "sustainable, long-term, antipoverty strategy," we cannot place all hope in the government.[136] Even if all problems could be solved "from above," given gridlock in Congress, those on the left are not likely to realize their policy vision anytime soon. It would be irresponsible not to try other ways to strengthen families, not to replace efforts for structural reform but to complement them.

Those who work with poor families know that even the best outcome at structural levels would not solve problems overnight. The "internalization of poverty" is a kind of brokenness, and it is every bit as real and debilitating as the internalization of privilege that plagues those who are "better off."[137] West rightly questions patronizing rhetoric suggesting that poor people somehow need churches to "fix" them.[138] However, people who live in poverty are often, though not always, beaten down by the stress and struggle against structural forces they cannot be expected to conquer alone. Because they have been "sinned against by systematic and systemic disempowerment, violence, and deception," there is often "a deep wounding of the heart" that manifests itself in "self-denigration, low self-esteem, self-withdrawal, resignation, and self-hatred."[139] Human beings who live in privilege similarly have a distorted identity due to their insulation from suffering, which manifests itself in a failure to recognize their true spiritual poverty. Privilege is accompanied by indifference, self-satisfaction, and a conviction that those with means should be "playing god in the lives of the poor."[140]

Both the nonpoor and the poor are wounded in ways that politics cannot heal. In *Before Midnight*, Celine and Jessie desperately want depth in their lives, and their desires to "save the world" lead them to careers in writing and environmental activism. But they are not willing to marry each other, commit to sexual fidelity, or open up their lives to something larger than their ongoing, intimate conversation, and parenting project. When distress hits, it is not clear that love alone will save them. Theirs are the problems of the privileged: cynicism, isolation, self-centeredness, and an unwillingness to embrace vulnerability or live in solidarity with those who have less.

In contrast, in a series of profoundly moving stories, the *New York Times* journalist Andrea Elliott portrayed the life of a girl named Dasani and her family, who lived in public housing in New York City.[141] The series inspired justifiable rage at a system that allows families to live in truly awful shelter conditions and offers no realistic way up to low-income people who live blocks from shops catering to the whims of New York's wealthy elite. But the story also tells us something about why Chanel, Dasani's mother, has eight children. At eleven, Dasani, though fiercely loyal to her siblings, sees children as her mother's problem; but her mother sees them as her only accomplishment. The story ends with the family moving into a decent apartment in a neighborhood where they have some community ties and a school that nurtures the children's hopes; but knowing the family's history, the reader can only be so optimistic. Will the parents overcome their drug addiction, find steady work, and construct a child-centered home life? Will Dasani believe enough in herself and her dreams to escape the single motherhood that the vast majority of poor women say they do not want? Will she ever have the quiet house of her dreams? Here, too, despite moments of beauty, hope, and joy, there is brokenness, isolation, and something less than the ideal.

To be promarriage is to take marriage seriously and provide support for its flourishing. Most people want lifelong marriage, understand its benefits, and experience its everyday ups and downs as challenging and fulfilling. Christians say less than we ought to about how the fullness of love over time fulfills human beings' deepest longings. Of course, we also need to say that sometimes commitment brings great suffering. We stay faithful to another person, finally, not because we have managed to "keep the spark alive" but because in doing so we find a deeper joy. This is not always the case, but it often is; and it could be more often, if we gave marriage the sustained attention it deserves. Because we want the joy of committed love for each other, we need to support good policies on marriage, divorce, jobs, and wages. But we also need to work at the local level to help each other develop the virtues of fidelity, humility, hope, and courage that make long-lasting relationships possible. By communicating the best of contemporary theology, preparing couples for marriage, providing MRE, working to increase good employment opportunities, and ministering to those in troubled marriages and broken families, Christians can make their belief in marriage concrete. Through their communal practices, they can nurture virtue and make it a little easier for the privileged and the not-so-privileged to find what they seek.

NOTES

1. See, e.g., Sherif Girgis, Ryan T. Anderson, and Robert P. George, *What Is Marriage? Man and Woman: A Defense* (New York: Encounter, 2012).

2. In the section of the US Conference of Catholic Bishops' (USCCB) website devoted to "defense of marriage," efforts to ensure that same-sex marriage is

not legalized predominate; see http://www.usccb.org/issues-and-action/marriage
-and-family/marriage/promotion-and-defense-of-marriage/index.cfm.

3. USCCB, *Marriage: Love and Life in the Divine Plan*, 2009, http://www
.usccb.org/issues-and-action/marriage-and-family/marriage/love-and-life/.

4. See "Why Marriage Matters" and "Marriage Rx," available at www.for
yourmarriage.org/marriage-resources.

5. National Fatherhood Initiative, *With This Ring: A National Survey on Marriage in America*, 2005, http://www.smartmarriages.com/nms.pdf. The top reasons for divorce identified by divorced people included a lack of commitment, conflict, infidelity, marrying too young, unrealistic expectations, domestic violence, inequality, conflicts over housework, a lack of preparation, and financial problems.

6. Gail Risch, L. Riley, and Michael Lawler, "Problematic Issues in the Early Years of Marriage: Content for Premarital Education," *Journal of Psychology and Theology* 31, no. 1 (2003): 253–69.

7. See the Knights of Columbus, www.kofc.org/un/en/public_policy/marriage
.html; the National Organization for Marriage, www.nationformarriage.org; the Heritage Foundation, www.heritage.org/issues/family-and-marriage; the Family Research Council, www.frc.org/Marriage-and-Family; and ProtectMarriage.com, http://protectmarriage.com/.

8. Adam Liptak, "Supreme Court Bolsters Gay Marriage with Two Major Rulings," *New York Times*, June 26, 2013, http://www.nytimes.com/2013/06/27
/us/politics/supreme-court-gay-marriage.html; *Pew Research Center*, June 6, 2013, "In Gay Marriage Debate, Supporters and Opponents See Legal Recognition as 'Inevitable,'" http://www.people-press.org/2013/06/06/in-gay-marriage
-debate-both-supporters-and-opponents-see-legal-recognition-as-inevitable/. Thirty-seven states and the District of Columbia have legalized gay marriage; see "The Changing Landscape of Same-Sex Marriage," *Washington Post*, April 27, 2015, http://www.washingtonpost.com/wp-srv/special/politics/same-sex
-marriage/. Opinion polls show rapid movement to approval of same-sex marriage in all age groups, with Millennials leading the way; see Pew Research Center, "Changing Attitudes on Gay Marriage," September 24, 2014, http://www.pew
forum.org/2014/09/24/graphics-slideshow-changing-attitudes-on-gay-marriage/.

9. See, e.g., Center for American Progress, www.americanprogress.org; CLASP, www.clasp.org/; the Brookings Institution, www.brookings.edu/research
/topics/economics; the Voice of the Faithful, www.voiceofthefaithful.org; DignityUSA, www.dignityusa.org; and Catholics in Alliance for the Common Good, http://www.catholicsinalliance.org.

10. "A Call for a New Conversation on Marriage," Institute for American Values, http://www.americanvalues.org/search/item.php?id=102.

11. Ron Haskins, "Marriage Debate Still Vital," 2013, Institute for American Values, http://www.americanvalues.org/search/item.php?id=2466; Ron Haskins,

"Fighting Poverty the American Way," Brookings Institution, June 20, 2011, http://www.brookings.edu/research/papers/2011/06/20-fighting-poverty-haskins.

12. Chuck Donovan, "A Marshall Plan for Marriage: Rebuilding Our Shattered Homes," Heritage Foundation, June 7, 2011, http://www.heritage.org/research/commentary/2011/06/a-marshall-plan-for-marriage-rebuilding-our-shattered-homes.

13. Jon Corvino, "Evidence and Humility in the Marriage Conversation," Institute for American Values, 2013, http://www.americanvalues.org/search/item.php?id=2466.

14. Isabel V. Sawhill, "Family Structure: The Growing Importance of Class," Brookings Institution, January 2013, http://www.brookings.edu/research/articles/2013/01/family-structure-class-sawhill.

15. Despite a decrease in fertility, most adults still want children. See Frank Newport and Joy Wilke, "Desire for Children Still Norm in US," Gallup, September 25, 2013, http://www.gallup.com/poll/164618/desire-children-norm.aspx. A small but growing percentage of married women in their early forties have no children. See Esther Lamidi and Krista K. Payne, "Change in Proportion of Childless Women, 1995–2010," Bowling Green State University, http://www.bgsu.edu/content/dam/BGSU/college-of-arts-and-sciences/NCFMR/documents/FP/FP-13-20.pdf.

16. Barbara Dafoe Whitehead and David Popenoe, "Who Wants to Marry a Soulmate," in *The State of Our Unions 2001: The Social Health of Marriage in America* (New Brunswick, NJ: National Marriage Project, 2001), http://www.stateofourunions.org/pdfs/SOOU2001.pdf.

17. Andrew Cherlin, *The Marriage Go-Round: The State of Marriage and Family in America Today* (New York: Alfred A. Knopf, 2009), 139.

18. Ibid., 140.

19. Pope Paul VI, *Gaudium et Spes*, no. 48, http://www.vatican.va/archive/hist_councils/ii_vatican_council/documents/vat-ii_const_19651207_gaudium-et-spes_en.html. Compare the gendered language used by the USCCB, *Marriage: Life and Love in the Divine Plan*, 2010, http://www.usccb.org/issues-and-action/marriage-and-family/marriage/love-and-life/index.cfm.

20. See, e.g., Richard R. Gaillardetz, *A Daring Promise: A Spirituality of Christian Marriage* (New York: Crossroad, 2002), David Matkzo McCarthy, *Sex and Love in the Home*, new edition (London: SCM Press, 2004); and John S. Grabowski, *Sex and Virtue: An Introduction to Sexual Ethics* (Washington, DC: Catholic University Press of America, 2003).

21. D'Vera Cohn, Jeffrey S. Passel, Wendy Wang, and Gretchen Livingston, "Barely Half of US Adults Are Married: A Record Low," *Pew Research*, December 14, 2011, http://www.pewsocialtrends.org/2011/12/14/barely-half-of-u-s-adults-are-married-a-record-low/. The vast majority of Americans still marry at some

point in their lives, and most of those who do not wish they could. Frank Newport and Joy Wilke, "Most in US Want Marriage, but Its Importance Has Dropped," Gallup, August 2, 2013, http://www.gallup.com/poll/163802/marriage-impor tance-dropped.aspx.

22. Cherlin, *Marriage Go-Round*, 9.

23. Ibid., 20. I take up this issue in more depth later in the chapter.

24. Stephanie Coontz, *Marriage, A History: How Love Conquered Marriage* (New York: Penguin, 2006), 287.

25. Ibid., 289.

26. Ibid.

27. Ibid., 301.

28. See, e.g., David Cloutier, *Love, Reason, and God's Story: An Introduction to Catholic Sexual Ethics* (Winona, MN: St. Mary's Press, 2008), 174–75.

29. Scott Coltrane and Michele Adams, *Gender and Families*, 2nd ed. (Lanham, MD: Rowman & Littlefield, 2008), 331.

30. Kathryn Edin and Maria Kefalas, *Promises I Can Keep: Why Poor Women Put Motherhood before Marriage and Adoption* (Berkeley: University of California Press, 2005), 203.

31. Paul R. Amato, Alan Booth, David R. Johnson, and Stacy J. Rogers, *Alone Together: How Marriage in America Is Changing* (Cambridge, MA: Harvard University Press, 2009), 31, 215–17.

32. Ibid., 261–62.

33. John Paul II, *Familiaris Consortio*, 1981, http://w2.vatican.va/content /john-paul-ii/en/apost_exhortations/documents/hf_jp-ii_exh_19811122_familiaris -consortio.html. The reality of dual career families and the challenges they present is, however, often not acknowledged in marriage preparation programs. See Risch, Riley, and Lawler, "Problematic Issues," 263.

34. Lisa Sowle Cahill, *Sex, Gender and Christian Ethics* (Cambridge: Cambridge University Press, 1996), 119.

35. Ibid., 205.

36. McCarthy, *Sex and Love*, 283.

37 Ibid., 83.

38. Ibid., 93–94. Margaret Farley also calls for "fruitfulness," broadly defined, in her sexual ethics; see Margaret Farley, *Just Love: A Framework for Christian Sexual Ethics* (New York: Continuum, 2006), 226–28.

39. Some Protestant theologians today are questioning the need for fidelity and exclusivity in marriage, but Catholics rarely make arguments like these. Compare Marvin M. Ellison, "Reimagining Good Sex: The Eroticizing of Mutual Respect and Pleasure," and W. Scott Haldeman, "A Queer Fidelity: Reinventing Christian Marriage"—both in *Sexuality and the Sacred: Sources for Theological Reflection*, ed. Marvin M. Ellison and Kelly Brown Douglas (Louisville: Westminster, 2010), respectively, 245–46 and 304–16—with Farley, *Just Love*, 259–71.

40. Lisa Sowle Cahill, *Family: A Christian Social Perspective* (Minneapolis: Fortress Press, 2000), 111–29; Gloria H. Albrecht, *Hitting Home: Feminist Ethics, Women's Work, and the Betrayal of "Family Values"* (New York: Continuum, 2004), 145–54; Christine Firer Hinze and Mary Stewart Van Leeuwen, "Whose Marriage? Whose Health: A Christian Feminist Ethical Response," *Marriage, Health, and the Professions* ed. John Wall, Don S. Browning, and William J. Doherty (Grand Rapids: William B. Eerdmans, 2002), 145–66.

41. Traci C. West, "The Policing of Poor Black Women's Sexual Reproduction," in *God Forbid: Religion and Sex in American Public Life*, ed. Kathleen M. Sands (New York: Oxford University Press, 2000), 135–54.

42. Donovan, "Marshall Plan"; Family Research Council, "Why Marriage Should Be Privileged in Public Policy," April 30, 2003, http://www.frc.org/insight /why-marriage-should-be-privileged-in-public-policy.

43. In addition to Donovan, "Marshall Plan," see the National Organization for Marriage website, https://www.nationformarriage.org/; and Family Research Council, "Why Marriage Should Be Privileged in Public Policy," http://www.frc .org/insight/why-marriage-should-be-privileged-in-public-policy.

44. Derek Thompson, "How Motherhood Is Changing Dramatically— in 11 Graphs," *The Atlantic*, May 12, 2013, http://www.theatlantic.com /business/archive/2013/05/how-motherhood-is-changing-dramatically-in-11 -graphs/275778/. The data are from the Pew Forum. A total of 61 percent of unmarried mothers have not completed high school, and only 9 percent have a college degree. Gretchen Livingston and D'Vera Cohn, "Record Share of New Mothers are College Educated," Pew Research, May 10, 2013, http://www .pewsocialtrends.org/2013/05/10/record-share-of-new-mothers-are-college -educated/.

45. Isabel Sawhill and Quentin Karpilow, "Strategies for Assisting Low-Income Families," June 28, 2013, http://www.brookings.edu/research /papers/2013/07/01assisting-low-income-families-sawhill. The authors consider several strategies for increasing the income of a targeted group of low-income families (i.e., single-mother heads of household earning below minimum wage) and find that high school graduation, raising the minimum wage to $9 per hour, and an economy of full employment would help, but adding a partner who is a second earner to the household would help the most. The most significant differences between middle-class households and poor households are the full-time employment of the head of household and the presence of a second earner.

46. One of the first to point to this problem was William Julius Wilson, *The Truly Disadvantaged: The Inner City, the Underclass, and Public Policy* (Chicago: University of Chicago Press, 1990).

47. Eighty percent of poor women believe that people should marry before having children and that children raised by two parents will be better off, but they marry later and less often and have more children before marrying, because

they believe that "it is better to have children outside of marriage than to foolishly marry and risk divorce." Edin and Kefalas, *Promises I Can Keep*, 207.

48. Joy Moses, "Improving the Poverty Numbers through Wedded Bliss?" Center for American Progress, September 20, 2102, https://www.americanpro gress.org/issues/poverty/news/2012/09/20/38433/improving-the-poverty-numbers -through-wedded-bliss/. "Most men who are live-in partners, 67 percent, have a high school diploma or less and typically have higher rates of unemployment than men who choose to marry."

49. *Getting It Right: Marriage Preparation in the Catholic Church* (Omaha: Center for Marriage and Family at Creighton University, 1995), http://www .usccb.org/issues-and-action/marriage-and-family/marriage/marriage-preparation /getting-it-right-marriage-preparation-in-the-catholic-church.cfm.

50. CARA, *Marriage in the Catholic Church: A Survey of US Catholics*, 2007, http://cara.georgetown.edu/MarriageReport.pdf.

51. Cited by Risch, Riley, and Lawler, "Problematic Issues," 253.

52. Ibid., 254.

53. Ibid., 255, 258.

54. "Divorce Still Less Likely among Catholics," CARA, 1964, republished September 26, 2013, http://nineteensixty-four.blogspot.com/2013/09/divorce-still -less-likely-among.html.

55. Risch, Riley, and Lawler, "Problematic Issues," 263–64.

56. National Fatherhood Initiative, *With This Ring*.

57. Risch, Riley, and Lawler, "Problematic Issues," 264.

58. On Catholics cohabiting, see USSCB, "Marriage Preparation and Cohab-iting Couples," http://www.usccb.org/issues-and-action/marriage-and-family /marriage/marriage-preparation/cohabiting.cfm. On premarital sex, see Frank Newport, "Americans, Including Catholics, Say Birth Control Is Morally OK," Gallup, May 22, 2012, http://www.gallup.com/poll/154799/americans-including -catholics-say-birth-control-morally.aspx

59. CARA, *Marriage in the Catholic Church*, 4, 5.

60. In addition, couples exposed to counseling options may be predisposed to seek counseling when they need it later on. See Risch, Riley, and Lawler, "Problem-atic Issues," 253.

61. Gail Risch and Michael Lawler. "The First Five Years of Marriage: Resources and Programs for Ministry," *Family Ministry* 15, no. 4 (January 1, 2001): 22–28.

62. CARA, *Marriage in the Catholic Church*.

63. Ibid.

64. Theodora Ooms, "The New Kid on the Block: What Is Marriage Educa-tion and Does It Work?" 2005, http://www.clasp.org/resources-and-publications /archive/0183.pdf. See also Theodora Ooms, "Strengthening Couples and

Marriage in Low-Income Communities," 2002, http://research.policyarchive.org/14013.pdf.

65. It is worth considering whether marriage preparation could be formally extended to cohabiting couples. See Todd A. Salzman and Michael G. Lawler, *The Sexual Person: A Renewed Catholic Anthropology* (Washington, DC: Georgetown University Press, 2008), 211–13. Salzman and Lawler argue that both risk factors, which are common to cohabiting partners, and the instability often created by cohabitation itself, suggest the need for church-sponsored marriage preparation programs geared to cohabiting couples (p. 212).

66. Ooms, "New Kid on the Block."

67. Stanley Hauerwas, *A Community of Character: Toward a Constructive Christian Social Ethic* (Notre Dame, IN: University of Notre Dame, 1981), 172.

68. Ibid., 165.

69. Ibid.,166.

70. Elisabeth Donahue, Irwin Garfinkel, Ron Haskins, Sara McLanahan, and Ronald B. Mincy, "Strengthening Fragile Families," Brookings Institution, October 2010, http://www.brookings.edu/research/reports/2010/10/27-fragile-families-foc.

71. Ibid.

72. Ibid. See also Ooms, "New Kid on the Block." In addition, Oklahoma's Family Expectations Program is an interesting case study. Early research found that its emphasis on relationship skills education, family support, and support services increased the likelihood that couples would remain romantically involved, faithful to each other, and more effective co-parents, even if they did not marry. See Barbara Devaney and Robin Dion, "15-Month Impacts of Oklahoma's Family Expectations Program," Mathematica Policy Research, 2010, http://www.mathematica-mpr.com/~/media/publications/PDFs/Family_support/BSF_15month_impacts.pdf. Other studies have found strong evidence of higher relationship satisfaction and modest evidence of lower likelihood of divorce, better engaged fathers, reduced domestic violence, and improved child well-being. See Courtney Harrison, Dana Alfred, Kristin Bugbee, and Rachel Derrington, "What Policymakers Should Know about Marriage and Relationship Education," National Healthy Marriage Resource Center, January 8, 2011, http://www.healthymarriageinfo.org/resource-detail/index.aspx?rid=3942.

73. David P. Gushee, *Getting Marriage Right: Realistic Counsel for Saving and Strengthening Relationships* (Grand Rapids: Baker, 2004), 110.

74. Ibid.

75. Moses, "Improving the Poverty Numbers."

76. Robert Rector, "Marriage Reduces Child Poverty in Kansas," Heritage Foundation, September 28, 2012, http://www.heritage.org/research/commentary/2012/09/marriage-reduces-child-poverty-in-kansas.

77. Robert Rector, "Before Marriage: America's Greatest Weapon against Child Poverty," Heritage Foundation, September 5, 2012, http://www.heritage.org /research/reports/2012/09/marriage-americas-greatest-weapon-against-child-poverty.

78 See Institute for American Values, *When Marriage Disappears: The New Middle America* (New York and Charlottesville, VA: Institute for American Values and National Marriage Project, 2010), http://americanvalues.org/catalog/pdfs /state_of_our_unions_2010.pdf. Although Americans of varying education and income levels value marriage equally in the abstract, "Middle Americans' growing distance from a bourgeois ethos that stresses self-control in service of the success sequence makes it more difficult for them to avoid a nonmarital childbirth, to get married, and to steer clear of divorce court." Their high ideals of marriage are less obtainable because their economic prospects are less bright. The reality that less educated men have experienced lower wages and more unemployment since the 1970s is a key factor in the decline of marriage.

79. Eduardo Porter, "In the War on Poverty, a Dogged Adversary," *New York Times*, December 17, 2013, http://www.nytimes.com/2013/12/18/business /economy/in-the-war-on-poverty-a-dogged-adversary.html?hp&_r=2&.

80 Moses, "Improving the Poverty Numbers."

81. See, e.g., Gerald Beyer, "The Continuing Relevance of Brothers and Sisters to Us to Confronting Racism and White Privilege," *Josephinum Journal of Theology* 19, no. 2 (2012): 246–53.

82. See Colin Gordon, *Mapping Decline: St. Louis and the Fate of the American City* (Philadelphia: University of Pennsylvania Press, 2009).

83. Though some argue that not all retailers can pay higher wages and still serve their clientele, others maintain that investing in employees is good business in the long run. See Zeynep Ton, "Why 'Good Jobs' Are Good for Retailers," *Harvard Business Review*, January–February 2012, https://hbr.org/2012/01 /why-good-jobs-are-good-for-retailers.

84. Leo XIII, *Rerum Novarum* (1891), no. 44, http://w2.vatican.va/content /leo-xiii/en/encyclicals/documents/hf_l-xiii_enc_15051891_rerum-novarum.html.

85. Although employers do not bear full responsibility for paying just wages, they have an obligation, in recognition of the dignity of the worker and the principle of subsidiarity, to do the best they can in this regard. See John Paul II, *Laborem Exercens* (1981), no. 17, http://w2.vatican.va/content/john-paul-ii/en/encyclicals /documents/hf_jp-ii_enc_14091981_laborem-exercens.html; and Matthew Shadle, "Reflections on a Just Wage," *Political Theology Today*, September 12, 2013, http://www.politicaltheology.com/blog/reflections-on-a-just-wage/.

86. Benedict XVI, *Caritas in Veritate*, 2009, no. 66, http://w2.vatican.va /content/benedict-xvi/en/encyclicals/documents/hf_ben-xvi_enc_20090629 _caritas-in-veritate.html.

87. Steve Greenhouse, "Movement to Increase Minimum Wage Broadens Its Tactics," *New York Times*, March 30, 2015, http://www.nytimes.com/2015/03/31/business/movement-to-increase-mcdonalds-minimum-wage-broadens-its-tactics.html.

88. See, e.g., Chalmers Center, "US Church Training," https://www.chalmers.org/our-work/us-church-training/.

89. Nothing in this section should be understood as acceptance of claims about lack of virtue among the unemployed or rejection of the reality that globalization and racism have contributed to unemployment in poor communities. See, e.g., William Julius Wilson, "When Work Disappears: New Implications for Race and Urban Poverty in the Global Economy," *Ethnic and Racial Studies* 22, no. 3 (December 7, 2010).

90. The term "soft skills" can be code for racist assumptions and judgments; see Wilson, "When Work Disappears." It is important to be aware of how racism might color perceptions of job readiness. Still, some unemployed people struggle with nontechnical skills necessary for sustaining employment. At the policy level, work to rectify injustice must continue, but this is a long-term strategy. At the local level, it is possible to help individuals gain skills they can use to succeed in the workplace now.

91. See St. Francis Community Services, "Midtown Center," http://www.midtowncc.org/programs.htm.

92. Bryant L. Myers, *Walking with the Poor: Principles and Practices of Transformational Development*, rev. ed. (Maryknoll, NY: Orbis, 2011), 127.

93. Ibid., 129.

94. Elizabeth Marquardt, *Between Two Worlds: The Inner Lives of Children of Divorce* (New York: Crown, 2005), xiv, 10.

95. Cherlin, *Marriage-Go-Round*, 17, 97.

96. Gretchen Livingston and D'Vera Cohn, "The New Demography of American Motherhood," Pew Research Center, May 6, 2010, http://www.pewsocialtrends.org/2010/05/06/the-new-demography-of-american-motherhood/.

97 Americans break off cohabiting relationships more often than those in other Western countries and children born to married or cohabiting partners are more likely in the United States than elsewhere to see their parents break up; see Cherlin, *Marriage-Go-Round*, 17. Twice as many children experience cohabitation as divorce and those children are at greater risk for abuse, drug use, depression, and dropping out of high school. See Institute for American Values, "New Report: Cohabitation, Not Divorce, Is Now Driving Rising Rates of Family Instability in America," August 16, 2011, http://www.globenewswire.com/news-release/2011/08/16/453980/229607/en/New-Report-Cohabitation-Not-Divorce-is-Now-Driving-Rising-Rates-of-Family-Instability-in-America.html.

98. For a comprehensive overview of the literature, see Paul Amato, "Children of Divorce in the 1990s: An Update of the Amato and Keith (1991) Meta-Analysis," *Journal of Family Psychology* 15 (2001): 355–70; and Robert E. Emery, Christopher Beam, and Jenna Rowen, "Adolescents' Experiences of Parental Divorce," in *Encyclopedia of Adolescence*, ed. B. Bradford Brown and Mitchell Prinstein (Salt Lake City: Academic Press, 2011).

99. Marquardt, *Between Two Worlds*, 54. I group together those who agreed or agreed strongly, except where noted.

100. Ibid., 53.

101. Ibid., 212.

102. Ibid., 38.

103. Ibid., 53.

104. Ibid., 32.

105. John H. Harvey and Mark A. Fine, *Children of Divorce: Stories of Loss and Growth* (Mahwah, NJ: Lawrence Erlbaum Associates, 2004), 153.

106. See also Emery, Beam, and Rowen, "Adolescents' Experiences."

107. Coontz, *History of Marriage*, 308.

108. Ibid., 310.

109. Ibid., 313.

110. Amato et al., "Children of Divorce."

111. Linda Waite, Don Browning, William J. Doherty, Maggie Gallagher, Ye Luo, and Scott M. Stanley, *Does Divorce Make People Happier?* (New York: Institute for American Values, 2002), http://www.americanvalues.org/search/item.php?id=13.

112. Amy L. Stewart, "Covenant Marriage: Legislating Family Values, " *Indiana Law Review* 32, no. 2 (1999), http://journals.iupui.edu/index.php/inlawrev/article/view/3348.

113. See, e.g., Oklahoma State University Bureau of Social Research, "Marriage in Oklahoma: 2001 Baseline Statewide Survey on Marriage and Divorce," 10, http://www.okmarriage.org/downloads/media/survey_report.pdfQ1. A majority of Oklahomans surveyed believe that divorce is problematic but is justified when parents are no longer in love or children are being exposed to conflict.

114. William J. Doherty and Chief Justice Leah Ward Sear, *Second Chances: A Proposal to Reduce Unnecessary Divorce* (New York: Institute for American Values, 2011), http://www.americanvalues.org/search/item.php?id=83.

115. Elizabeth Marquardt, ed., *Does the Shape of Families Shape Faith? Calling the Churches to Confront the Impact of Family Change* (New York: Broadway Books, 2012).

116. Marquardt, *Between Two Worlds*, 208.

117. Ibid., 210.

118. See Cardinal Walter Kasper, *The Gospel of the Family* (Mahwah, NJ: Paulist Press, 2013), 25–33; Machteld Reynaert, "Somewhere in Between: Children with Divorced Parents as a Challenge for Pastoral Theological Thinking," *INTAMS Review* 16 (2010): 208–15; and Julie Hanlon Rubio, "Divorce and the Faith of Children: A Challenge for the Church," in *Family's Many Faces*, ed. Karlijn Demasure (Leuven: Peeters, 2014), 113–30. On Eucharistic exclusion, see James Coriden, "What's a Remarried Catholic to Do?" *Commonweal*, January 27, 2012, reprinted in *The Furrow* 63 (2012): 205–11; and Laura Arosio, "A Ceremony for Divorce? Emerging Practices for a New Rite of Passage," *INTAMS Review* 17 (2011): 14–24.

119. See "Retrouvaille: A Lifeline for Marriages," http://www.retrouvaille.org/.

120. Ibid.

121. See Catholic Divorce Ministry, http://www.nacsdc.org/. The USCCB's website, foryourmarriage.com, offers links to marriage support services available in every state, but the offerings vary considerably; see http://www.foryourmarriage.org/marriage-resources/marriage-help-and-support/find-support.

122. Emily Simpson, "The Church's Divorce Dilemma," *Our Sunday Visitor*, May 22, 2011, https://www.osv.com/TabId/735/ArtMID/13636/ArticleID/9448/.

123. "Symposium: Raising Catholic Kids: The Challenge of Rooting Family in Faith," *Commonweal*, November 25, 2013, https://www.commonwealmagazine.org/symposium-raising-catholic-kids.

124. Hauerwas, *Community of Character*, 190–93.

125. Damon Linker, "Is Monogamy on the Way Out?" *The Week*, http://theweek.com/articles/444787/monogamy-way.

126. Girgis, Anderson, and George, *What Is Marriage?* 55.

127. Ibid., 60.

128. Ibid., 61–62.

129. Ibid., 87. The theological question of same-sex marriage is, of course, more complex, and I do not attempt to address it here.

130. West, "Policing," 151.

131. Ibid., 146–48.

132. Ibid., 150–51.

133. Ibid., 151.

134. Keri Day, "Saving Black America: A Womanist Analysis of Faith-Based Initiatives," *Journal of the Society of Christian Ethics* 33, no. 1 (2013): 76. See also West, "Policing," 150.

135. Day, "Saving Black America," 77–79.

136. Ibid., 77.

137. Meyers, *Walking with the Poor*, 129, 124.

138. West, *Disruptive Christian Ethics*, 110; she quotes President George W. Bush: "You don't fix the crack in the wall until you fix the foundation."

139. Meyers, *Walking with the Poor*, 140.

140. Ibid., 145.

141. Andrea Elliott, "Invisible Child," *New York Times*, December 9, 2013, http://www.nytimes.com/projects/2013/invisible-child/#/?chapt=1.

CHAPTER 5

Poverty Reduction

A Social Virtue Ethic

Catholic Social Teaching (CST) is known for its prophetic teachings on poverty. Concepts such as the option for the poor, the universal destination of material goods, and the social mortgage on private property are widely viewed as radical calls to limit indulgence and prioritize the needs of the less fortunate. A strong practice of charity in most Catholic parishes aims to respond to these callings. Through clothing drives, branches of the Saint Vincent de Paul Society, soup kitchens, food pantries, and Christmas gift collections, parishes encourage giving to the poor. Some parishes even offer basic health care, tutoring, legal help, and assistance in obtaining employment. Most dioceses have an office of peace and justice, and many parishes have social ministry committees of some kind. Organizations like Catholic Charities and the Catholic Campaign for Human Development go even further in working to empower underprivileged populations. One might argue that plenty is being done.[1]

At the political level, Catholics work through advocacy and community organizing to change structures. The US Conference of Catholic Bishops utilizes pastoral letters and statements, public campaigns, and traditional lobbying, and other Catholic groups (e.g., Catholics in Alliance for the Common Good and the Catholic League for Religious and Civil Rights) do the same. At the personal level, most ordinary Catholics participate in antipoverty efforts through their local parishes, schools, and community organizations, and most of this activity can be characterized as charity or relief. This "both-and" approach to poverty, a combination of attention to structural change and personal charitable efforts, shows the strong commitment of the church as an institution and of ordinary Catholics to aiding the poor.

However, politics and charity may be insufficient. With a gridlocked US Congress, it is no longer clear that placing most of one's hope in national politics is justifiable. There is little political will either for the sweeping entitlement reform that many conservatives would like to see or for the additional discretionary funding for antipoverty programs favored by many liberals. Though progress is sometimes more possible at the local and state levels, similar problems often impede real reform. Churches most often respond to poverty with charity. Yet some who study the effectiveness of charitable efforts conclude that "one of the biggest mistakes that North American churches make—by far—is in applying relief in situations in which rehabilitation or development is the appropriate intervention."[2] When relief in the form of money, food, or presents is provided, the weakness of the poor and the strength of the well-off can be reinforced; the problem of poverty is rarely overcome. As Maureen O'Connell writes, relief "ultimately traps people in cycles of charity that perpetuate mutually exclusive relationships of givers and receivers of aid rather than foster mutually beneficial relationships of collaborators or partners in social justice."[3] Instead of empowering people to take charge of their own lives, by concentrating on relief, churches can unintentionally underwrite the status quo. No one desires this outcome, yet most contribute to it. When it comes to politics, those on the right tend to argue for less government intervention, those on the left argue for more intervention, and few are satisfied with the status quo. Yet both tend to channel their own time, energy, and money into charitable activities that help those in need live a little more comfortably. Most also know that those efforts fall short of what is actually needed. Though there are success stories, often the same families receive gifts, food, or tutoring each year, and the same neighborhoods continue to struggle.

Today, a new interdisciplinary literature on "poverty reduction" is emerging, which is allowing scholars to identify best practices for moving people out of poverty. Practitioners working on global poverty issues in various cultural contexts have new information, embodied in the development literature, that can enable communities in the United States to approach poverty more effectively. Catholic parishes, with their long history of serving immigrants and the poor, are uniquely situated to learn from this literature and to translate it for use in their own particular contexts. This new direction is neither personal nor political but local.

This chapter aims to (1) briefly describe the problem of poverty in the United States, (2) identify overlaps between CST and the development literature in order to outline key principles and strategies for poverty reduction, (3) argue for a new approach to poverty that moves beyond charity and politics to retrieve some forgotten practices of early-twentieth-century Catholic parish life that challenge the standard ways in which Catholic organizations approach poverty, and (4) adapt these practices for current contexts. With poverty, as with all the other social problems addressed in this book, I affirm the need for continued work both "from above" (through policy reform) and "from below" (through personal conversion). Most Christian social ethics has concentrated on what can be done from either above or below, and I do not question the need for either structural change or personal initiative.[4] However, I do argue that it is also important to translate the wisdom of the Catholic tradition into better practices that effectively address the problem of poverty by empowering people in the space between the personal and the political. Here, those on the right and left can join together in imagining new possibilities.

NEW PROBLEMS, NEW POSSIBILITIES

Global poverty has received much more attention in the last few decades, and the focus has shifted from good intentions to beneficial outcomes.[5] On the ground, the Millennium Development Goals agreed upon by the United Nations focused on key problems and inspired many more groups to begin evaluating programs based on outcomes so that progress toward these goals can accelerate.[6] Powerful individuals, such as Bill and Melinda Gates and Warren Buffet, seem to believe that major progress is more possible now than ever before, if only we approach poverty with the same rigor with which we approach business.[7] Theologians, too, urge Christians not to be content with charity for its own sake but to think of effectiveness as a key measure of true compassion.[8]

Both declines in poverty and its persistence inspire the current drive to reduce it. On one hand, global extreme poverty declined significantly in the twentieth century—by the World Bank's estimate, from 52 percent in 1980 to 43 percent in 1990 and to 17 percent in 2010.[9] Although capitalism is credited with much of this progress, income transfers, social safety nets, and social programs have also contributed to declining inequality.[10] Knowledge of such significant progress inspires hope that poverty can be further reduced. However, though many fewer people in the world exist on less than $1 a day today than in 1980, the percentage of those living below $2 a day has not moved significantly in decades.[11] The 2014 Millennium Development Goals report shows that though several targets have already been met, others have proven elusive.[12] There is still much work to do, but there is greater hope that intelligently designed programs can end the scourge of extreme poverty.

Theologians share both the hope and despair of social scientists and aid workers, and in recent years, they have turned their attention to global poverty.[13] In contrast, relatively little attention has been focused on domestic poverty. Both major political parties' 2012 campaigns emphasized the plight of the middle class. Searches in social science indexes on poverty reduction yield virtually no titles on domestic poverty. Far fewer theologians are studying the issue.[14]

This is somewhat surprising, because though the global financial and economic crisis of 2007–9 has ended, poverty remains deeply problematic. About 15 percent of people in the United States remain poor, though if one includes the "near poor," the figure can rise to as high as one-third.[15] It is true that real household income has *risen* slightly for all income groups (and has risen much more for the top 1 percent) in the last several decades, but the progress has been concentrated in the highest income levels and poverty has not gone away.[16]

The need to focus on domestic poverty holds, even if poor people here are better off than the 40 percent of the world's population who live on less than $2 a day. In 2010, as liberals mourned the increase of poverty in the United States, conservative think tanks controversially reminded everyone that the poor in the United States were far better off than poor people in other parts of the world.[17] We can and should acknowledge this reality without abandoning the cause of poverty reduction. It is true that only a small percentage of poor people in the United States live with constant hunger, severe overcrowding, or a lack of access to health care and education, but it is also true that a persistent number deal with food insecurity, inadequate health care, and a substandard education.[18] Although it is important not to understate the extent of suffering in the United States, any analysis of domestic poverty must keep in mind the gross disparities between all US citizens and the very poor in the developing world. Yet knowing that the United States, unlike many other nations, has the infra-structure and financial resources to solve this problem should make us all the more anxious to do so. Moreover, the goal should be not simply to make poverty more bearable or to subsidize incomes so they rise above the poverty line but also to reduce poverty.

PRINCIPLES OF POVERTY REDUCTION

Most Catholics agree that having a special concern for the poor is central to their faith, but disagreement about how to act on this concern is widespread.[19] Although, in principle, all Catholics should be able to agree on the need for poverty reduction, questions of guiding principles and strategy need to be clarified. I propose that the principles of solidarity, subsidiarity, participation, and frugality that are central to contemporary Christian thinking about poverty have a great deal in common with the strategies for poverty reduction recommended by social scientists and aid workers today. Seeing the overlap between the two discourses is a crucial step toward developing concrete local responses as alternatives to charity and politics.

Solidarity

Solidarity is the appropriate starting point for any Catholic discussion of poverty. First of all, we acknowledge that we are inescapably connected as human beings created by one God. In the well-known words of Pope John Paul II, "We are all responsible for all."[20] The problems of those who suffer should matter to us; their needs make claims on our lives. Of course, some are uncomfortable with the sweeping nature of this declaration and worry that it says too much to mean anything.[21] It is necessary to point out how vagueness and a lack of attention to structural issues can limit the usefulness of solidarity defined this way, but a strength of John Paul II's claim is its very Catholic anthropology; "we are all responsible for all" because we are related. This is precisely what Christine Firer Hinze brings forward in a wonderful analysis of the communion of the saints as a resource for social ethics. This communion of persons includes "all souls who have loved and suffered in poverty of body and spirit, in hunger, in thirst for justice, in meekness and mercy, and all who have been abused and persecuted for loving what and whom God loves."[22] More than the option for the poor (an obligation to do "for" others), solidarity is a description of what is—our interconnectedness. Right from the beginning, Christians recognize that to be a person is to be in relation to others. As Pope Benedict XVI writes, *the human race is a single family working together in true communion, not simply a group of subjects who happen to live side by side* (emphasis in the original).[23] This is both an anthropological claim and an ethical norm: "It is not by isolation that man establishes his worth, but by placing himself in relation with others and with God."[24] The obligation flows right from the reality.

Something like solidarity lies at the root of the mission of many organizations that work in the field of human socioeconomic development. Paul Farmer's Partners in Health, for instance, speaks of a mission that is "both medical and moral," "based on solidarity rather than charity alone."[25] It is this sense of connectedness to other human beings that leads Partners in Health to commit to bringing the best health care to its patients, with a priority on the very sick and very poor, because their needs are the greatest. It is the force behind their assessment that technological progress may seem like a solution to poverty, but in practice it more often increases the gap between rich and poor, and thus "our structural sin deepens."[26] Because they believe that all human beings are connected, they mourn the gap between rich and poor and work for the structural changes that will level the ground on which we stand, erasing the wounds of inequality.

Subsidiarity

Sometimes, strong defenders of solidarity subtly challenge the centrality of subsidiarity to a Catholic social ethic, or at least they raise questions when subsidiarity is used to support lower levels of government intervention. If we are all connected, it can seem that increased government spending for the needy among us should almost always be viewed positively. Yet the tradition of CST does have a preference for the thriving of smaller groupings. As I noted in chapter 3, Pope Pius XI famously argued, "Just as it is gravely wrong to take from individuals what they can accomplish by their own initiative and industry and give it to the community, so also it is an injustice and at the same time a grave evil and disturbance of the right order to assign to a greater or higher association what a lesser and subordinate organizations can do."[27] The principle of subsidiarity is not radically antigovernment or anticorporation. However, it does hold that though government has an irreplaceable role in recognizing and protecting human rights, the "right order" of society is much richer than the state and individuals. In community associations of all kinds, solidarity can be experienced and enacted, and often we can make better decisions about how to live together.

In *Centesimus Annus*, John Paul II worries about two sources of alienation: the market and "the Social Assistance State." Although he celebrates "the modern business economy's respect for freedom and creativity," he argues that "many people, perhaps the majority today, do not have the means which would enable them to take their place in an effective and humanly dignified way within a productive system in which work is truly central."[28] The market can marginalize those who cannot participate, but an overly aggressive state can also threaten the humanity of society:

> By intervening directly and depriving society of its responsibility, the Social Assistance State leads to a loss of human energies and an inordinate increase of public agencies, which are dominated more by bureaucratic ways of thinking than by concern for serving their clients, and which are accompanied by an enormous increase in spending. In fact, it would appear that needs are best understood and satisfied by people who are closest to them and who act as neighbours to those in need. It should be added that certain kinds of demands often call for a response which is not simply material but which is capable of perceiving the deeper human need.[29]

This Catholic preference for local participation is echoed by many who study international development. Analysts claim that aid money is often wasted because local organizations are not consulted about major projects.[30] Aid agencies come in with ideas and because they have power, confidence, and resources, their offers are accepted, and their plans are implemented. However, it is not uncommon for these plans to unravel. Local organizations have knowledge of culture, resources, the physical environment, and religion that outsiders lack. The best programs advocate not only consulting with local people but also involving them in planning and working alongside them.

The philosopher Peter Singer questions traditional forms of aid but argues for continued giving to developing nations: "Huge shipments of food can indeed destroy local markets and reduce incentives for local farmers to produce a surplus to sell, but we should instead give to organizations which will work to develop social structures 'to make it possible for people to earn their own money, or to produce their own food and meet their other needs in a sustainable manner and by their own work.'"[31]

Catholic development organizations have learned this lesson from experience, as Charles Camosy points out in his description of how Catholic Relief Services (CRS) changed after the Rwandan genocide: "This unspeakable tragedy happened despite CRS having worked in the country since 1960 and having spent millions of dollars on education, maternal and child health and in agricultural development work. CRS workers were so close with the people that several even married Rwandans. The utter failure of their aid effort to avoid the genocide caused the agency to engage in a period of 'prolonged period of prayer, reflection, planning and policy development.'"[32] They found that their top-down focus limited their effectiveness on the ground. After the tragedy, they began working more closely with local organizations, making concrete the subsidiarity they affirmed in theory.[33] If poverty reduction efforts are to be humane and effective, adherence to this principle is crucial.

Participation

In the introduction to this chapter, I briefly alluded to distinctions between relief, rehabilitation, and development approaches. I suggested that a common mistake of US churches is providing relief when rehabilitation or development is needed. A key claim of the writers Steve Corbett and Brain Fikkert in *When Helping Hurts* is that because people are created to contribute to the world and want to provide for themselves, development should be directed to helping them achieve this goal.[34] CST makes a similar, though not identical point. In *Laborem Exercens*, John Paul II calls work "a fundamental dimension of man's existence on earth" and claims that through work we "subdue" or "dominate" the earth.[35] "However true it may be that man is destined for work and called to it," he cautions, "in the first place work is 'for man' and not man 'for work.'"[36] Work is important because it is how human persons make their mark upon the earth or co-create the world. It is essential to life, though it is not the only essential thing or the only way to contribute to society.[37]

Work is important because it is a dimension of participation, which is a key principle in Catholic social thought. When people are not able to participate in society, their sociality—a fundamental dimension of their personhood—is denied. Unemployment is one important aspect of the social marginalization that results from poverty. Restoring people to work allows them to contribute to the life of a community. Thus, John Paul II writes that "a person is alienated if he refuses to transcend himself and to live the experience of self-giving. . . . A society is alienated if its forms of social organization, production, and consumption make it more difficult to offer this gift of self."[38] Ideally, a society enables the self-giving participation of all persons. The Catholic tradition acknowledges the role of relief but privileges efforts that enable people to contribute to the common good and support their families by giving themselves to something for the sake of others.[39] In its preference for participation, CST is very much in line with the literature of poverty reduction.

Frugality

Frugality is not usually included in lists of the key principles of CST.[40] I contend, however, that it is a key dimension of many social papal encyclicals, from *Rerum Novarum* to *Caritas Veritate*. A full discussion is impossible in this chapter, but a few points are crucial. First, frugality is the flipside of the just wage. An employer is obligated to pay a wage that enables a worker to live *in frugal comfort*.[41] Pope Benedict, in *Caritas in Veritate*, calls for social transformation and for new lifestyles marked by simplicity and gratuity of time and money.[42] Though CST has not developed this idea in sufficient depth, it seems an underutilized resource with a great deal of importance—both for the poor, who need it to live on small incomes while accumulating assets; and for the better off, who can use it to control expenses so they have more money to give to domestic and international development organizations. Frugality (spending less by questioning the standards of one's reference group) is a necessary virtue for all people.[43]

Aid organizations also acknowledge the need for training in frugality. New research on the effects of poverty has documented the extreme stress to which it subjects adults and the way it diminishes cognitive resources and has a negative impact on decision making.[44] Researchers are careful to note that poor individuals are not inherently less able to make good decisions. Rather, living in poverty has a negative impact on their abilities. Given this situation, training in fiscal discipline and structures that make saving easier are crucial for those who seek to climb out of poverty. The current development literature affirms the important place of education and assistance with saving and asset building.[45]

Though the virtue of frugality may be construed in narrowly individualistic or paternalistic ways, it need not be. In the context of CST, Christians are called into a community where we practice these virtues together so that we can better care for each other. Imagine, for example, if a Catholic high school were to hold discussions for groups of parents and students about the costs of senior year (e.g., graduation announcements, pictures, and parties; prom attire, hair and make-up packages, bids, limousines, and party buses)? What if the community—out of a concern for inclusivity, a desire to not encourage less-well-off students to take on levels of spending they cannot afford, and a concern to enable its middle- and upper-class families who tend to spend the most to maintain generous levels of charitable giving—discerned together a better, simpler approach to senior year that enabled students and their families to mark important occasions without excessive luxury? Or what if a local nonprofit offered classes on frugality open to both clients and supporters? How might the resulting conversations and connections shape the lives of all the attendees? This communal approach to frugality begins to look a lot more like solidarity.

The principles of solidarity, subsidiarity, participation, and frugality are all crucial to the Catholic approach to poverty reduction. Although one could certainly argue for the inclusion of several others (e.g., the option for the poor, justice, human dignity, the common good, rights and responsibilities, and the priority of labor), those I have chosen are essential to formulating better strategies for poverty reduction. Solidarity grounds our concern in the reality of relationship and gives priority to the needs of a community's least privileged members. Subsidiarity reminds us to work as locally as possible, involving and empowering people in need. Participation places work at the center of antipoverty plans, and frugality allows the poor to build assets while encouraging the rich and middle class to give as much as they should to poverty reduction efforts. These principles are not only central to Catholic thought; they cohere with what social scientists and aid workers are saying about best practices for poverty reduction, as I show in the next section.

STRATEGIES FOR POVERTY REDUCTION

It is impossible to deny that poverty is not only personal but also structural. The policies that perpetuate the privileges and liabilities of race, class, and gender give context to individual lives and shape possibilities.[46] For this reason, Catholics have long supported political advocacy in support of better policies, including just wages, Social Security, education, and health care.[47] Moreover, economic growth is essential to moving people out of poverty, though insufficient in itself.[48] However, though efforts to increase growth and encourage advocacy for just policies should continue, we should also consider what research suggests about how local groups can best help poor people move out of poverty.[49] The strategies I consider next constitute a set of proposed "best practices" for economic empowerment in the space between the personal and the political.

Asset Mapping

Charity groups often begin by asking about needs, but John Kretzmann and John McNight, of Asset-Based Community Development, recommend instead beginning with asking questions about the strengths of communities and individuals that enable those involved to construct an asset map.[50] If the goal is reducing poverty, it makes sense to focus on the community's advantages—its assets—by asking "What do we have?" and "What can we do well?" This map can include the skills of individuals (e.g., cooking, gardening, mathematics, computers, organizing) as well as physical resources (e.g., land where produce can be grown, abandoned buildings that could be bought cheaply and rehabilitated) and community organizations. Corbett and Fikkert contend that especially when people are marginalized, questions about gifts and talents can be a crucial part of helping them think positively about their future. Moreover, people may be able to build on their assets, and increased assets are associated with movement out of poverty.[51]

Needs Assessment

Later, needs must be assessed. Often, charity groups do not formally assess the needs of the people they wish to help; they assume they know what they are. The behavioral economists Dean Karlan and Jacob Appel decry this approach, saying, "If we want to solve poverty, we need to know what it is in real—not abstract—terms. We need to know how it smells, tastes, and feels to the touch."[52] In many parish-based programs, this knowledge is lacking. A participant in a parish Christmas gift tree program buys a basketball for "an eight-year-old boy," but the ball may sit in a closet if the child prefers puzzles to sports. A parish group collects food that may be thrown away because it does not match a family's preferences or dietary needs. Those in charge of clothing drives lament both the arrival of bags of clothing in very poor condition and the mismatch in the tastes of givers and receivers. The sorts of charitable activities that middle-class parishioners enjoy (e.g., Thanksgiving baskets, clothing, and canned food drives) may be the least needed, and, like international food aid initiatives, they keep economic activity strong in wealthy communities rather than generating activity where it is most needed. Even helping with utility bills, which is central to the work of the Saint Vincent de Paul Society, does not attempt to deal with the underlying problem of insufficient income. Churches and other community groups need more information about what poor people in their area really need to move out of poverty. An assessment of needs might uncover some of the following: tutoring, better schools, a safe playground, a bank that will provide loans for home repair and small businesses, a grocery store, a health clinic, and jobs. Community groups may not be able to address every need, but knowing how people perceive their situation is key.

Relationship Building

Building trust with a community before serving the people within it is crucial, as most development groups know well.[53] Yet this strategy is routinely overlooked by religious charities. The Society of Saint Vincent de

Paul, for instance, sends parishioners on home visits to clients. The vast majority of visits are one-time only.[54] The idea, which dates back to the 1800s, is to bring food but also to try to have a conversation, give advice on job training and budgeting, and pray with people. This personalist approach has advantages over the alternative of simply dropping off food, yet it is also limited. The group can only offer so much help to each client. Most of the situations of clients are unsustainable; they simply do not have enough income to meet their expenses. Yet what can parishioners do in one visit to a family they do not know and may never see again? This work of charity is rooted in compassion. It provides crucial help for many who cannot make it through the month on their own. Yet it is not the full vision of CST, which encourages relational solidarity.

Christians who have studied development argue that we can do much more if we place relationships at the center of development work. Partners in Health (PIH), for instance, identifies four principles as foundation to its work: "We go," "We make house calls," "We build health systems," and "We stay."[55] Central to PIH's approach is the training of health advocates from the communities it serves. It has been successful in improving health because it trains and empowers local residents. PIH's health advocates are "members of the communities they serve, and their patients know and trust them. They embody the PIH ethos of accompanying patients through their illnesses, treating them like family, and doing whatever it takes to help them get well."[56] The poverty reduction literature echoes the heart of contemporary CST, which calls for empowerment and a sharing of lives.

Job Training and Job Creation

Charitable organizations in the United States would do well to sharpen their ability to help poor adults find regular employment. In developing countries, aid groups must often contend with a lack of infrastructure (e.g., roads, clean water, power, and land appropriate for agriculture) and available jobs. Education and industry are insufficient to guarantee adequate income. Microfinance is a strategy that is being touted as the next best thing in global poverty reduction, because it gives people the seed they need to create work that otherwise simply would not exist. It has been enormously successful in some areas, and some argue that there is great potential for developing it in the United States.[57]

However, development experts are aware of the limits of microfinance.[58] Not everyone is an entrepreneur. In a poor economy, people sometimes opt to use investment funds for other purposes. In group plans, risk is shared, but weaker members can drag down stronger ones. Some communities lack an outside market, and people in poor communities rarely have much money to spend on new products or services. Unequal wealth brought about by successful clients can destabilize communities. Microfinance is a good but limited tool for increasing participation in the economy.

Preparing people for existing jobs is the more important strategy in the United States, where many potential job applicants lack the skills necessary to compete for or hold down the available jobs. Here, programs that focus on job preparedness and adult education are key to development.[59] Currently, the United States has rebounded from the global financial and economic crisis of 2007–9, and the official unemployment rate is under 6 percent.[60] Yet it is important to remember that those who are poor in the United States have a far greater chance of finding work than many in the developing world.[61] Although there is some debate on the effectiveness of job retraining programs, many available jobs go unfulfilled because of a lack of employees with the necessary skills.[62] The recent recession stemmed in part from a larger transition from an industrialized economy to an economy with many more service jobs.[63] It is harder now for those without college degrees to find jobs with living wages. Job-specific training is crucial to prepare men and women for skilled jobs that do pay more. However, as discussed in chapter 4, the development of "soft skills"—such as organizing child care, getting to work on time, restraining anger, and dressing professionally—is at least as important.[64] Moreover, this sort of skill development may be something that community groups can address better than government agencies.

Asset Accumulation

Helping people accumulate assets is another best practice. Because those who are poor need to concentrate their resources on just getting by, they are unable to deal with unexpected events. Problems such as illness and job loss, along with the need to spend large amounts of money on weddings and funerals, can wipe out gains and send people into a downward spiral of increasing poverty.[65] Asset accumulation is key to helping individuals and families weather crises.[66] In addition, having savings increases the ability of poor people to take risks (e.g., investing in education) to increase their earning power.

Just offering people the opportunity to save money is effective at increasing savings rates, and incentives such as automatic savings programs that encourage "people to bind themselves . . . to doing the right thing" are also helpful.[67] Matched savings programs, such as individual development accounts, combine incentives for saving with goal setting and financial literacy training; using savings from these accounts to complement microfinance is a strategy with potential to help people build their assets with assistance from donors.[68] Many development experts see asset accumulation through savings as at least as important as income generation.[69]

In sum, the new literature on poverty reduction suggests the importance of knowing a community's assets and needs, helping people find work, and encouraging them to save in order to help them manage risk. The approaches that experts see as most effective cohere with Catholic principles. Solidarity can be realized in long-term, demanding relationships between affluent and marginalized communities. Subsidiarity is respected because community organizations are seen as the key agents of development. Participation is encouraged through job training and job creation, and frugality is nurtured through asset building and savings programs. The fit between CST and the poverty reduction literature seems clear; but as the next section shows, historically, most Catholic antipoverty efforts have not been aimed at poverty reduction, though they are beginning to move in this direction.

ADAPTING CONTEMPORARY CATHOLIC RESPONSES TO POVERTY

Examining the Effectiveness of Current Programs

The Society of Saint Vincent de Paul was founded in Lyon in 1833. Today, the society's conferences in many parishes attempt to fill the gaps left by social service agencies by delivering food, running thrift stores, providing help with utility bills, collecting and fixing used cars, and the like. Their mission is to join with others in the work of "relieving need and addressing its causes, making no distinction in those served, because in them, Vincentians see the face of Christ."[70] Much of this work is necessary to prevent vulnerable people from experiencing more suffering and falling even more deeply into poverty. However, these efforts are, with some exceptions, responsive and reactive—they are effective at alleviating poverty but not at getting to its roots. The majority of data collected in the organization's standardized reports are about services provided rather than movement out of poverty.[71] Only recently has the organization begun to identify poverty reduction as a goal.[72] New resources for "ending poverty through systemic change" will require local conferences to adapt the traditional home visit model and begin mentoring clients, with the goal of accompanying them as they journey out of poverty.[73] It is not clear how many conferences are early adopters of the new model. The shift in focus is a relatively new attempt to work on the problem of poverty at a deeper level.

Catholic Charities, which was founded in 1910 in Washington, DC, has been actively committed not just to poverty alleviation but also to poverty reduction since 2006, when it introduced its "Campaign to Reduce Poverty in America," which has served as a road map for subsequent efforts.[74] The organization traditionally focused on providing direct services, supporting successful public policies (e.g., the minimum wage; Social Security; the Earned Income Tax Credit; Pell Grants; the Supplemental Nutrition Assistance Program, food stamps; Medicaid; and Medicare), and advocating for structural changes that would increase the supply of good jobs, affordable housing, health care, and social benefits.

Until relatively recently, Catholic Charities spoke about "poverty reduction" as the way government benefits help people live above the poverty line when their earnings alone would be insufficient to get them to this level. For instance, according to a 2006 report, "the poverty rate for individuals in 2004 would nearly double if it weren't for the income security programs that we have in place."[75] Catholic Charities also sponsored local efforts to help people move out of poverty, but the organization seemed to place its hope in government action to increase jobs and wages and provide more social welfare.[76] It described its commitment this way: "Because we know that poverty is a systemic problem and requires a systemic response, we pledge ourselves to attack the structural roots of poverty by advocating in Washington and state capitals," as well as informing the public about poverty, and providing social services.[77] To attack poverty at the systemic level was to advocate for political change.

Recently, however, Catholic Charities has deepened its emphasis on poverty reduction. Though its focus remains on policy change, its guiding principles are "results driven," "market-based," and "systems-changing," and its "#End45" campaign aims to better the prospects of the 45 million people in the United States who are living in poverty.[78] As with the Saint Vincent de Paul Society, the emphasis on real poverty reduction is encouraging though still relatively new. The gap between traditional service provision to individuals and advocacy at the state and federal levels is just beginning to be bridged.

The Catholic Campaign for Human Development (CCHD), founded in 1969, is the official domestic antipoverty program of the US Conference of Catholic Bishops. It forms partnerships with local community development organizations in order to carry out its mission. To this end, the CCHD funds groups that "work to change social structures and policies that undermine life and dignity, especially for the poor and powerless."[79] The examples of CCHD in action shown on its website are concentrated in the area of community organizing, which can be considered a local strategy.[80] Catholic parishes are sometimes directly involved in funded work, but many grants go to nonprofit groups.[81] CCHD is the most serious Catholic attempt to deal with poverty at its root and could be a model for future engagement. Its community development grants, which range from $25,000 to $75,000, are a significant tool for reducing poverty at the local level by empowering poor people and "nurturing solidarity between the poor and nonpoor."[82]

All US antipoverty groups need to face the difficult reality of a stubbornly flat poverty rate. Fifty years after President Lyndon B. Johnson declared the War on Poverty, it is far more pervasive than it ought to be in such a rich nation.[83] So soon after the end of a recession, one must view the poverty rate of 15.1 percent with some caution.[84] However, though it is unsurprising that poverty reduction has not advanced in the last several years, the fact that it has hovered between 11 and 15 percent since 1965 should be troubling.[85] Surely, the work of structural change is long term, and many factors that are out of any organization's control can have an impact on its effectiveness. In particular, the racist policies that have denied African Americans equal opportunities for work and asset accumulation cannot be ignored.[86] A retreat from political advocacy is certainly not warranted.

However, what is still largely missing from this snapshot of Catholic antipoverty work are parish-based efforts to help people move out of poverty. On one hand, the efforts of the Saint Vincent de Paul Society and Catholic Charities to move their organizations to an empowerment model are encouraging. On the other hand, realistically, it will take years for results to trickle down to these organizations' local branches. In the spring of 2014, I attended a conference for nonprofit organizations led by Robert Lupton, the author of *Toxic Charity: How Churches and Charities Hurt Those They Help—and How to Reverse It*.[87] The room was filled with hundreds of people who had given their lives to helping the poor. Some became angry at Lupton, even as they recognized the patterns he described. Others were intrigued, but wondered aloud how they could possibly change the direction of programs that are designed to serve rather than to empower. Most continued to listen because they could see that Lupton was totally committed to his cause, having lived and worked in the inner city for years. It was both frustrating and exciting to hear so many good, committed, knowledgeable people begin to imagine how to do antipoverty work differently. In the next subsection, I suggest that Catholics have wisdom to offer to this conversation that comes from their past.

Retrieving Wisdom from the Past

Most contemporary parish-based antipoverty efforts stand out in the history of US Catholicism because they are largely directed toward people who do not live within the parish boundaries. Ever since most Catholics migrated into the middle classes in the mid–twentieth century, social justice has moved from its place at the center of parish life because most Catholics no longer come to a parish seeking social support. Instead of "helping our own," parishes began to serve others.[88] Half of all parishes still engage in at least some direct social ministry, and one-third engage in some advocacy, and Catholics generally support this. [89] However, middle- and upper-class parishes tend to focus their energy on charitable activities benefiting children and the elderly who live elsewhere in town or abroad.[90]

In contrast, from the early 1800s until the early 1900s, Catholic parishes in the United States functioned as indispensable subcultures for urban, immigrant, working-poor Catholics. They provided community, social welfare, education, and spiritual sustenance. Priests, women religious, and parishioners contributed to the provision of services such as visiting the sick, operating food pantries, and staffing nurseries.[91] Many parishes also ran organizations such as building-and-loan associations, insurance groups, and burial societies that helped poor people make it through difficult times and save for the future.[92] At the same time, many Catholic social service institutions arose—such as hospitals, schools, orphanages, and Catholic Charities itself.[93] It is the second kind of response to poverty that interests me most; but sadly, it is this model that has all but disappeared.

The forms of parish organizations varied by ethnic group and region of the country, but all were ways for communities of working-poor immigrants to survive and progress. For instance, in the Northeast, the typical Italian American parish "made itself part of the Italian community and developed relations with Italian neighborhood institutions, including the family, mutual benefit societies and entrepreneurs."[94] The parish built relationships with people by celebrating with families and providing opportunities for entrepreneurs to promote their businesses. It also sponsored "mutual benefit societies," to which dues were paid in and from which benefits were paid out for members who were sick or unemployed.[95] In the Midwest, German Catholics formed societies called "*verein*," through which parish families supported each other in times of need.[96]

Immigrant parishes in the United States were far from perfect. The historian Jay Dolan points out that part of the reason for the rise of parish-based ethnic groups was the conservative vision of social reform prominent in the nineteenth century, when most Catholics believed that poverty should be embraced as God's will and countered with faith, self-denial, and moral living.[97] It was only later that Catholics would begin to challenge unjust social structures and join in social reform movements. In addition, part of the impetus for forming Catholic mutual aid societies was the concern to avoid proselytizing Protestant missionaries. For instance, a community of sisters founded the House of Mercy to care for immigrant Catholic girls in New York City who might otherwise succumb to the evil city or non-Catholic reformers.[98] Most important, the lack of Catholic concern for poor people outside their communities, especially African Americans, is egregious and inexcusable.[99] As the historian John McGreevy has shown, parish boundaries intentionally excluded African Americans, and charity was directed to "our own" rather than to those outside the lines the parish had drawn.[100] Instead of resisting segregation, the church was complicit in social sin, because it "related to African Americans in the same patterns of domination, segregation, and racism as the social institutions within our nation."[101] These serious problems limit the usefulness of the early immigrant model for our modern context.

Nonetheless, the strengths of immigrant parishes are still worth considering. They responded to the real assets and needs of a community. They set in place structures that reduced the sorts of risks that throw working-class people into poverty. They placed members of the community in service to one another. Instead of waiting for the government to act, Christian communities took charge of their own situation. Today's Catholics find themselves in a very different situation, with a much better consciousness of race and class. The old models cannot simply be lifted from the past. However, we can learn from those local responses that helped people move out of poverty and empowered them to live decent lives, even within the limits of relatively small incomes. By combining this forgotten aspect of the Catholic tradition with the evidence-based best practices of development experts today and the best principles of CST, it is possible to forge a better Catholic response to poverty that is fitting for today's context.

Toward a New Model

The interplay of solidarity and subsidiarity in Catholic social thought, outlined above, should bring Catholics to question current practices and explore new approaches. Solidarity both motivates social concern and grounds a more relational approach to poverty. Clothing, food, and present drives, though well intentioned, do not draw people into relationship with anyone but their own neighbors. More important, they do not get to the root of the problem. Instead, parishes could explore strategies of resource/needs mapping in their own community (or one nearby) and begin building relationships with the people of that community. By focusing on development instead of relief, programs would be honoring the value of subsidiarity, which encourages communities to work together to meet their own needs first. Subsidiarity stands as an important check on paternalistic social assistance and puts a priority on grassroots participation in economic development.[102]

If work is a form of human participation in community and the way that most people actualize their capacities, it is key to the social question. Most Catholics can do little about job creation from above, but even in the face of relatively higher levels of unemployment, they can participate in programs that help people acquire soft job skills, acquire the support they need to work full time, and receive mentoring that will help them through rough times.[103] Earlier Catholic communities fostered connections with other community institutions and supported local entrepreneurs and small businesses.[104] Parishes today are well suited to take up a contemporary version of this activity by bringing their considerable resources to bear on helping people find and keep suitable jobs.[105] If they can form partnerships with local businesses or draw on government resources while keeping their grassroots identity, so much the better.[106]

Promoting saving is just as necessary as fostering work capability. In the past, immigrant parishes had savings-and-loan associations that encouraged what is now called asset building. It may be possible to revive this model in order to help those who are poor save more of what they earn. Offering matched savings programs, such as individual development accounts, or forming partnerships with a local nonprofit to provide financial literacy training is an approach that religious organizations are adopting with some success.[107]

Of course, saving requires frugality—which, I have argued, is a virtue in need of retrieval. Some worry that the promotion of frugality is paternalistic and inappropriate. It can be. In the past, particularly when linked with a belief that poverty is God's will, it certainly was.[108] However, today the Catholic tradition advocates a simple lifestyle for everyone for much better reasons. If this vision were promoted via parish-sponsored presentations on saving money or small groups in which participants could help each other build better budgets, parishioners of all incomes could live on less. Growth in this virtue might open up all kinds of possibilities that are now closed to those who adopt the typical middle-class American model as ideal. If, instead, we take as our models communities such as the Catholic Workers, Jesuit Volunteer Corps, Amate House in Chicago, L'Arche, and women religious, more options emerge. Even with recent increases in the minimum wage, a single mother living with two small children and working a part-time service job has a nearly impossible task if she is trying to live in an apartment and cook for herself. She is similarly handicapped living in a home with other adults who are not working. Unless her income significantly increases, she will need to rely on government subsidies. However, if three working single moms share a rental house, child care, and cooking, and participate in an asset-building program at their local parish, they have a much better shot at independent living and saving for the future.[109]

Parishes themselves can promote frugality by adopting it in their own practices. CST should be lived as well as preached.[110] For instance, by looking to the past and to some developing countries today, we can find models for weddings and funerals that are far less costly and promote these alternative practices. Because weddings and funerals are life-cycle events that often send a marginal family into poverty for years, promoting more frugal alternatives can make a real difference in their lives.[111] In addition, promoting frugality for everyone could free up the incomes of middle-class families to contribute to parish-based development efforts. Communal shared sacrifice for the sake of poverty reduction could be the key to the success of the whole project. A transformational model with roots in the past could offer those on both the left and the right room to develop different kinds of antipoverty projects for a new era.

FROM ABOVE, FROM BELOW, AND IN BETWEEN

I have argued that both progress in eliminating poverty and its persistence should compel those in the United States to commit to further poverty reduction. There is a great deal of overlap between the principles of CST, what development experts are saying about best practices for poverty reduction, and the practices of early American Catholic parish-based mutual aid societies. Contemporary Catholic parishes that follow a synthesis of the wisdom from these sources have the potential to move to the forefront of poverty reduction efforts.

One might argue that the Christian tradition ought not be used to promote poverty reduction because results are not really our concern. Christians are called to embrace spiritual and material poverty and to feed the hungry rather than to try to stop hunger.[112] The salvation of souls is contingent precisely on this kind of work rather than on empowerment. The church's tradition upholds those who are dependent, vulnerable, and not at all self-sufficient. Many Catholic saints have shown great love for the poor, accepting their brokenness and the reality that many will remain unempowered. Perhaps all this focus on results is fundamentally at odds with what the tradition teaches about poverty.

In part, I must concede that it is at odds. The early church tradition includes radical sayings about the poor, but most writers were much more worried about how giving affected the giver than the receiver.[113] Historically, Catholic organizations did not adopt the goal of ending poverty. Even today, some argue that beggars deserve our kindness whether or not our help is effective. Moreover, it is no doubt true that some percentage of the poor will never be self-sufficient. Thankfully, Catholic theology has a place for them, and the church should also have one. Theologies that place too much emphasis on efficiency and self-sufficiency can paint a distorted picture of what it means to be a human person and what it means to be a faithful Christian.

However, unlike in many other periods of history, today it is possible to make a real difference in people's lives. Now may be the moment to say that charity is not solely or even primarily about the salvation of the givers; it is about the liberation of the oppressed. Effectiveness matters because to be a Christian is to care about the suffering of others and want to alleviate it. It only makes sense to care about the impact of charitable efforts on the most vulnerable. This is what it means to have true compassion today. Efforts to alleviate poverty are crucial to salvation broadly conceived, for the liberation and salvation of rich and poor alike.[114]

Making a real difference will involve changing the way we approach poverty. In *Caritas in Veritate* Pope Benedict asserts that gratuity is an ethic both for "peoples in hunger" and "peoples blessed with abundance."[115] It applies to people in both worlds, because "every life is a vocation" and all people deserve the chance to use their freedom to create their own lives.[116] This welcome emphasis on participation should direct us to support development projects that empower people. "Reciprocity," the pope says, "is the heart of what is it is to be a human being."[117] People who are poor want to own their duty to shape their destiny and find their own way of gratuity. People who live in abundance want to own their duty to give out of their substance and practice gratuity more radically. Empowerment, then, is a better framework for authentic human development than charity.[118]

I saw this approach in action when I was in Nicaragua in 2008. Together with an organization called AKF and a group of wealthy Midwestern Rotary Club donors, I visited two small rural communities.[119] I watched our leader, Elena Hendricks, engage in community organizing. She began by asking the people in the community to divide into groups and make a list of their strengths and dreams. The Rotarians were interested in helping the villagers start sewing cooperatives and a large vegetable garden that would help stabilize their food supply. First, Elena asked the community what they celebrated and what their resources were. Some spoke of wells they had built by hand and illnesses they had survived. The discussion then turned to needs. The villagers spoke of their desire for musical instruments for their church services and of a possible expansion of their church. Later, they articulated needs for a school and health clinic. They named clay soil and the river as assets. Elena drew pictures on butcher paper of what the villagers told her their dreams would look like. We played games that erased distinctions between the helpers and the helped. Later, the Rotarians would process what they had heard. Only after several similar visits would AKF allow them to begin funding projects.

Aid agencies are not always this committed to process. Elena told of another group that built a concrete play area right in the middle of what had been the community's soccer field. When it rains, the village center now floods, and no one plays soccer there anymore. All this the villagers could have told the aid group that installed the playground, but the group had its own idea; they did not take the time to build the relationships necessary for real dialogue, and they missed an opportunity to meet real needs and empower those they sought to help.

Catholic social reform efforts should center on poverty reduction rather than poverty relief. Although it is impossible to identify in advance which detailed strategies will work in a given community, a focus on identifying strengths and acknowledging weaknesses, building relationships, encouraging participation, cultivating the frugality needed for savings and asset building, and developing community networks of support is broadly applicable. It is a strategy that draws upon the best of the Catholic social tradition and translates principles and practices in order to seize hold of the possibilities of the contemporary situation. Because it entails a strong commitment to bettering the lives of the poor through empowerment, it cuts across the liberal/conservative divide. It does not in any way negate the need for political advocacy or personal conversion, but it does give us another space to come together and work for what we all want: if not an end to poverty, at least much less of it.

NOTES

1. For a fairly comprehensive overview of Catholic social justice and charity efforts from the 1800s until the present, see Charles E. Curran, *The Social Mission of the US Catholic Church: A Theological Perspective* (Washington, DC: Georgetown University Press, 2011).

2. Steve Corbett and Brain Fikkert, *When Helping Hurts: How to Alleviate Poverty without Hurting the Poor . . . and Yourself* (Chicago: Moody, 2009), 105. Corbett and Fikkert are connected with the Chalmers Center (https://www.chalmers.org/). Though there are important theological differences between Catholics and evangelicals, the Chalmers Center provides effective tools for churches interested in poverty reduction efforts that have proven to be effective.

3. Maureen O'Connell, *Compassion: Loving Our Neighbor in an Age of Globalization* (Maryknoll, NY: Orbis, 2009), 24.

4. For a fuller analysis of Christian social ethics, see Julie Hanlon Rubio, *Family Ethics: Practices for Christians* (Washington, DC: Georgetown University Press, 2010), 37–65.

5. See, e.g., Charles Kenny, *Getting Better: Why Global Development in Succeeding—and How We Can Improve the World Even More* (New York: Basic Books, 2011); Dean Karlan and Jacob Appel, *More Than Good Intentions: How a New Economics Is Helping to Solve Global Poverty* (New York: E. P. Dutton, 2011); Jeffrey D. Sachs, *Common Wealth: Economics for a Crowded Planet* (New York: Penguin, 2008); Jeffrey D. Sachs, *The End of Poverty: Economic Possibilities for Our Time* (New York: Penguin 2006); Caroline Moser, ed., *Reducing Global Poverty: The Case for Asset Accumulation* (Washington, DC: Brookings Institution Press, 2007); Deepa Narayan and Patti Petesch, eds., *Moving Out of Poverty: Cross-Disciplinary Perspectives on Mobility* (New York: Palgrave Macmillan and World Bank, 2007); and Peter Singer, *The Life You Can Save: Acting Now to End World Poverty* (New York: Random House, 2009).

6. See United Nations, "Reports," http://www.un.org/millenniumgoals/reports.shtml.

7. See Bill & Melinda Gates Foundation, "A Call for Global Citizens," http://www.gatesfoundation.org/, especially, "What We're Learning," which best illustrates the research-based approach that is central to the foundation.

8. In addition to O'Connell, *Compassion*, see Charles C. Camosy, *Peter Singer and Christian Ethics* (Cambridge: Cambridge University Press, 2012).

9. World Bank, "Poverty Overview," April 6, 2015, http://www.worldbank.org/en/topic/poverty/overview. See also the discussion of progress by Joe Pettit, "A Defense of Unbounded (but Not Unlimited) Economic Growth," *Journal of the Society of Christian Ethics* 30, no. 1 (2010): 183–204.

10. "Towards the End of Poverty," *The Economist*, June 1, 2013, http://www
.economist.com/news/leaders/21578665-nearly-1-billion-people-have-been-taken
-out-extreme-poverty-20-years-world-should-aim.

11 See World Bank, "Poverty Reduction and Inequity," http://web.world
bank.org/WBSITE/EXTERNAL/TOPICS/EXTPOVERTY/EXTPA/0,,content
MDK:20040961~menuPK:435040~pagePK:148956~piPK:216618~theSite
PK:430367~isCURL:Y,00.html.

12. See United Nations, *Millennium Development Goal 8: The State of the
Global Partnership for Development—MDG Gap Task Force Report 2014*
(New York: United Nations, 2014), http://www.un.org/millenniumgoals/2014
_Gap_Report/MDG%20Gap%20Task%20Force%20Report%202014_full%20
report_English.pdf. For all the annual Millennium Development Goals reports,
see http://www.un.org/millenniumgoals/reports.shtml.

13. See, e.g., James F. Keenan, ed., *Catholic Theological Ethics: Past, Present,
and Future* (Maryknoll, NY: Orbis, 2011). The volume includes selected published
papers from the second annual meeting of moral theologians from all over the
world. In the sections gathering important voices from "the present" and "the
future," two-thirds of the essays focus on the social, economic, and health problems of the developing world.

14. On economic justice issues, a search of major theological journals in the
last five years yields virtually no articles on domestic poverty issues. Books in
the last ten years are similarly scarce. An exception is by Mark J. Allman, ed., *The
Almighty and the Dollar: Reflections on Economic Justice for All* (Winona, MN:
Anselm, 2012). For a comprehensive review of recent research, which also has an
emphasis on global rather than domestic poverty, see Christine Firer Hinze, "Economic Recession, Work, and Solidarity," *Theological Studies* 72 (2011): 150–69.

15. Jason DePartle, Robert Gebeloff, and Sabrina Tavernise, "Older, Suburban,
and Struggling, 'Near Poor' Startle the Census," *New York Times*, November 18,
2011, http://www.nytimes.com/2011/11/19/us/census-measures-those-not-quite-in
-poverty-but-struggling.html?r=2&pagewanted=2&nl=todaysheadlines&emc
=tha23.

16. US Census Bureau, *Income, Poverty, and Health Insurance Coverage in the
United States: 2010*, http://www.census.gov/newsroom/releases/archives/income
_wealth/cb11-157.html. The poverty threshold for a family of four in 2010 was
$22,314. The 15.1 percent poverty rate was the highest since 1993, but lower than
in 1959.

17. See, e.g., Robert Rector and Rachel Sheffield, "Understanding Poverty
in the United States: Surprising Facts About America's Poor," Heritage Foundation, September 13, 2011, http://www.heritage.org/research/reports/2011/09
/understanding-poverty-in-the-united-states-surprising-facts-about-americas
-poor.

18. Comparative studies show the United States lagging behind other developed nations in the percentage of people who move out of poverty. In addition, a greater percentage of Americans remain poor overall. See Stefan Dercon and Joseph S. Shapiro, "Moving On, Staying Behind, Getting Lost: Lessons on Poverty Mobility from Longitudinal Data," in *Moving Out of Poverty*, ed. Narayan and Petesch.

19. William D'Antonio et al., *American Catholics Today: New Realities of Their Faith and Their Church* (Lanham, MD: Sheed & Ward, 2007), 93.

20. John Paul II, *Solicitudo Rei Socialis* (1987), no. 38, http://w2.vatican.va /content/john-paul-ii/en/encyclicals/documents/hf_jp-ii_enc_30121987_sollicitudo -rei-socialis.html.

21. Christine Firer Hinze, "Over, Under, Around, and Through: Ethics, Solidarity, and the Saints," in *CTSA Proceedings* 66 (2011), 40. Hinze prefers a more concrete definition.

22. Hinze, "Ethics, Solidarity, and the Saints," 48.

23. Benedict XVI, *Caritas in Veritate* (2009), no 53, http://w2.vatican.va /content/benedict-xvi/en/encyclicals/documents/hf_ben-xvi_enc_20090629_caritas -in-veritate.html.

24. Ibid.

25. Paul Farmer, "A Doctor's Tribute to Gustavo Gutierrez," in *In the Company of the Poor: Conversations with Dr. Paul Farmer and Fr. Gustavo Gutierrez*, ed. Michael Griffin and Jennie Weiss Block (Maryknoll, NY: Orbis, 2013), 21.

26. Ibid., 22.

27. Pius XI, *Quadragesimo Anno* (1931), no. 79, http://w2.vatican.va/content /pius-xi/en/encyclicals/documents/hf_p-xi_enc_19310515_quadragesimo-anno .html.

28. John Paul II, *Centesimus Annus* (1991), no. 33, http://w2.vatican.va /content/john-paul-ii/en/encyclicals/documents/hf_jp-ii_enc_01051991_centesimus -annus.html.

29. Ibid., no. 48.

30. See e.g., Peter Buffett, "The Charitable-Industrial Complex," *New York Times*, July 26, 2012, http://www.nytimes.com/2013/07/27/opinion/the-chari table-industrial-complex.html?r=0.

31. Camosy, *Peter Singer*, 153.

32. Ibid., 154.

33. Ibid., 155.

34. Corbett and Fikkert, *When Helping Hurts*, 78–79.

35. John Paul II, *Laborem Exercens* (1981), no. 4, http://w2.vatican.va/content /john-paul-ii/en/encyclicals/documents/hf_jp-ii_enc_14091981_laborem-exercens .html. Contemporary Catholic thinkers are more likely to emphasize stewardship.

36. Ibid., no. 6. The gender-exclusive language here is, of course, problematic.

37. E.g., caring work in the home is valuable, as is time away from work for family, leisure, and the spiritual life. Ibid., no 19.

38. John Paul II, *Centesimus Annus*, no. 41.

39. Of course, some people, because of mental illness, ongoing substance abuse issues, or other problems will not be able to work. Relief will always be needed. Communities such as the Catholic Worker and L'Arche allow for participation in community when it is not possible in the economic sector.

40. There are different lists of key themes but this one from the USCCB is fairly standard: www.usccb.org/beliefs-and-teachings/what-we-believe/catholic -social-teaching/seven-themes-of-catholic-social-teaching.cfm. William Byron, SJ, has identified ten themes, including subsidiarity; see William Byron, "The Ten Commandments of Catholic Social Teaching," *OSV Newsweekly*, n.d., https:// www.osv.com/TabId/735/ArtMID/13636/ArticleID/9770/.

41. Leo XIII. *Rerum Novarum* (1891), no 34, http://w2.vatican.va/content /leo-xiii/en/encyclicals/documents/hf_l-xiii_enc_15051891_rerum-novarum .html.

42. Benedict XVI, *Caritas in Veritate*, no. 51.

43. See David Cloutier, "The Problem of Luxury in the Christian Life," *Journal of the Society of Christian Ethics* 32:1 (2012): 3–20; and James A. Nash, "Toward the Revival and Reform of the Subversive Virtue: Frugality," *Journal of the Society of Christian Ethics* (1995): 137–6.

44. See, e.g., Evan Nesterak, "The Cognitive Burden of Poverty," *Psychreport*, September 2, 2013, http://thepsychreport.com/research-application /featured-research/the-cognitive-burden-of-poverty/.

45. See Abhibit Banerjee et al., " A Multifaceted Program Causes Lasting Progress for the Very Poor: Evidence from Six Countries," *Science* 348, no. 6236 (May 2015), http://www.sciencemag.org/content/348/6236/1260799.full. In theological ethics, see James P. Bailey, *Rethinking Poverty: Income, Assets, and the Catholic Social Justice Tradition* (Notre Dame, IN: University of Notre Dame Press, 2010).

46. For a brief summary of structural factors shaping the African American experience, see Bryan N. Massingale, *Racial Justice and the Catholic Church* (Maryknoll, NY: Orbis, 2010), 37–40; and Gerald Beyer, "The Continuing Relevance of Brothers and Sisters to Us to Confronting Racism and White Privilege," *Josephinum Journal of Theology* 19, no. 2 (2012): 235–64.

47. See, e.g., Ernie Cortes, "Reflections on the Catholic Tradition of Family Rights," in *One Hundred Years of Catholic Social Teaching: Celebration and Challenge*, ed. John A. Coleman (Maryknoll, NY: Orbis, 1991), 155–73.

48. In listing five key conclusions emerging from data on poor people's mobility, Deepa Narayan and Patti Petesch note that "as many studies have concluded,

growth alone is not enough—especially when inequalities are large." Deepa Narayan and Patti Petesch, "Agency, Opportunity Structure, and Poverty Escapes," in *Moving Out of Poverty*, ed. Narayan and Petesch, 31.

49. For the developing world, structural changes, not individual changes, "most often facilitate escapes from poverty," as noted by Charles Tilly, "Poverty and the Politics of Exclusion," in *Moving Out of Poverty*, ed. Narayan and Petesch, 45–75, at 63. However, even there, innovative strategies at the individual and community levels can be important complements to structural programs.

50. Corbett and Fikkert, *When Helping Hurts*, 133–35. Participatory approaches to development begin with focusing on assets rather than needs.

51. Stefan Dercon and Joseph S. Shapiro, "Moving On, Staying Behind, Getting Lost: Lessons on Poverty Mobility from Longitudinal Data," 77–126, cited in *Moving Out of Poverty*, ed. Narayan and Petesch, 109. The authors caution that correlation is not causality.

52. Karlan and Appel, *More Than Good Intentions*, 37. They recommend randomized control trials to determine the impact of programs on participants (pp. 30–31).

53. Trust is crucial to getting poor communities to buy into programs. Ibid., 48.

54. See, e.g., Society of Saint Vincent de Paul–Archdiocesan Council of Saint Louis, https://svdpstlouis.org/. This local chapter offers legal assistance, utility assistance, free lunches, assistance for fire victims, repairs for seniors, housing for disabled persons, a veterans' program, a released prisoners' program, used cars, pharmaceutical vouchers, medical screening, and thrift stores.

55. See Partners in Health, "We Make House Calls," http://www.pih.org/blog/we-make-house-calls?subsource=AR2014_nav_widget.

56. Ibid.

57. See Opportunity Fund: Working Capital for Working People, http://www.opportunityfund.org/learn/microloans. The Aspen Institute estimates that only 2 percent of potential US microfinance customers are being served, compared with the 17 percent in the developing world. A growing percentage of Americans are "unbanked."

58. Karlan and Appel, *More Than Good Intentions*, 82, claim that microcredit can work but is not a "one-size-fits-all solution to poverty"; see, especially, chapters 5 and 6.

59. Brian Nolan and Robert Erikson summarize longitudinal data showing that "poverty exits" in the United States are most closely associated with increases in the number of persons in a household who work, an increase in the number of months worked, and an increase in earnings. Brian Nolan and Robert Erikson, "Intragenerational Income Mobility: Poverty Dynamics in Industrial Societies," in

Moving Out of Poverty, ed. Narayan and Petesch, 127–64, at 142. Jobs are more closely associated with movement into and out of poverty in the United States than in other countries. The likelihood of persistent poverty in the United States "was most affected by the number of workers in the household" (p. 143).

60. US Bureau of Labor Statistics, "Labor Force Statistics from the Current Population Survey," http://data.bls.gov/timeseries/LNS14000000.

61. E.g., in 2012 unemployment rates in many countries in Africa, the Middle East, and India were far higher than in the United States—consider Haiti, at 40.6 percent. Even in Central and South America, where official unemployment rates are high, underemployment and low wages are far more serious problems than in the United States; see http://www.indexmundi.com/g/r.aspx?t=100&v=74.

62. See Chris Arnold, "A Labor Mismatch Means Trucking Jobs Go Unfilled," NPR, October 13, 2011, http://www.npr.org/2011/10/13/141325299/a-labor-mismatch-means-trucking-jobs-go-unfilled, which cites the work of the economists Giorgia Topa and Aysegul Sahin.

63. Rebecca Todd Peters, "Considering a Solidarity Economy as a Framework for Justice," in *Almighty and the Dollar*, ed. Allman, 129–31.

64. Nick Schulz, "Hard Unemployment Truths about 'Soft' Skills," *Wall Street Journal*, September 19, 2012, http://www.aei.org/publication/hard-unemployment-truths-about-soft-skills/. See also Corbett and Fikkert, *When Helping Hurts*, 191–94.

65. Dercon and Shapiro, "Moving On," 91, find a strong correlation between health problems and movement into poverty.

66. Dercon and Shapiro, "Moving On," 93, claim that "risks and shocks are a factor that hinders people from escaping poverty or even pushes them into poverty," though they caution that more evidence is needed on the role of assets in protecting them from risk. Karlan and Appel, *More Than Good Intentions*, 151, are more positive about the role of savings in changing lives. Michael Carter argues that assets are linked to capabilities and are more important for measuring and reducing poverty than income; Michael Carter, "Learning from Asset-Based Approaches to Poverty," in *Reducing Global Poverty*, ed. Moser, 51.

67. Karlan and Appel, *More Than Good Intentions*, 157, 160.

68. See Accion, "Microloans in the United States," 2015, http://www.accioneast.org/home/support-accion/learn/microlending-in-the-united-states.aspx.

69. Karlan and Appel, *More Than Good Intentions*, 145–46.

70. See Society of Saint Vincent de Paul–Archdiocesan Council of Saint Louis, "Who We Are," https://svdpstlouis.org/who-we-are.

71. See National Council of the US Society of Saint Vincent de Paul, "Annual Report," https://www.svdpusa.org/members/Membership/Annual-Report.

72. See National Council of the US Society of Saint Vincent de Paul, "Systemic Change: Hope in Action," http://www.svdpusa.org/systemicchange/.

73. See National Council of the US Society of Saint Vincent de Paul, "End Poverty through Systemic Change Vision Statement—FAQ," http://www.svdpusa .org/systemicchange/General-Information/FAQs.

74. On the history, see J. Bryan Hehir, *Catholic Charities USA: 100 Years at the Intersection of Charity and Justice* (Collegeville, MN: Liturgical Press, 2010); and Fred Kammer, SJ, *Faith, Works, Wonders: An Insider's Guide to Catholic Charities* (Eugene, OR: Pickwick, 2009). On current programs, see Catholic Charities, "What We Do," https://catholiccharitiesusa.org/what-we-do.

75. Catholic Charities, *Poverty in America: A Threat to the Common Good* (Washington, DC: Catholic Charities, 2006), 14, 16. Charts show how the United States compares to other countries in the "[poverty] reduction factor" or the percentage change in the poverty rate after government assistance.

76. Ibid., 15–16.

77. Ibid., 26.

78. See Catholic Charities, "#End45: Raise a Hand to End Poverty in America," https://catholiccharitiesusa.org/c/end45.

79. See US Conference of Catholic Bishops, "Catholic Campaign for Human Development," http://www.usccb.org/about/catholic-campaign-for-human-devel opment/upload/cchd-gospel-in-action-handout.pdf.

80. See US Conference of Catholic Bishops, "Catholic Campaign for Human Development: Success Stories," http://www.usccb.org/about/catholic-campaign -for-human-development/grants/success-stories.cfm.

81. On community organizing in Catholic organizations, see Curran, *Social Mission*, 138–39.

82. See US Conference of Catholic Bishops, "Catholic Campaign for Human Development: Grants," http://www.usccb.org/about/catholic-campaign-for-human -development/grants/index.cfm.

83. Debate over the impact of the War on Poverty continues. See, e.g., Annie Lowrey, "50 Years Later, War on Poverty Is a Mixed Bag," *New York Times*, January 2, 2014, http://www.nytimes.com/2014/01/05/business/50-years-later-war -on-poverty-is-a-mixed-bag.html; and Peter Ferrera, "Ryan Leads on Welfare Reform and Fighting Poverty," *Forbes*, September 13, 2014, http://www.forbes .com/sites/peterferrara/2014/09/13/ryan-leads-on-welfare-reform-and-fighting -poverty/.

84. Hinze, "Economic Recession," 155–64.

85. See "Income and Poverty Rates at 1990s Levels," *New York Times*, September 13, 2011, http://www.nytimes.com/interactive/2011/09/13/us/income -poverty-rate-at-1990s-levels.html. The article shows real median household income growing from $40,000 to just under $50,000 during the same period, though income was slightly higher in the late 1990s and early 2000s, and grew much faster for the top 10 percent than for all other groups. In 2012, the last year

for which data are available, the poverty rate remained 15 percent, about the same as in 1965, the year the War on Poverty began. See Carmen DeNavas-Walt, Bernadette D. Proctor, and Jessica C. Smith, "Poverty and Health Insurance Coverage in the United States: 2012," US Census Bureau, September 2013, www.census.gov /prod/2013pubs/p60-245.pdf.

86. See Bailey, *Rethinking Poverty*, 18–24.

87. Robert D. Lupton, *Toxic Charity: How Churches and Charities Hurt Those They Help—and How to Reverse It* (New York: HarperCollins, 2011).

88. Curran, *Social Mission*, 81–82.

89. Philip Murnion, "Catholic Parish in the Public Square," in *American Catholics and Civic Engagement: A Distinctive Voice*, ed. Margaret O'Brien Steinfels (Lanham, MD: Sheed & Ward, 2004), 84. Poor parishes have much more to offer in this area (p. 85).

90. Mary Beth Celio, *Celebrating Catholic Parishes* (Seattle: Archdiocese of Seattle, 2001), 10. Celio notes that the average parish supports 6.1 ongoing programs, but this figure includes teen activities, altar guild, prayer groups, etc. The majority of ongoing service opportunities (averaging 4.1) that are provided are to the elderly and sick, with a significant number of parishes also providing cash or voucher for people in need. The proportion of parishes offering ongoing service involving contact with the poor is much lower, at 11 percent.

91. Jay P. Dolan, *The Immigrant Church: New York's Irish and German Catholics, 1815–65* (Baltimore: Johns Hopkins University Press, 1975), 130–32.

92. Gerald P. Fogarty, "The Parish and Community in American Catholic History," reprinted in *Building the American Catholic City*, ed. Brian C. Mitchell (New York: Garland, 1988), 9.

93. For a critical history of Catholic Charities, see Dorothy M. Brown and Elizabeth McKeown, *The Poor Belong to Us: Catholic Charities and American Welfare* (Cambridge, MA: Harvard University Press, 1997). Of course, Catholic Charities, like many nonprofit organizations, receives a good chunk of its resources from the federal government. My quarrel is not with federal funding but with the methods of addressing poverty.

94. Mary Elizabeth Brown, "The Network of Community Life," *US Catholic Historian* 14, no. 3 (1996): 31–56, at 31.

95. Ibid., 37.

96. Dolan, *Immigrant Church*, 128.

97. Ibid., 123.

98. Ibid., 132.

99. Mary J. Oates, *The Catholic Philanthropic Tradition in America* (Bloomington: Indiana University Press, 1995), 28.

100. John T. McGreevy, *Parish Boundaries: The Catholic Encounter with Race in Twentieth-Century Urban North America* (Chicago: University of Chicago Press, 1998).

101. Jamie T. Phelps, OP, "Joy Came in the Morning: Confronting the Evil of Social Sin and Socially Sinful Structures," in *A Troubling in My Soul: Womanist Perspectives on Evil and Suffering*, ed. Emily M. Townes (Maryknoll, NY: Orbis, 1993), 57.

102. Pope Benedict XVI, *Caritas in Veritate*, no. 58.

103. Corbett and Fikkert argue that churches are especially well placed to help people prepare for work and find jobs. Corbett and Fikkert, *When Helping Hurts*, 190–94.

104. Brown, "Network," 40.

105. The Chalmers Center provides training and resources for churches that want to move in this direction; see Chalmers Center, "Why Faith & Finances?" https://www.chalmers.org/our-work/us-church-training/why-faith-and-finances.

106. See, e.g., Rana Foroohar, "The School That Will Get You a Job," *Time*, February 13, 2014, http://time.com/7066/the-school-that-will-get-you-a-job/.

107. Corbett and Fikkert, *When Helping Hurts*, 196–98. Voices for Women, a nonprofit women's group that has its roots in Midtown Catholic Charities in Saint Louis, has matching savings programs for adult and children, as well as a loan program that the women created after learning about microlending programs abroad; see Voices of Women Community Development Corporation, "VOW STL: Community Women in Action for a New Direction," http://www.vowstl.org/.

108. Dolan, *Immigrant Church*, 124.

109. Most families will need more than one working adult to move out of poverty. See Nolan and Erikson, "Intragenerational Income Mobility," 127–64; and Isabel Sawhill and Quentin Karpilow, "Strategies for Assisting Low-Income Families," Brookings Institution, July 1, 2013, http://www.brookings.edu/research/papers/2013/07/01assisting-low-income-families-sawhill.

110. Curran, *Social Mission*, 134–35, 139–42.

111. Corbett and Fikkert, *When Helping Hurts*, 207.

112. See Kent J. Lasnoski, *Vocation to Virtue: Christian Marriage as a Consecrated Life* (Washington, DC: Catholic University of America Press, 2014), 58–63, 179–88.

113. See Roman Garrison, *Redemptive Almsgiving in Early Christianity* (Sheffield, UK: Journal for the Study of the New Testament, 1993); and Gary Anderson, *Charity: The Place of the Poor in the Biblical Tradition* (New Haven, CT: Yale University Press, 2014).

114. See Dean Brackley, SJ, *Call to Discernment in Troubled Times: New Perspectives on the Transformational Wisdom of Ignatius of Loyola* (New York: Crossroad, 2004).

115. Pope Benedict XVI, *Caritas in Veritate*, no. 17.

116. Ibid., nos. 16–17.

117. Ibid., no. 57.

118. Ibid., no. 43.

119. See Escuela AKF: Escuela Asociación Kairós para la Formación, http://escuelaakf.org/Home.html.

CHAPTER 6

Abortion

Toward Cooperation with Good

In a local diocesan newspaper, a fifteen-year-old young woman named Kayla is pictured holding her baby. She is living in an immigrant family headed by a single father, and she does not have enough money to care for her newborn child. However, with the help of Catholic Charities and a local archdiocesan fund for pregnant women, she is making it. Her own courage and her family's support led her to keep the baby; the Christian community is helping her care for him. She and her family did not consider adoption or abortion. Her dad is committed to family: "I want to stay 100 percent with my kids. She's my daughter, and I have a big heart. It's not easy, but you have to try."[1]

In another time, Kayla might have been taken away in secret to a maternity home, or perhaps she would have had to carry her child to term without community support. However, today the situation is different. Each year, 40 percent of children are born outside marriage, and 1.2 million babies are aborted. A majority of women who choose abortion are unmarried, in their twenties, and black or Hispanic, and also already have at least one child; relatively large proportions are poor (42 percent) and low income (27 percent).[2] However, it is important to know that groups that make up a plurality of abortion patients are also more likely to give birth to children they did not intend to conceive.[3] Women who have abortions typically cite several reasons for their choice: responsibility to other individuals, financial concerns, fear that having a baby would interfere with work or school, and a lack of support from a partner.[4] Most women who have children outside marriage are similarly constrained. Although women with higher levels of education and income tend to follow a traditional script, saving childbearing for after marriage, those with less education and income have a higher share of unintended pregnancies and a disproportionate share of both abortions and unwed births.[5] Unintended pregnancy, abortion, and childbearing outside marriage are all more common today among those on the margins of society and, increasingly, among the less-educated portion of the middle class.

Few would disagree with the idea that it is just, compassionate, and pro-life to provide support for pregnant women with insufficient resources. In the story about Kayla, the reporter quotes the director of Respect Life, the pro-life apostolate in Saint Louis, who says, "We're pro-life in a whole-life way. We're . . . about protecting women and children, but we have the resources to help you choose life, despite difficult circumstances."[6] Yet liberals and conservatives tend to disagree about which pro-life strategies are most important. Liberals favor social and economic support to make abortion less necessary, whereas conservatives focus on legal remedies to make abortion less available. Charitable help for vulnerable pregnant women is lauded by everyone, even if most would probably agree that the situation of the young mother profiled above is hardly ideal. We do what we can, given our commitment to life.

Typically, the ethical debate centers on the morality of abortion, but recently there has been more discussion on strategies for reducing abortion. Adoption would likely result in better outcomes for a vulnerable mother and child, but it is only rarely the choice of women in crisis pregnancies.[7] A large percentage of women who have abortions were not using contraception, and most of those who have children outside marriage also say their pregnancies were "unintended." But how much would better access to contraception reduce abortion? The evidence is not conclusive.[8] Recent progress in promoting abstinence among teens has encouraged advocates of chastity movements, but abstinence until marriage is the choice of a small percentage of all US adults, and the long-term effects of abstinence education are unclear.[9] Efforts to overturn *Roe v. Wade* (1973) or to pass a human life constitutional amendment have proven unsuccessful, though small victories at the state level in recent times have energized pro-life advocates who favor legal remedies, while clearly showing just how hard the route to making abortion illegal would be.[10] Those who care deeply about unborn life and vulnerable women are left with an almost impossible problem: how best to discourage abortion and ensure that fewer women are faced with the kinds of difficult choices that Kayla and others like her have had to make.

In this chapter I argue that reducing the abortion rate in the United States depends on identifying effective strategies that can be pursued by both liberals and conservatives working together at the grassroots level. There are no easy answers, but if those on both the left and the right put less energy into political battles, become less concerned about coopera- tion with evil, and attend to local strategies, it may be possible to signifi- cantly reduce abortion. By building a consensus on their shared concern for unborn children and the women who carry them, they can do more working together than fighting apart. First, I establish that though reduc- ing the abortion rate is not the ultimate goal for Christians committed to protecting the dignity of unborn life, it is a realistic goal given the realities of public opinion. Next, I locate my proposed strategy in the context of theological discussions on abortion. The heart of the chapter is an analy- sis of the situations of women who have abortions and women who give birth outside marriage. This is followed by an assessment of how well local strategies can respond to the realities on the ground. Finally, I ask whether a reduction in the abortion rate is a moral goal for Christians who continue to hope for full respect for all human life.

LAW AND PUBLIC OPINION: WHERE ARE WE? WHAT IS POSSIBLE?

In chapter 1 I discussed Catholic realism about politics, claiming that though Catholics prize good citizenship, strive for the common good, and oppose immoral laws, the tradition also makes room for some toleration or even material cooperation with evil in pluralistic societies. John Court- ney Murray made the case for limiting aspirations for the state, and others since have made an even stronger case for increasing expectations for what the church itself ought to do. Cathleen Kaveny argues for a richer under- standing of the many different levels on which law operates, so we can appreciate how law can teach virtue not just by prohibiting actions but also by encouraging or discouraging a range of choices. While affirming the tradition's hope in government, I argued that in light of growing cynicism about politics (especially among the young), the difficulty of taking pluralism seriously, and the first duty of the church to "be the church," greater realism and humility with respect to politics are necessary.

The question of realism lies at the heart of the Christian public debate over abortion. In an important article, the law professor Susan Stabile attempts to carve out a common ground approach to this contentious issue. Stabile characterizes a realist position as one that is rooted in factual accuracy about the status of unborn life and the actual effectiveness of various approaches; one that is viable ("it has to work"); and one that is consistent with Catholic teaching, which includes some room for material cooperation with evil.[11] She begins by arguing that a realist approach would acknowledge that belief in the human dignity of women should make us wary of forced pregnancy and thus of illegal abortion.[12] She hopes that if pro-choice advocates understand that abortion will still be legal, they will be more likely to acknowledge abortion as a "tragic choice" and work with pro-lifers to make abortion safe and rare.[13] Realists would then evaluate the efficacy of legal restrictions at the state level (e.g., requiring informed and parental consent, banning partial birth abortions, and regulating abortion providers). Stabile reports conflicting studies, but she sees restrictions as one part of an effective strategy to reduce the abortion rate.[14] In addition, she argues that because such a large percentage of those who seek abortion are economically disadvantaged, attempting to provide more support for at-risk populations is a sound strategy.[15] She does not believe that Catholic teaching allows for public advocacy of contraception, even in the context of a realist strategy.[16] Instead, she advocates working with others to "try to effect a shift in the cultural expectation of sexual activity among the young," though she offers no data on the effectiveness of such efforts in reducing the abortion rate.[17]

Thinking about realistic approaches to reduce abortion is in its early stages, but Stabile is in good company. Advocates generally share three assumptions: (1) Public opinion in the United States is firmly pro–legal access to abortion (at least in the first trimester), and a reversal is unlikely. (2) Given this situation, attempts to reduce rather than outlaw abortion are not only more realistic but also more pro-life (i.e., they have the potential to save more babies than do efforts to overturn *Roe*). (3) Realist strategies are more in keeping with Catholic political philosophy since Murray.

The second assumption (effectiveness) is taken up below, but here I briefly take up the first and third assumptions.

Is public opinion solidly pro-choice? It is complicated. In a recent study by the Pew Forum, a solid majority (63 percent) said that they do not want *Roe* overturned, and this number has not changed much in twenty years.[18] In the same survey, only 47 percent of Americans (but 58 percent of Catholics) said that having an abortion is morally wrong.[19] However, the answers are more complex when the questions get more specific. When asked if abortion should be legal in all circumstances, some circumstances, or never, the majority answer is "some circumstances."[20] Support for the answer "all circumstances" peaked in the 1990s.[21] There is some indication that the Millennial generation (which favors *Roe* just as much as everyone else) is more morally conflicted about abortion (51 percent believe it is morally wrong).[22]

However, general questions about legality and morality fail to capture the complexity of public opinion. When asked if abortion should be legal in cases when a woman "has a very low income and cannot afford any more children" or "is not married and does not want to marry the man," most Americans say no, though they approve of legal availability when a woman's physical or mental health is in danger, the pregnancy is the result of rape, or "there is a strong chance of a serious defect in the baby."[23] It appears that the relatively low proportion that labels abortion "morally wrong" in a general question is thinking about those cases in which they would approve it. The majority of women who obtain abortions normally give several reasons for their decision, but they generally fall into the category of economic and family concerns. According to the Guttmacher Institute (the research organization associated with Planned Parenthood), "The reasons women give for having an abortion underscore their understanding of the responsibilities of parenthood and family life. Three-fourths say they cannot afford a child; three-fourths say that having a baby would interfere with work, school, or the ability to care for dependents; and half say they do not want to be a single parent or are having problems with their husband or partner."[24]

Though Americans' answers to survey questions suggest that they morally oppose most abortions in the United States, in most cases they still support leaving the decision to a woman and her doctor. This does not mean that most are comfortable with the pro-choice label; 50 percent now call themselves pro-life, while 41 percent call themselves pro-choice, a new record and a striking change from 1995, when only 33 percent called themselves pro-life while 56 percent identified with the pro-choice label.[25] A study that allowed people to choose both labels found that more people (43 percent) preferred both over one or the other.[26] In sum, Americans remain conflicted about the morality of abortion, even as they hesitate to impose legal barriers on women's choices.

In this context, it is difficult to imagine that even if *Roe* were overturned and the regulation of abortion were returned to the states (an unlikely prospect in itself), a majority of states would make abortion illegal. In fact, Joseph Wright estimates that overturning *Roe* would result in a decrease of fewer than 100,000 abortions, whereas other strategies would result in much greater decreases.[27] I discuss the possible effects of legal changes in greater depth below. But assume for a moment that this analysis is correct—that is, that support for legal access to abortion is solid and support for a total ban on abortion is weak, even though Americans view abortion as a morally complex issue. Does the goal of reducing the abortion rate then become acceptable? Although some argue that to retreat is to fail to acknowledge the moral evil involved, Kaveny presents a convincing case that a complex approach is justifiable. First, it recognizes the moral complexity of the issue: "Abortion is a heart-wrenching and difficult problem because the most vulnerable class of human beings—the unborn—are totally dependent on human beings who are themselves very vulnerable—women facing crisis pregnancies."[28] Second, compromise at the legal level is appropriately practical, in that it acknowledges that "human law must attempt to lead people to virtue, . . . [but] it can only do so gradually. On the one hand, human law ought to point toward and encourage virtuous action; on the other hand, it ought never to engage in coercion or manipulation to secure it."[29] And third, agreeing to a reduction of the abortion rate as a goal frees those who oppose abortion unilaterally to work with the more conflicted majority on a combination of reasonable restrictions and enabling supports. If, as Kaveny argues, the law teaches virtue both by what it restricts *and* what it discourages, protects, regulates, and encourages, those who are concerned about abortion should unite in working for a comprehensive legal response.[30] I would add that a full ethical response cannot only be legal. If we want to build a "supportive society" and a "culture of life," much of our work will need to be at the grassroots level.[31] Though I am supportive of ongoing work to restrict the legal availability of abortion, in the remainder of this chapter,

I want to broaden the ethical conversation by focusing on what can be accomplished at the local level. First, however, I situate my argument for local strategies in the context of the broader theological discussions.

HUMAN LIFE, WOMEN'S AGENCY, AND COOPERATION WITH EVIL

From the 1980s to the mid-2000s, the ethical debate about abortion was not a major focus of moral theology, perhaps because each side in the debate had little hope of persuading the other of its claims.[32] Though there were no major developments, some new emphases should be noted. In the world of academic theological studies, the stronger recognition of women's agency is a key theme among more liberal thinkers. For instance, Lisa Sowle Cahill has pushed for a greater recognition of women both in the church and outside it, arguing that without such an affirmation of women, Catholics cannot credibly participate in the debate over abortion; she has also argued for some flexibility in the earliest weeks of pregnancy.[33] Tina Beattie goes much further, claiming that between an extreme pro-choice ethic and an extreme pro-life ethic lies a view that "woman and foetus become mother and child through the mother's recognition of the other as another self and her welcome of that person into the world of human language and consciousness."[34] She conceives of the early months of pregnancy as a time of "ensoulment," for "the developmental process allows a period of grace between conception and the emergence of the human form, when the woman's freedom to decide whether or not to accept the responsibility of motherhood takes precedence over any hypothetical conjecture about the moral status of the embryo."[35] However, the majority of Christian moral theologians, though conscious of the uniqueness of pregnancy, are wary of arguments allowing one class of persons to determine the personhood of another. Liberal Catholic theologians seek ways to give more attention to women's agency without denying the rightful claims of the fetus.

Charles Camosy's book *Beyond the Abortion Wars* attempts to find a way forward by emphasizing the ambiguity of American moral evaluation of abortion.[36] If one looks beyond typical survey questions that mask the complexity of people's views, it seems that moral ambivalence continues, and young adults are among the most conflicted. In this complicated space, Camosy makes a persuasive case for the humanity of the fetus and the obligation to rescue the vulnerable. Recognizing the difficulties that women face, however, he wisely advocates policy recommendations that combine restricting the availability of an abortion to twenty weeks, with increased social support for pregnant women. His provocative proposal could unite people with different views, and thus it would represent significant progress. Still, even if his proposed legislation would pass, assuming he is right about the limited impact of necessary social policy and given that the great majority of abortions occur in the first twelve weeks, this move would leave most abortions untouched.

Among virtue ethicists, there is more of a focus on what churches can do. Thus Stanley Hauerwas, who is characteristically unwilling to engage in traditional political debates, calls on Christians to oppose abortion by focusing on becoming the sort of people who welcome children. He insists that Christians should embrace children because they are members of a community of hope that trusts in God.[37] The key response to the tragedy of abortion is for Christians to live into the faith they profess. Similarly, Joseph Kotva argues that the practice of abortion leads Christians away from their true end: "Each abortion slowly and gradually shapes us, making it less likely that we will greet each new life with the expectation that here is one who might join in the worship of God."[38] Instead, he argues that Christians should engage in pro-children practices, such as child dedications, reflecting on the biblical infancy narratives about Jesus, children's worship, day care, and adoptions.[39] He also suggests opposing abortion because it harms women and advocates engaging in practices that empower women, such as encouraging leadership roles, using inclusive language, and promoting strong women as role models in sermons and sacred art.[40] He allows that formation for practices of "burden bearing" will also be necessary to prepare Christians for situations in which carrying a pregnancy to term will be difficult.[41] Legislation is not the focus; virtue formation within the Christian community is.

Theologians' best arguments seem to be reaching for common ground. They recognize the compelling claims of the fetus during its early development, the need for the social recognition of women's agency, and the importance of supportive communities to help women in crisis pregnancies carry babies to term. These arguments are characterized by clarity about what is at stake in the lives of two vulnerable groups of persons and a strong sense of how the entanglement of these two makes finding solutions to this problem so very difficult.

However, political questions have not gone away. The US Conference of Catholic Bishops (USCCB) has taken its traditional strong opposition to abortion to a new level by naming voting as a potential source of cooperation with evil.[42] As I noted in chapter 1, the bishops left room for the conscientious voter to choose a pro-choice candidate, but they drew attention to the potential for material cooperation with evil, depending on the intentions of the Catholic voter. And when the USCCB put more of its energy into political debate, theologians and ordinary Catholics followed. Kaveny published a series of essays in *Commonweal* questioning the USCCB's use of the categories "intrinsic evil" and "material cooperation with evil," while calling for greater attention to traditional staples of modern Catholic political discourse, such as toleration and respect for pluralism.[43] Liberal Catholic organizations began arguing that a vote for a Democrat was a more pro-life vote.[44] As evidence, they noted that abortion rates most often fell under Democratic presidents and rose under Republican ones.[45] They asked social scientists to calculate the effects of economic stability and social support, while reminding people that though politicians may hold pro-life positions, it is crucial to know what they can and will actually do to limit abortion.

This move to consider the practical question of how best to reduce abortion echoed the influential speech of former New York governor Mario Cuomo at the University of Notre Dame in 1984. Although not a theologian, Cuomo touched a nerve with his speech. Proclaiming that he and his wife Matilda followed church teaching on birth control, believed abortion was the taking of a potential human life, and had the right to advocate for their views in the public square, he insisted that the key question was not "May I?" but "Should I?"[46] Pointing to the lack of consensus among the American public and recalling the US bishops' historical reticence on the issue of slavery, he concluded that the time was not right to push for restrictive laws and instead advocated supportive programs for women and children.[47] Though many rightly question whether Cuomo gave sufficient weight to the duty to shape a consensus and to the pedagogical function of the law, his questions about political strategy remain very much in play.

Whether contemporary theologians focus on personal, communal, or political reform, their work is marked by a sensitivity to the moral complexity of abortion and a desire to find solutions that work.[48] Most thinkers see abortion as a tragic choice that Christians should be committed to either eliminating or reducing.[49] Whether pro-life or pro-choice in the political realm, they converge in concern for women and the developing human life in the womb. They are conscious that cooperation with evil may be at stake in voting decisions, but also seek positive ways of cooperating with the goods of minimizing unwanted pregnancies and helping women bring babies to term. This is a crucial new moment, but more information about the most effective ways to reduce abortion at the local level is still needed. Moreover, there is a need to think about the myriad of ways in which, whether by action or inaction, Christians cooperate with a culture that has come to see abortion as a too-common solution to an unwanted pregnancy. The first step toward better practical solutions is trying to understand why some women in less-than-ideal situations have abortions while others have children.

LISTENING TO YOUNG, UNMARRIED PREGNANT WOMEN

In the beginning of her book *Real Choices: Listening to Women, Looking for Alternatives*, Frederica Mathewes-Green writes that though Americans are uneasy about abortion, they will want it to be legal until they can answer the question "How could we live without [it]?"[50] "The key" to finding a credible answer, she says, "lies in recognizing why women have abortions."[51] If we do not want vulnerable pregnant women to suffer, we need to find alternatives to abortion. But unless we know what the problems are, we will not be able to provide solutions. For instance, the pro-life movement has been good at offering shelter for pregnant women, baby supplies, counseling, and connections to government social services.[52] Three thousand crisis pregnancy centers "provide over 2.3 million women in difficult pregnancies with alternatives to abortion."[53] Of course, many argue that providing contraception or better social support is more crucial to reducing the abortion rate, and they work to provide these options. But without knowledge of why women make the choices they do, it is difficult to figure out what will actually make a difference.

Two types of organizations have a good amount of information on why women have abortions: abortion clinics and crisis pregnancy centers. The Guttmacher Institute completes extensive surveys every few years. There are fewer data from crisis pregnancy centers, but Mathewes-Green's work is significant. The overlap between the two is striking. Despite some differences, both sources attest to the complex nature of women's decisions. Women who have abortions, both sources attest, do so for a combination of factors involving instability in their personal, familial, economic, and work lives.

The most recent study from the Guttmacher Institute relies on a large quantitative survey and a smaller number of qualitative interviews with women conducted at clinics. The two methods yielded similar results, with the exception that "women's responses often did not fit the categories of the structured survey; the reasons tended to overlap between the domains of unplanned pregnancy, financial instability, unemployment, single motherhood and current parenting responsibilities."[54] Since 1987, when similar surveys were completed, abortion patients have become somewhat older, more likely to cite concern for other children as a reason for their decisions, and less likely to cite "fear of single motherhood" or interference with work or school.[55] Overwhelmingly, "women in every age, parity, relationship, racial, income and education category cited concern for or responsibility to other individuals as a factor in their decision to have an abortion."[56] This does not mean that women find the decision easy. Abortion "was not something they desired," and many even saw it as sinful or wrong, but they thought that bearing a child they could not properly care for was also potentially wrong and concluded that abortion was "a responsible choice."[57] It is worth noting that this narrative from pro-choice sources contradicts the more radical story promoted by some radical activists, who insist that abortion is "a great decision" that "should be as common as possible."[58] According to Guttmacher, abortion is a difficult but necessary choice for most women.

In contrast, Mathewes-Green is convinced that abortion is not just a difficult decision but also a tragic choice for many women. Her data may be distinct, in part because she has information from qualitative interviews and case histories of women who have seen post-abortion grief counselors. Though one might see this source of information as biased, it coheres with the other available data. Most women with whom Mathewes-Green spoke did not focus on the practical problems that kept them from having a baby. Rather, they told her about "pressures in relationships" with parents and fathers.[59] The information that Mathewes-Green obtained from pregnancy resource centers affirmed this (the second-most-important reason women gave for having an abortion was that "the husband or partner was absent, undependable, or insufficiently supportive"), though financial difficulties and problems with work or school were also highlighted.[60] Of course, these problems are interrelated. Women have a need for housing, child care, and financial assistance because their families are unable or unwilling to help them.[61] Mathewes-Green includes more survey items that refer to relationship pressures and groups together as the second most common reason for abortion; several items refer to the partner's lack of support. Guttmacher, however, highlights economic issues and characterizes relationship issues under the category "responsibility to others."[62]

In essence, what Guttmacher characterizes as a reasonable, free choice made by a woman for the sake of others, Mathewes-Green portrays as a desperate decision born of a failure of community. She describes women who

> felt bound to please or protect some other person, and abortion was the price she had to pay, who felt isolated, endangered, and sad. Loneliness and fear of abandonment pushed them toward this choice, decked out in its first-person-singular bunting. . . . The woman choosing abortion doesn't feel autonomous, but enmeshed in relationships which bind and constrain her decision, now this way, now that . . . her choice will reverberate through many lives, and she fears provoking anger or pain.[63]

Mathewes-Green notes that those who are close to women in these situations see their pain and want to help. Abortion seems the easiest way to do this, so they assist with a compassionate affirmation of this difficult choice.[64]

However, every day many women in similarly challenging circumstances nonetheless choose to have their babies. They do not, ordinarily, give them up for adoption; they raise them despite imperfect situations. More than 40 percent of children in the United States are born outside marriage, most into circumstances that are far from ideal. In their study of poor single mothers, the psychologists Kathryn Edin and Maria Kefalas found that unlike upper- and middle-class women, poor women had strong reasons to want children, even if marriage was not likely in the near future. Children were central to their understanding of a meaningful life, and if life denied them other sources of meaning, these young women did not want to miss out on children. Edin and Kefalas conclude that "the daily stresses of an impoverished adolescence lived out in the environs of East Camden or West Kensington breeds a deep sense of need for something positive to 'look to.' The strong sense of anomie, the loneliness, the rootlessness, the lack of direction, the sense that one's life has little meaning or has spun out of control . . . create a profound drive to make life more meaningful."[65]

This same lack of control and support that leads some women to have an abortion leads others to have children outside marriage. Though poor women tell researchers that people should marry before having children, if they cannot find a mate they feel sure will be a good partner, they are more likely than other women to have children outside marriage. In their eyes, marriage is a luxury but children are a necessity.[66] Poor women worry about domestic violence, crime, substance abuse, and infidelity destabilizing their families.[67] They worry that men will fail to measure up—not just because of a lack of a job, but also due to a lack of commitment to a job, a propensity to spend money on himself, partying, womanizing, and so on.[68] When they insist on being "set" before marrying, they are seeking control within a marriage, and potentially after if it breaks up.[69] Even if a man is in the picture, they are willing to wait for marriage because they see pregnancy as a test for a man and for their relationship, whereas middle-class couples see their relationship as the core of the family and more often welcome children only after that relationship is secure.[70]

Of course, as I noted in chapter 4, the attitudes of the middle class are changing, so neat distinctions between poor and middle-class couples are not quite accurate anymore. As Bradford Wilcox has shown, there is a convergence among all less-educated Americans, so the middle class is coming to share the attitudes previously associated with the lower classes.[71] This is why births outside marriage and abortions are concentrated among both the poor and the lower middle class. Women in both groups experience instability in their personal and financial lives that is much less prevalent in the lives of those with at least some college education and socioeconomic resources. In this context, some choose to have babies but others choose abortion. It is not simply poverty, or personal unreadiness, or relationship issues that determine these choices. Rather, it is all these mixed together; and we have no good comparative data that can tell us why women in very similar circumstances make very different choices.[72]

As childbearing outside marriage becomes more and more normative, at least in certain subgroups, it seems that the term "crisis pregnancy" is becoming less and less accurate. The prospect of scandal for an unmarried pregnant woman has greatly decreased. Yet the problem of vulnerable women making difficult choices about abortion and lone child rearing remains. Edin and Kefalas tell us that "in the social world inhabited by poor women, a baby born into such conditions represents an opportunity to prove one's worth. The real tragedy, these women insist, is a woman who's missed her chance to have children."[73] Although they may dream the same dreams as their middle- and upper-class peers, they are far less confident that they can reach their goals, and thus they "grab eagerly at the surest source of accomplishment within their reach: becoming a mother."[74] Perhaps this is why researchers continue to find high numbers of pregnancies outside marriage, even with the widespread availability of contraception and, when they dig deeper, ambivalence about whether a pregnancy was planned or unplanned.[75] Listening to unmarried pregnant women allows us to see a complex world where decisions about sex and childbearing are made—a world of unstable relationships, uncertain plans, and unrelenting tensions about how best to love others and take care of one's self.

THE LIMITS OF TRADITIONAL STRATEGIES

In this context, how should Christians aim to reduce abortion? Traditional strategies focus either on reducing the rate of unwanted pregnancies (via increasing access to contraception or providing abstinence education) or providing alternatives once a woman is pregnant (by encouraging adoption or increasing social support for lower-income families). Though these strategies all have some positive effects, none is sufficient to seriously reduce the number of abortions in the United States.

Contraception

A representative article on abortion from a pro-choice perspective concludes, "Although the focus of this study was women's reasons for having abortions, our findings have broader implications regarding the burden of unwanted pregnancy and the need for increased access to and use of contraceptive services. . . . The fact that an increasing proportion of women having abortions are poor underscores the importance of public assistance for family planning programs as an effective means of reducing the incidence of both unintended pregnancy and abortion."[76] However, evidence for the claim that increasing the availability of contraception reduces the abortion rate is mixed. The Guttmacher Institute estimates that contraception has prevented 20 million unplanned pregnancies in the last twenty years, 9 million of which would have ended in abortion. They emphasize that the 7 percent of women who do not use contraception account for about half of unintended pregnancies and abortions.[77] Researchers at Washington University saw a 20 percent drop in the number of abortions during the years of their Contraceptive Choice Project, in which more than 9,000 women were given information about different kinds of contraception and offered the choice of implant methods (75 percent choose them).[78] Teenage participants in the study had lower rates of births and abortions. The number of repeat abortions also decreased during this period. Because "half of all pregnancies in this country are unintended and, of those, half end in abortion," the Center for American Progress argues that providing women with comprehensive sex education, health insurance coverage for contraception, and better access to emergency contraception would lead to a reduction of the abortion rate.[79]

However, others argue that contraception is not an easy solution. Both Guttmacher and the Centers for Disease Control and Prevention find that only a small portion of women who have abortions say that a lack of access to contraception was the reason they became pregnant; the vast majority were either using contraception or had used it in the past but were not using it at the time they got pregnant.[80] Moreover, the policies and programs recommended by contraception advocates do not necessarily yield the expected results; birthrates are lower but abortion rates are often higher in states where access to contraception is easy than in states with more restrictions.[81] Abortion, not contraception, lowers teen pregnancy rates in the so-called blue states. Access to contraception has not been a silver bullet in the United States.[82] Worldwide, though Guttmacher claims that restrictive contraception and abortion laws are associated with higher abortion rates, critics contend that wealth makes the difference, so comparisons between Western Europe and Southeast Asia or Sub-Saharan Africa are flawed.[83] A thorough analysis of global laws and rates does not yield easy answers.[84]

It seems that accessible, affordable, reliable contraception can be a factor in the prevention of unwed pregnancies and abortions, but cultural factors in poor and, increasingly, middle-class communities make things very complicated. A striking graph in a 2010 report from the Institute for American Values, "When Marriage Disappears," shows the proportion of never-married young adults who said that they had used contraceptives "all the time" in their last relationship. Only 19 percent of the least educated, 35 percent of the moderately educated, and 55 percent of the highly educated answered positively.[85] Similarly, Edin and Kefalas explain that though free contraception was easily available to young women in their study of poor communities, a rigorous use of contraception was not a top priority. Many used it regularly for a time and then became less careful about getting pregnant. As one woman told them, "It wasn't like I cared if I did or didn't. It wasn't like a matter of, 'Oh my God, if I get pregnant, I'm *dead*.' It was just—if I did, I did."[86] Openness to childbearing outside marriage may also play a role in reducing perfect use, even if some women find themselves choosing abortion when they actually become pregnant. Furthermore, when contraception is used, less effective methods like condoms are often chosen over implants, which reduces the chance of avoiding pregnancy.[87] Although campaigns to encourage hormonal methods of contraceptive like the pill or implants may yield somewhat better results, contraception alone cannot solve the problem of unintended pregnancies.

Abstinence Education

Many conservative Christians believe that because the majority of women who have abortions are young and unmarried, reducing sexual activity outside marriage is an important key to reducing the abortion rate. Advocates of abstinence education (AE) have been encouraged by significant drops in teen sexual activity in the last twenty years; now fewer than half of older teens say they have ever had sexual intercourse.[88] Those who believe that the abstinence-only focus of the George W. Bush administration played a role in this drop argue that communicating the expectation that sexual activity is to be reserved for marriage is far more responsible and effective than handing adolescents information about contraception, especially given widespread evidence that when they do use contraception, teens are likely to use it inconsistently.[89]

There is limited evidence that abstinence-only education is effective in delaying sexual activity. Two researchers from the Heritage Foundation reviewed twenty-two studies of AE programs. Five of these studies found significant gains in reducing and delaying sexual activity.[90] The programs varied significantly in structure and outcomes. Some studies found that students in AE programs were half as likely to report sexual activity in the follow-up period, whereas others found lower rates of sexually transmitted diseases, fewer partners, and/or lower pregnancy rates. The researchers note that their positive findings are limited because true control studies are relatively rare and programs vary significantly.

It is these kinds of limitations that lead the sociologist and AE advocate Bradford Wilcox to more cautious conclusions.[91] In his review, Wilcox uses only peer-reviewed studies published in scientific journals. He concludes that there is significant evidence that abstinence benefits adolescents, particularly girls. Although it is not clear that public AE programs influence teens' behavior, privately funded programs, "such as the virginity pledge movement led by groups such as True Love Waits, have increased rates of virginity among adolescents, and they have also reduced the onset of teenage sex, the number of sexual partners, and sexual infidelity among adolescents. Studies also suggest that they have played an important role in driving down the teenage pregnancy rate in the last decade or so."[92]

Wilcox acknowledges that most teens who receive AE, including those who take a virginity pledge, do go on to have sex before marriage, but they do so about eighteen months later than average and have lower teen pregnancy rates.[93] He cautions that it is often difficult to ascertain the significance of AE initiatives versus selection effects that would predict for lower levels of sexual activity.[94] In addition, though he credits AE with about half the decline in teenage pregnancy, he sees evidence that contraception (which he personally opposes on moral grounds) accounts for a sizable proportion of the remaining half.[95]

Other researchers are even more skeptical about the benefits of AE. In a comparative review of abstinence-only programs versus more broadly based sexual risk reduction programs, researchers found that though the latter resulted in decreases in sexual activity and pregnancy, it was much more difficult to prove that AE programs yielded similar results because there are too few well-designed studies and there is far too much variation among programs.[96] The robust results claimed by advocates are simply not evident in the peer-reviewed research.[97]

This does not necessarily mean that AE is not helpful. It is possible that the messages of abstinence-only education, along with sexual education that provides information on contraception instead of or in addition to a message of abstinence, have both contributed to a cultural shift toward waiting a little later to initiate sexual activity and trying harder to avoid teenage pregnancy.[98] Lower teen abortion rates in the 1990s and 2000s likely resulted both from less sexual activity and more contraceptive use. Even AE advocates admit that they have not achieved their stated goal of reducing the number of people who have sex before marriage.[99] Abstinence education, like contraception, is but a partial strategy for reducing the abortion rate.

Adoption

Theologians and activists frequently describe adoption as an important response to crisis pregnancy. Adoption is viewed in increasingly favorable terms in the Christian community, and efforts to encourage adoption have increased since the 2000s.[100] In recent years theologians have argued that given the large number of children in need, both in the US foster care system and internationally, adoption should be considered not simply as a last resort for infertile couples but also as a potential choice or even a moral duty for any couple.[101] Others claim that adoption should be second nature for Christians, because they are all adopted sons and daughters of God.[102]

However, among women who become pregnant outside marriage, adoption is rarely viewed positively. A Guttmacher survey reported that "more than one-third of interview respondents said they had considered adoption and concluded that it was a morally unconscionable option because giving one's child away is wrong."[103] In an essay in *America*, Timothy O'Malley explains, "When my wife and I decided to adopt, we were surprised to learn from our social worker that many birth mothers cease considering adoption as an option when their parents express disgust at the possibility that another couple would raise their child."[104] Higher percentages of Latino and black women have unplanned pregnancies, and adoption has historically been less common in these groups.[105] Though precise statistics are unavailable, approximately 135,000 adoptions are approved in US courts every year, and only about 14,000 of these involve newborns.[106] Twenty percent of babies born to unwed white mothers were adopted in the early 1970s (and the rate was likely higher in previous decades) versus 1.3 percent in 2002; and for all unmarried mothers the proportion fell from 8.7 percent to 1 percent during the same period.[107] Mathewes-Green's survey of pregnancy center staff members lists the difficulty of adoption as the number one "most common problem" and "most difficult problem to solve."[108] Edin and Kefalas report that in the poor, urban communities they studied, women and girls who give up their babies to strangers are often condemned.[109] Adoption is a very difficult choice for most birth mothers, no matter how unprepared for parenthood they might feel.

It might seem that this situation is changing. Adam Pertman suggests that we are in the midst of an adoption revolution, in which the stigma of adoption is decreasing, legal changes are making adoption faster and easier, and the movement toward open records is making the choice of adoption more plausible for birth parents.[110] As American families become increasingly diverse through interracial marriage, divorce, single parenting, and remarriage, adoption has become less remarkable.[111] However, Pertman also acknowledges that adoption "has always been an emotionally wrenching and legally complicated process, because, by its nature, it must balance the rights and needs of vulnerable people. . . . It's incomprehensible that there are people who believe that a woman, especially, can relinquish a child and then put the experience aside, forget about it, pretend she didn't part with a piece of herself."[112] This is especially true because those seeking to adopt are typically quite different by race, class, and education from those who would potentially be able to give their children up for adoption.[113] Though broad-based efforts to facilitate and encourage adoption should continue, it seems unlikely that adoption will be more than a small factor in the movement to reduce the abortion rate.

Health and Social Welfare

Pro-life liberals who are reluctant to push for restricted access to abortion place their hope in creating a world where a woman would never need to worry about health care, maternity leave, or support during her pregnancy. This seems to cohere with what we know about why women have abortions.

According to Mathewes-Green, among the most common problems are fears that pregnancy and child rearing will interfere with job or school, necessitate health care, or cost too much money.[114] Guttmacher reports a very similar list of top reasons.[115] Pregnancy centers seem to believe this is true, which is why they provide women with health care, financial resources, and housing during, and sometimes even after, pregnancy.[116] Some recent studies suggest that states that offer health care, including coverage for contraceptives and obstetrics, see a reduction in abortion rates.[117]

The most comprehensive case for an economic/social method for reducing abortion is made by Joseph Wright of Catholics in Alliance for the Common Good, who calculates that "increasing economic support for low-income families and pregnant women would decrease the number of abortions by over 300,000 per year"—200,000 more than overturning *Roe v. Wade*.[118] Wright notes the lower abortion rates in Belgium, Ireland, the Netherlands, France, Germany, and Switzerland—all countries with more social services.[119] He compares these countries with several in South America with restrictive laws, economic difficulties, and higher abortion rates, while admitting that not all Western European countries fit his model.[120] And he cites an earlier study by Catholics in Alliance for the Common Good that calculates how many abortions would occur if there were increases in employment and changes in the social welfare system.[121] In response to criticism, he later revised his findings, emphasizing mainly the connection between poverty and abortion.[122] Clearly, poverty has some effect. Abortion rates in the United States have decreased in times of prosperity and high employment rates, and women with more socioeconomic resources have more options and get fewer abortions.

Still, it does not seem as if we yet have robust evidence to show that social support will result in a large reduction in the abortion rate. The reasons women give for having an abortion are complex; the most common concern is that the baby will radically change her life.[123] Women with education and plans have fewer unplanned pregnancies and abortions but abort a higher percentage of unplanned pregnancies than do poor women, because the cost of pregnancy in their lives in so clear. Poorer women sometimes choose an abortion in desperation, but are more likely to reject it, for "a pregnancy offers young women who say their lives are 'going nowhere fast' a chance to grasp at a better future."[124] Social welfare policies can help and ought to be pursued; but given this highly complex context, they are insufficient tools.

BUILDING A CULTURE THAT WELCOMES NEW LIFE

This chapter advocates a shift in focus from cooperation with evil (e.g., trying to change permissive laws allowing abortion) to cooperation with good (working toward reducing abortion by preventing unwanted pregnancies and enhancing options when unwanted pregnancies occur). Yet the strategies considered thus far (contraception, abstinence education, adoption, and social welfare) seem insufficient for a serious campaign to reduce the abortion rate. As with poverty and marriage, work from above is necessary but difficult due to ongoing disagreements about policy and insufficient attention given to the complex roots of the problem. The most important work to be done lies at the local level—in particular, in efforts to empower young adults to see themselves and their relationships differently and in efforts to encourage caregiving in communities.

The Self in Relation

Talking about abstinence education is difficult because turning back to earlier norms about premarital sex seems nearly impossible and so far no program has been able to show long-term success. The best that such programs have been able to do is delay sexual activity for a few years and reduce teen pregnancy rates. These are important gains. But when rates of pregnancy outside marriage remain high, it is important to ask if it is possible to do better. What would it take to convince older teens and twenty-somethings (high-risk groups for abortions) that pregnancy is not something they want to risk?[125] According to Wilcox, research suggests five elements of successful programs: "a clear and compelling normative message," inclusion of trusted young adults and peers, a focus on how abstinence connects with hopes for the future, involvement in service activities, and cooperation with other institutions in the community.[126] This is an interesting list. Effective sex education does not simply provide information and guidance in ethical decision making; it also puts forth norms, just as effective social justice education does. Research suggests that the norm should be saving sex for highly committed relationships or marriage. This norm needs to be communicated not just by adults but also by peers who can be trusted. Young adults need to see abstinence as a practice connected to their future—as spouses, parents, and workers.

Their hopes and dreams and their perceptions of what makes life meaningful need to go beyond the pleasures of sex or the hoped-for joy of
having a baby right now. Engaging in service allows young adults to love
and be loved, to connect with a community and feel purposeful. Finally,
young adults need to hear the message about saving sex and childbearing
for later from many different players in their communities so that the
message is reinforced.

Still, there will always be unplanned pregnancies. Mathewes-Green
writes, "There are many practical problems that must be solved in the
course of an unplanned pregnancy. But the primary need appears to be
to forge connections to other people, people that she can lean on through
the difficult months ahead, . . . [she and her baby need] someone who
would care for them personally and who wouldn't let them down."[127]
Glen Stassen describes an effective program in Louisville that tried to
offer teens this kind of support.[128] The program provided continuing
education, health care, and counseling for pregnant teens. A total of 99
percent of the girls in the program chose to have their babies, versus 75
percent of younger teens and 40 percent of older teens nationally in the
year of the study. The girls were able to stay in school, have their babies
cared for in a nursery, and receive education in parenting and planning
for the future. Most of the girls did not become pregnant again, and they
had lower than average rates of drug addiction, suicide, and dropping
out. Stassen also recounts how a supportive church and community gave
his own family the strength to bear and raise a child with severe disabilities. He argues for public funding of programs like this one, while
underlining the need for strong support at the community level.

The effective prevention of unwanted pregnancies seems to hinge on
helping young adults see themselves as unique persons with gifts and
futures. It involves surrounding them with love and giving them something worthwhile to do. It entails helping them see what is good about
marriage and sex in committed relationships and challenging them to be
accountable to their communities by avoiding childbearing outside marriage. It is important to celebrate the many single mothers and fathers
in poor communities who do their very best to raise their children in
difficult environments. However, as I argued in chapter 4, it is crucial to
acknowledge that, on average, children born to single mothers will be
disadvantaged. Some affirm the "responsible" choice of single mothers
to have abortions in order to avoid going on public assistance.[129] But if,

instead, we want to reduce the abortion rate, we need to raise more young adults who value themselves, see how they can make a contribution in their community, and worry enough about their potential children not to risk pregnancy before they are ready to become parents.

Adoption and Community

Mathewes-Green tells us that most women have abortions not because they lack money or health care but because they lack strong support from people close to them.[130] Without this support, they simply cannot envision bringing a child into their lives. And yet many couples long for a child to adopt. They stand ready to help, but most are living a world apart from those who are most likely to find themselves unexpectedly pregnant. Stanley Hauerwas localizes the imperative of social support for pregnant woman, saying that Christians must "in their own communities, make clear that the role of parent is one we all share. Thus the woman who is pregnant and carrying a child need not be the one to raise it."[131] If the world says "You can have a child only if you have everything set—that is, if you are in a good 'relationship,' if you have your finances in good shape, the house, and so on," Christians must say something else entirely.[132] We need to "learn to be a people dependent on one another. We must learn to confess that, as a hospitable people, we need one another because we are dependent on one another. The last thing that the church wants is a bunch of autonomous, free individuals. We want people who know how to express authentic need, because that creates community. So, the language of abortion is a reminder about the kind of community that we need to be. Abortion language reminds the church to be ready to receive new life *as church*."[133]

What Hauerwas is calling for is radical. Most churches today are not communities of this kind, but surely more churches could be. By engaging in child-centered practices (e.g., providing day care, tutoring, and parenting classes and by sending volunteers to pregnancy resource centers), Christian communities can become more open to children. Perhaps they will then become more ready to take responsibility for children whose biological parents cannot raise them or to give children up to the care of others when necessary.[134] Through theological rethinking and concrete practice, we can prepare to be the kind of people who can give babies up and receive them. Both those who give and those who receive offer a profound self-gift and are, in an important sense, model parents who love selflessly not for their own good but for the good of their children.[135]

However, there may also be other communities that are just as capable or even more capable of cultivating this kind of love. If parents of babies for whom they could not care turned to local communities in the past—and if even today this practice continues, especially in black and Latino communities—this plan may be more realistic than a general call for adoption and social support.[136] There is a need for programs like the one Stassen describes, which create communities within social institutions. Advocacy for better benefits for low-income women is necessary. As Cahill affirms, "access to basic social goods as the precondition of meaningful decision making in relation to motherhood and family," and certainly this is the ideal. Yet many young women, both in the United States and around the world, make decisions to bring children into the world even though they lack the resources that many middle-class people would consider necessary.[137] The pregnant women in Mathewes-Green's study consistently said that what they needed most was support from a family member or friend. "Be that friend," she says. "There are no 'public policy' implications here; this is not an item for bureaucracy."[138] Support from a partner, friend, or family member is crucial in enabling a woman to keep and raise a child in difficult circumstances. A good number of adoptions already occur within extended families.[139] Adoption is much easier to consider when it occurs in close proximity. Cultivating openness to giving up and caring for children in neighborhoods and extended families is the key to making adoption an effective abortion reduction strategy.

Solutions like those outlined above are not simply personal. They need to be nurtured and supported by communities and sometimes sustained by government funding. Still, they differ profoundly from government-issued debit cards or laws restricting access to a clinic. One might call supportive friendship, ecclesial community, abstinence education, mentoring programs, and community adoption "middle axioms" or "the personal practice of social virtue."[140] They are all ways that people with different perspectives can come together to love young adults, aid expectant parents, and reduce abortion. In the space between, new possibilities can come to life.

WHAT ARE WE HOPING FOR?

At the end of her attempt to articulate a faithful, Catholic realist approach to abortion, Susan Stabile asks if it is even possible to be a Christian realist. That is, ought Christians to be asking questions about what will do the most good, given the limits of this world, and should we be resigning ourselves to not trying to get the law to recognize all that we believe to be true? She believes that it is possible, but admits that affirming realism "raises questions about what is the role of Catholics in the world and what it means to bear faithful witness to the Gospel, which are beyond the scope of my inquiry."[141] If the pro-life side could manage to limit their expectations, Stabile believes that pro-choice advocates would be more willing to discuss alternative measures to make abortion more difficult and less necessary. Conversely, if the pro-choice side could acknowledge abortion as a tragic choice that we ought to work to avoid, that might make it easier for pro-life advocates to live with *Roe*.[142]

Some would argue that this is not what Christian ethics is all about. In her book *Hitting Home: Feminist Ethics, Women's Work, and the Betrayal of "Family Values,"* Gloria Albrecht calls for a total transformation of capitalist society. She cites her "faith in and expectation of ongoing social re-creation. In Christian terms this occurs when women and men strive to embody more fully the meaning of divinity which they equally image by working to embed its inclusive and egalitarian values in social institutions."[143] She refuses to domesticate Christian ideals to make them fit into the world. Similarly, Camosy argues that pro-life liberals are wrong to give up on legal change because justice demands "equal protection of the laws for our prenatal children."[144]

If we accept Kaveny's reading of Aquinas, however, expectations like these for civil society may be overdrawn. The law teaches virtue but can only go so far beyond the people's consent before it gets into trouble, even when it comes to securing fundamental rights.[145] Realism is inherent to good politics in a pluralistic society. We need not abandon our most deeply held beliefs, but we do need to adjust our expectations for the state. As Cahill says, "Religious traditions and participatory theology can contribute to the creation of local networks of transformation through dialogue and experimentation with better alternatives."[146] She calls not for big dreams or moral absolutes but for modest hopes. This is particularly difficult with the issue of abortion, because Catholics believe that each abortion takes an innocent human life. Yet if we accept that pluralism is our political situation, Christians can still "insert themselves as one voice among many into public life to promote their own vision of human flourishing and serve the common good."[147]

If we take seriously the Catholic understanding of a complex society in which the state plays a limited role, it is possible to reluctantly accept political compromise, while continuing to engage in work for cultural change. In the space between the personal and political, it may be possible to build a deeper consensus about human life from the ground up. Catholics with different views on abortion law can model humility, patience, and hope in God, as well as in fellow human beings, as they work together to lower the abortion rate, while continuing to envision a future in which abortion is eliminated altogether.

NOTES

1. Jennifer Brinker, "Finding Their Way," *St. Louis Review*, October 7–13, 2013, 2.

2. Rachel K. Jones, Lawrence B. Finer, and Susheela Singh, "Characteristics of US Abortion Patients, 2008," Guttmacher Institute, 2010, available at www.guttmacher.org.

3. Ibid.

4. "Fact Sheet: Induced Abortion in the United States," Guttmacher Institute, July 2014, http://www.guttmacher.org/pubs/fb_induced_abortion.html.

5. National Marriage Project and Center for Marriage and Institute for American Values, "When Marriage Disappears: The Retreat from Marriage in Middle America," 2010, http://stateofourunions.org/2010/when-marriage-disappears.php.

6. Brinker, "Finding Their Way," 3.

7. Adam Pertman, *Adoption Nation: How the Adoption Revolution Is Transforming Our Families—and America*, rev. and updated ed. (Boston: Harvard Common Press, 2011), 28.

8. "Teenagers in the United States: Sexual Activity and Contraceptive Use, and Childbearing, 2006–2010, National Survey of Family Growth," *Vital and Health Statistics* 23, no. 1 (October 2011), http://www.cdc.gov/nchs/data/series/sr_23/sr23_031.pdf.

9. Bradford W. Wilcox, "A Scientific Review of Abstinence and Abstinence Programs," February 2008, http://www2.cortland.edu/dotAsset/de4f7ac5-0057-4ce5-ac8c-0ac5fd370c8f.pdf.

10. Laura Colarusso, "Why Anti-Abortion Groups Are Struggling at the Ballot Box," *The Week*, November 26, 2013, http://theweek.com/articles/455956/why-antiabortion-groups-are-struggling-ballot-box.

11. Susan J. Stabile, "An Effort to Articulate a Catholic Realist Approach to Abortion," *University of St. Thomas Law Journal* 7, no. 2 (2010): 344–47.

12. Ibid., 351.

13. Ibid., 352.

14. Ibid. One study found little evidence that consent laws decreased abortion rates, whereas a study by the Heritage Foundation found that Medicaid restrictions, parental consent laws, and provider regulations affected only the number of abortion providers. Ibid., 358, 359n91.

15. Ibid., 362. Still, Stabile cautions that economics is not the whole problem. Abortion numbers decreased overall during the 1990s, when the economy was doing well but states that enacted restrictions saw a greater reduction than others (p. 361).

16. Ibid., 368.

17. Ibid.

18. "*Roe v. Wade* at 40: Most Oppose Overturning Abortion Decision," Pew Research Center, January 16, 2013, http://www.pewforum.org/2013/01/16/roe-v-wade-at-40/.

19. Ibid.

20. Lydia Saad, "Generation Differences on Abortion Narrow," Gallup Politics, March 12, 2010, http://www.gallup.com/poll/126581/generational-differences-abortion-narrow.aspx.

21. Ibid.

22. "A Generation in Transition: Religion, Values, and Politics among College-Age Millennials," Public Religion Research Institute, http://publicreligion.org/research/2012/04/millennial-values-survey-2012/. See also Robert D. Putnam and David E. Campbell, *Amazing Grace: How Religion Divides and Unites Us* (New York: Simon & Schuster, 2010), 131–32.

23. Amelia Thomson-DeVeaux, "Moving beyond 'Pro-Choice' and 'Pro-life,'" Public Religion Research Institute, http://publicreligion.org/2013/01/moving-beyond-pro-choice-and-pro-life/.

24. Jones, Finer, and Singh, "Characteristics of US Abortion Patients."

25. Lydia Saad, "'Pro-Choice' Americans at Record-Low 41 Percent," Gallup Politics, http://www.gallup.com/poll/154838/Pro-Choice-Americans-Record-Low.aspx.

26. Cristina Stanojevich, "Overlapping 'Pro-Choice' and 'Pro-Life" Identities," Public Religion Research Institute, http://publicreligion.org/2013/01/graphic-of-the-week-overlapping-pro-choice-and-pro-life-identities/.

27. Joseph Wright, "Reducing Abortion in America: Beyond *Roe v. Wade*," Catholics United, August 2008, 4, http://www3.nd.edu/~cdems/College

_Democrats_of_Notre_Dame/College_Democrats_of_Notre_Dame/Issues_files
/reducing-abortion-in-america.pdf.

28. Dennis O'Brien, Peter Steinfels, and Cathleen Kaveny, "Can We Talk about Abortion? An Exchange," *Commonweal*, September 23, 2011, 19.

29. Cathleen Kaveny, *Law's Virtues: Fostering Autonomy and Solidarity in American Society* (Washington, DC: Georgetown University Press, 2012), 86.

30. O'Brien, Steinfels, and Kaveny, "Can We Talk?" 18, 19.

31. Ibid., 19.

32. The major books are still the following: Patricia Beattie Jung and Thomas A. Shannon, *Abortion and Catholicism: The American Debate* (New York: Crossroad, 1988); and Sidney Callahan and Daniel Callahan, eds., *Abortion: Understanding Differences* (New York: Plenum, 1984).

33. Lisa Sowle Cahill, "Abortion, Autonomy, and Community," in *Abortion and Catholicism*, ed. Jung and Shannon, 85–97.

34. Tina Beattie, "Catholicism, Choice, and Consciousness: A Feminist Theological Perspective on Abortion," *International Journal of Public Theology* 4 (2010): 68.

35. Ibid., 70.

36. Charles E. Camosy, *Beyond the Abortion Wars: A Way Forward for a New Generation* (Grand Rapids: William B. Eerdmans, 2015).

37. Hauerwas, "Abortion, Theologically Understood," Task Force of United Methodists on Abortion and Sexuality, February 1991, http://lifewatch.org/abortion.html.

38. Joseph J. Kotva, "The Question of Abortion: Christian Virtue and Government Legislation," *Mennonite Quarterly Review* 79 (2005): 484.

39. Ibid., 484–85.

40. Ibid., 487–92.

41. Ibid., 493–96.

42. USCCB, "Forming Consciences for Faithful Citizenship," 2007, no. 22, http://www.usccb.org/issues-and-action/faithful-citizenship/forming-consciences-for-faithful-citizenship-document.cfm.

43. These essays became chapters 9 and 10 in the book by Cathleen Kaveny, *Law's Virtues: Fostering Autonomy and Solidarity in American Society* (Washington, DC: Georgetown University Press, 2012).

44. Catholics in Alliance for the Common Good, "Pro-Life Issues," http://www.catholicsinalliance.org/pro_life_issues.

45. Patrick Whelan, MD, "Which Party Does Better at Reducing the Number of Abortions?" Catholic Democrats, December 17, 2008, http://www.catholicdemocrats.org/news/2008/12/which_party_does_better_at_red.php.

46. Mario Cuomo, "Religious Belief and Public Morality: A Catholic Governor's Perspective," speech, University of Notre Dame, September 13, 1984, reprinted in *Abortion and Catholicism*, ed. Jung and Shannon, 209, 206.

47. Ibid., 210–13.

48. This does not mean that activists are seeking common ground. See, e.g., John Gehring, "What Ever Happened to the Common Ground on Abortion Reduction?" *Religion & Politics*, April 16, 2013, http://religionandpolitics .org/2013/04/16/what-ever-happened-to-the-common-ground-on-abortion-re duction/. As ever, the culture war is most intense among professionals. Still, in popular forums, calls for common ground can generate large numbers of positive comments; see, e.g., Kate Gordon, "Why Pro-Life and Pro-Choice Advocates Should Find the Common Ground," *Millennial Journal*, October 8, 2013, http://millennial journal.com/2013/10/08/ percentC2 percentAC percentC2 percentAC percentC2 percentACwhy-pro-life-and-pro-choice-advocates-should-find-the-common -ground/.

49. A minority of Catholic moral theologians could be considered strongly pro-choice. See, e.g., Daniel Maguire, *Sacred Choices: The Right to Contraception and Abortion in Ten World Religions* (Minneapolis: Fortress Press, 2009).

50. Frederica Mathewes-Green, *Real Choices: Listening to Women, Looking for Alternatives to Abortion* (Ben Lomond, CA: Conciliar Press, 1997), 11.

51. Ibid.

52. Ibid., 193. The pregnancy center survey shows that the least-difficult problems to solve are anxiety about pregnancy, help with obstetric care, and housing during pregnancy.

53. Jon A. Shields, "*Roe*'s Pro-Life Legacy," *First Things*, January 2013, http:// www.firstthings.com/article/2013/01/roes-pro-life-legacy.

54. Lawrence B. Finer, Lori F. Frohwirth, Lindsay A. Dauphinee, Susheela Singh, and Ann M. Moore, "Reasons US Women Have Abortions: Quantitative and Qualitative Perspectives," *Perspectives on Sexual and Reproductive Health* 37, no. 3 (September 2005), http://www.guttmacher.org/pubs/journals/3711005 .html.

55. Ibid.

56. Ibid.

57. Ibid. See also Meaghan Winter, "My Abortion," *New York*, November 10, 2013, which includes the stories of twenty-six women.

58. Sunsara Taylor, quoted by Penny Starr, "Activist: Abortion Is a 'Great Decision,' 'Should Be as Common as Possible,'" CNS News, August 11, 2014, http://cnsnews.com/mrctv-blog/penny-starr/activist-abortion-great-decision -should-be-common-possible.

59. Mathewes-Green, *Real Choices*, 14.

60. Ibid., 13.

61. Ibid., 190.

62. Ibid., 191–93.

63. Ibid., 22.

64. Ibid., 23.

65. Kathryn Edin and Maria Kefalas, *Promises I Can Keep: Why Poor Women Put Motherhood before Marriage and Adoption* (Berkeley: University of California Press, 2005), 207.

66. Ibid., 210. See also the report on a homeless family in Brooklyn by Andrea Elliott, "A Neighborhood's Profound Divide," *New York Times*, December 11, 2013, http://www.nytimes.com/projects/2013/invisible-child/#/?chapt=3: "It is Dasani's belief that she and her siblings are the cause of her mother's ruin. It never occurs to her that, for Chanel, the children represent her only accomplishment."

67. Edin and Kefalas, *Promises I Can Keep*, 203.

68. Ibid., 8.

69. Ibid., 204.

70. Ibid., 209.

71. National Marriage Project and Center for Marriage and Institute for American Values, "When Marriage Disappears."

72. Some researchers suspect that because a greater proportion of poor women with unplanned pregnancies carry those babies to term in spite of less-than-ideal circumstances, their more pro-life beliefs play a role. See Amber Lapp, "Why Poor Women with Unintended Pregnancies Are Less Likely to Get Abortions," Family Studies, March 10, 2015, http://family-studies.org/why-poor-women-with-unintended-pregnancies-are-less-likely-to-get-abortions/.

73. Edin and Kefalas, *Promises I Can Keep*, 6.

74. Ibid., 46.

75. Ibid., 47.

76. Finer et al., "Reasons US Women Have Abortions," 118.

77. Amy Deschner and Susan A. Cohen, "Contraceptive Use Is Key to Reducing Abortion Worldwide," *Guttmacher Report on Public Policy* 6, no. 4 (October 2003), http://www.guttmacher.org/pubs/tgr/06/4/gr060407.html.

78. Blythe Bernhard, "Contraceptive Study in St. Louis Coincides with Drop in Abortion, Teen Pregnancy," *Saint Louis Post-Dispatch*, October 5, 2012, http://www.stltoday.com/news/local/metro/contraceptive-study-in-st-louis-coincides-with-drop-in-abortion/article_9efe9196-b672-5f6a-9a6a-c094e7fe5546.html.

79. Jessica Ahrons and Shira Saperstein, "The Right Way to Reduce Abortion," Center for American Progress, January 20, 2006, https://www.americanprogress.org/issues/women/news/2006/01/20/1796/the-right-way-to-reduce-abortion/.

80. Ross Douthat, "The 'Safe, Legal, Rare' Illusion," *New York Times*, February 18, 2012, http://www.nytimes.com/2012/02/19/opinion/sunday/douthat-the-safe-legal-rare-illusion.html.

81. Ibid.

82. Ross Douthat, "More on Red and Blue Families," *New York Times*, May 11, 2010, http://douthat.blogs.nytimes.com/2010/05/11/more-on-red-and-blue

-families/. He notes that California, Maryland, and Rhode Island have teen pregnancy rates that are similar to those of West Virginia, Alabama, and Kentucky but have lower teen birthrates, due to abortion.

83. Ross Douthat, "What Reduces Abortion Rates," *New York Times*, February 21, 2012, http://douthat.blogs.nytimes.com/2012/02/21/what-reduces -abortion-rates/.

84. Ibid.

85. National Marriage Project and Center for Marriage and Institute for American Values, "When Marriage Disappears."

86. Edin and Kefalas, *Promises I Can Keep*, 39.

87. Jo Jones, William Mosher, and Kimberly Daniels, "Current Contraceptive Use in the United States, 2006–2010, and Changes in Patterns of Use since 1995," *National Health Statistics Reports* 60, October 18, 2012, http://www.cdc .gov/nchs/data/nhsr/nhsr060.pdf. The pill has an 8.7 percent failure rate within 12 months of typical use, and condoms have a 17.4 percent failure rate (p. 3). There has been a small shift away from condoms and toward hormonal methods, but the rate of unintended pregnancy has remained constant (p. 11). The increase of contraception use and especially of dual method use among teens is associated with lower teen pregnancy rates (p. 12). See also National Marriage Project and Center for Marriage and Institute for American Values, "When Marriage Disappears," which argues that 14.6 percent of adolescent girls who use contraception can expect to become pregnant in their first year of sexual activity. Rates are similar for women in their early twenties: "Pregnancy rates were even higher among adolescent girls and young adult women whose income fell below 200 percent of poverty."

88. A recent study by the Centers for Disease Control and Prevention shows that 57 percent of fifteen- to nineteen-year-old girls and 58 percent of fifteen- to nineteen-year-old boys have never had sexual intercourse. See "Teenagers in the United States: Sexual Activity and Contraceptive Use, and Childbearing, 2006–2010, National Survey of Family Growth," *Vital and Health Statistics* 23, no. 1 (October 2011), http://www.cdc.gov/nchs/data/series/sr_23/sr23_031.pdf.

89. National Marriage Project and Center for Marriage and Institute for American Values, "When Marriage Disappears": "Adolescents are less developed emotionally and cognitively than their adult peers; consequently, they have greater difficulty exercising self-control and are more likely to use contraception incorrectly or inconsistently." Only 55 percent of teens use contraception consistently in their first sexual relationship and rates are lower over time.

90. Christine Kim and Robert Rector, "Evidence on the Effectiveness of Abstinence Education: An Update," Heritage Foundation, February 19, 2010, http://www.heritage.org/research/reports/2010/02/evidence-on-the-effectiveness -of-abstinence-education-an-update.

91. Wilcox, "Scientific Review."

92. Ibid., 3.

93. Ibid., 6.

94. Ibid.

95. Ibid., 19.

96. Helen B. Chin, Theresa Ann Sipe, Randy Elder, Shawna L. Mecer, Sajal K. Chattopadhyay, Verughese Jacob, Holly R. Wethington, Doug Kirby, Donna B. Elliston, Matt Griffith, Stella O. Chuke, Susan C. Briss, Irene Ericksen, Jennifer S. Galbraith, Jeffrey H. Herbst, Robert L. Johnson, Joan M. Kraft, Seth M. Noar, Lisa M. Romero, and John Santelli, "Effectiveness of Group-Based Comprehensive Risk-Reduction and Abstinence Education Interventions," *American Journal of Preventive Medicine* 42, no. 3 (2012): 272–94.

97. For the arguments of advocates, see the National Abstinence Education Association's website, http://www.thenaea.org/docs/Abstinence_Works.pdf.

98. Wilcox, "Scientific Review," 20. See also Sarah Kliff, "The Mystery of the Falling Teen Birth Rate," Vox, August 20, 2014, http://www.vox.com /2014/8/20/5987845/the-mystery-of-the-falling-teen-birth-rate, which concludes that a number of factors contributed to the declining birthrate, including contraception, sex education, the recession, and reality television shows about teen moms.

99. Ibid., 18.

100. See "Christian Evangelical Adoption Movement Perseveres amid Criticism, Drop in Foreign Adoptions," Associated Press, October 27, 2013, http:// www.faithstreet.com/onfaith/2013/10/25/christian-evangelical-adoption-move ment-perseveres-amid-criticism-drop-in-foreign-adoptions/20628; and Maggie Jones, "God Called Them to Adopt, and Adopt, and Adopt," *New York Times*, November 14, 2013, http://www.nytimes.com/2013/11/17/magazine/god-called -them-to-adopt-and-adopt-and-adopt.html.

101. Tim P. Muldoon, "Adoption: A Life-Giving Choice," *America*, November 29, 2004, http://americamagazine.org/issue/510/article/life-giving-choice.

102. Stephen C. Post, "Adoption Theologically Considered," *Journal of Religious Ethics* 25, no. 1 (1997): 149–68.

103. Finer et al., "Reasons US Women Have Abortions," 117.

104. Timothy P. O'Malley, "Trinitarian Love: The Sacramentality of Adoption," *America*, September 23, 2013, 22.

105. Pertman, *Adoption Nation*, 28.

106. Ibid., 37.

107. Ibid., 28.

108. Mathewes-Green, *Real Choices*, 191–92.

109. Edin and Kefalas, *Promises I Can Keep*, 74.

110. Pertman, *Adoption Nation*, 6, 14–17, 32.

111. Ibid., 63.

112. Ibid., 23.

113. Ibid., 28.

114. Mathewes-Green, *Real Choices*, 191.

115. Finer et al., "Reasons US Women Have Abortions," 113.

116. Mathewes-Green, *Real Choices*, 189–90.

117. Brian Fung, "Increased Access to Health Care May Decrease Abortions," *The Atlantic*, August 24, 2012, http://www.theatlantic.com/health/archive/2012/08/increased-access-to-health-care-may-decrease-abortions/261463/#comments.

118. Wright, "Reducing Abortion in America," 2.

119. Ibid., 5.

120. Ibid., 5n7.

121. Rose Marie Berger and Amy Spaulding, "Making Abortion Rare," *Sojourners*, January 2009, https://sojo.net/magazine/january-2009/making-abortion-rare.

122. Wright defends his study and backs away from some claims about the family cap and the Special Supplemental Nutrition Program for Women, Infants, and Children (known as WIC); see Joseph Wright, "Researcher Defends 'Reducing Abortion in America,'" *Crisis*, February 12, 2009, http://www.crisismagazine.com/2009/researcher-defends-qreducing-abortion-in-americaq.

123. Finer et al., "Reasons US Women Have Abortions," 113.

124. Edin and Kefalas, *Promises I Can Keep*, 46–47.

125. Ross Douthat argues that success in preventing teen births has not translated into success in decreasing births outside marriage, and thus the latter problem still needs to be addressed—"wait" is an insufficient strategy. Ross Douthat, "Teen Births and the Complexities of Culture," *New York Times*, August 21, 2014, http://douthat.blogs.nytimes.com/2014/08/21/teen-births-and-the-complexities-of-culture/.

126. Wilcox, "Scientific Review," 21–22.

127. Mathewes-Green, *Real Choices*, 23–24.

128. Glen Stassen, "What Actually Works?" *Sojourners*, June 2009, https://sojo.net/magazine/june-2009/what-actually-works.

129. See, e.g., Finer et al., "Reasons US Women Have Abortions," 115, which quotes women who choose abortion in order not to burden taxpayers who contribute to welfare.

130. Mathewes-Green, *Real Choices*, 23–24.

131. Stanley Hauerwas, "Abortion: Why the Arguments Fail," in *A Community of Character: Toward a Constructive Christian Social Ethic*, by Stanley Hauerwas (Notre Dame, IN: University of Notre Dame Press, 1981), 229.

132. Stanley Hauerwas, "Abortion Theologically Understood," http://lifewatch.org/abortion.html.

133. Ibid.

134. Joseph J. Kotva, "The Question of Abortion: Christian Virtue and Government Legislation," *Mennonite Quarterly Review* 79 (2005): 498.

135. O'Malley, "Trinitarian Love," 23–24. See also Holly Taylor Coolman, "Tied Together by Love," *America*, April 13, 2015, http://americamagazine.org/issue/tied-together-love.

136. Pertman, *Adoption Nation*, 59, 28.

137. Lisa Sowle Cahill, *Theological Bioethics: Participation, Justice, Change* (Washington, DC: Georgetown University Press, 2005), 188.

138. Mathewes-Green, *Real Choices*, 175.

139. Pertman, *Adoption Nation*, 46.

140. Cahill, *Theological Bioethics*, 193; Paul Furfey, *Fire on the Earth* (New York: Macmillan, 1936), 94.

141. Stabile, "Effort to Articulate a Catholic Realist Approach," 369.

142. Ibid., 352–53.

143. Gloria H. Albrecht, *Hitting Home: Feminist Ethics, Women's Work, and the Betrayal of "Family Values"* (New York: Continuum, 2004), 154.

144. Charles C. Camosy, "Reducing Abortion," in *A New Evangelical Manifesto: A Kingdom Vision for the Common Good*, ed. David P. Gushee (Atlanta: Chalice, 2012), 9–10. Camosy believes that the Supreme Court could overturn *Roe* if Justice Kennedy changes his mind, which he considers possible, though he admits that this would change laws only in "some states." However, even if this were to happen, I still hold that substantial changes at the state level would be unlikely, given the division among voters.

145. Kaveny, *Law's Virtues*, 57–65.

146. Cahill, *Theological Bioethics*, 189.

147. Miroslav Volf, *Public Faith: How a Follower of Christ Should Serve the Common Good* (Grand Rapids: Brazos, 2011), 145.

CHAPTER 7

End-of-Life Care

Enabling Better Practices for Dying Well

Though people disagree on many issues related to the end of life, many would acknowledge that there is something wrong with the way we die. The feared scenario looks something like this: I am in a hospital bed, perhaps in the intensive care unit. It is taking a long time to die. My mental and physical capacities are diminished, and I fear losing more of my self. I am feeling pain that cannot be relieved with medication and the anguish of being a burden on others. Doctors and nurses seem to be controlling decisions about my care. Most of my friends have already died, and family rarely visits. I am alone much of the time, waiting for the agony to end.

In contrast, the movie *Amour* provided a more attractive vision of death without diminishing the difficulty of decline. In the movie we see a husband embracing his duty to care for his wife, who reluctantly but lovingly accepts his care. As she forgets more, becomes less mobile, and gradually loses her ability to speak, he attends to her needs, remembers their life together, sings with her, and stays with her until the end. His profound commitment to his wife is portrayed as the essence of compassionate love. Instead of dying alone in the intensive care unit, she dies at home, attended by her beloved. She is set free before disease ravages her completely and is laid to rest in a room filled with flowers.

Amour paints dying as a very intimate process. For most of the movie, we see only the two elderly lovers in their world of music, books, and conversation. In the end, only he can understand her, only he can bear to see her deteriorate. Caregivers come and are let go. When their daughter and son-in-law try to help, he first tolerates their presence but later hides when they knock at the door. A former piano student of his wife visits and recalls an earlier public life, but he is the last visitor; no friends, students, or family members can accompany these two to the end. This journey involves vulnerability, fear, pain, and the need to be cared for—and even a second childhood. It requires an asymmetrical and unflinching love that only the husband can provide. Finally, he can bear it no more; so he ends her life and, presumably, his own.

Though few would go as far as the husband in *Amour*, many worry about facing lonely, painful deaths after receiving unwanted treatment. Only one-third of Americans die at home surrounded by loved ones, though 75 percent express the desire to do so.[1] Instead, most die in nursing homes or hospitals, often in the intensive care unit. Many worry about pain, and some still experience severe pain near the end of life, though when good palliative care methods are used, most physical suffering can now be avoided.[2] Despite widespread fear about the dying process, most do not have frank conversations with relatives about their wishes.[3] With the availability of physician-assisted suicide (PAS), some fear increasing pressure on vulnerable sick and elderly people to end their lives.[4] At the same time, overtreatment in the last stages of life is common and costly; 17 percent of Medicare spending goes to patients' last six months, and 25 percent goes to only 5 percent of patients in the final year of life, even though spending at the very end rarely results in strong positive outcomes.[5] Despite the unprecedented amount of resources going to extend life and newer opportunities to end it, a "good death" remains an elusive goal for many.

Much of public conversation about end-of-life issues turns on questions of policy: Should physicians be allowed to assist dying patients who want to end their lives? Should Medicare cover everything dying patients want? Should patients be able to make their own decisions about the care they receive or reject? What kinds of decisions should families be able to make on behalf of patients who cannot decide for themselves? Should conversations about death be a regular feature of hospital care when people are close to death, or could that lead to coercion, especially for vulnerable populations?

Often, these conversations come to a head with controversial court cases—such as *Cruzan* (1990), *Schiavo* (2005), and the *Affordable Care*

Act (2010)—that capture the attention of the nation and divide left and right. The culture war seems to be in full force, as the right claims that sick people are victims of a society that only prizes life when it is healthy and self-sufficient but the left asserts that people should be able to make their own decisions about death.[6] Catholic spokespersons and institutions are frequently at the center of these storms, though their views do not always prevail.

The law may very well be moving in the direction of greater legal recognition of individual liberty, including PAS, which is legal in five states—California, Oregon, Washington, Vermont, and Montana—though in 2012 voters in Massachusetts voted down a ballot measure that would have now legalized PAS there.[7] According to a recent Pew Research survey, the right to PAS is supported by 62 percent of Americans, up from 55 percent in 1990. Most support it if a patient is experiencing pain, has an incurable disease, believes his or her life is no longer meaningful, or feels as if he or she is a burden to their family.[8] Recent Gallup Polls have found that nearly 70 percent of Americans approve if asked about doctors helping patients end their lives; and, unlike in previous years, similar percentages even say they approve if the language of "suicide" is used.[9] When autonomy and choice are prized, it seems difficult to deny people the right to choose the circumstances of their deaths.[10] At the very least, it is clear that the courts are allowing states to experiment with PAS; and though it is not yet a widespread practice, support is gaining ground.

The value of autonomy that, for some, underlines the right to die means, for others, the right to extend treatment. Problems of overtreatment are inevitable in a culture that prizes autonomy, especially in today's context of ever-improving medical capacity ("rarely is there *nothing* more that doctors can do") and the Medicare system that gives patients the right to ask doctors to "do everything."[11] The cultural ethos pushes in two directions—"do everything to make me well" or "let me die on my own terms." Underneath conflicts about PAS and overtreatment lies the strong valuation of individual choice. So what appears to be a pro-life/pro-choice divide is really an argument about how best to respect human beings in their freedom and individuality at the end of their lives. The only really important question then becomes, "What does he or she really want?"

In contrast, the Christian tradition offers a vision of death and suffering marked by a richer set of values, along with practices that can help to shape important conversations about how to die. Theologians, like so many others, struggle to discern how best to honor human freedom, but they do so within a tradition that values caregiving and interdependence, and finds meaning in suffering. Though theologians hold various views on end-of-life care, nearly all draw on the tradition's teachings about caregiving, suffering, and solidarity. However, the wisdom about how to die is getting buried in debates about controversial court cases and policies. Thus I suggest that with end-of-life care—as with marriage, poverty, and abortion—Catholics should shift some of their energy from politics to the local sphere. In addition to advocacy about laws governing death and striving for personal holiness, they can work on building communities capable of supporting virtuous dying.

This chapter begins with an analysis of theological conversations about dying—first examining arguments for respecting the dignity of the dying, while accepting the suffering and need for community that typically characterize the end of life; and then considering the arguments for greater consideration of autonomy and control over the dying process. I argue that although these two sides may appear to be hopelessly at odds, there is potential common ground in shared affirmations of autonomy and community, and common desires for a better way of dying. Next, I turn to medicine and bioethics, in order to describe the social context of dying and to identify roadblocks to progress. In the last section, I argue that at the local level, the wisdom of the Catholic tradition can contribute to better discernment if we learn to walk in the middle of the tension on end-of-life care, helping to shape conversations for all of those in the last stages of the journey to a good death.

HUMAN DIGNITY: FINITUDE, VULNERABILITY, AND COMMUNITY

The Catholic tradition tries to stake out middle ground in debates on end-of-life care by affirming the moral legitimacy of pain relief and the right to forgo unnecessary treatment while rejecting PAS. In doing so, it claims to respect the dignity of the person. The acceptance of patients' rights to avoid great physical pain and to discern when to discontinue lifesaving treatment or forgo additional tests, surgeries, or medicines is rooted in a clear recognition of the human dignity of the dying. Though some would argue that full recognition of this dignity also requires acceptance of a right to die, the Catholic tradition holds that dignity is not undermined by the weakness and dependence that many people experience near the end of life. Rather, the claim is that embracing human life even at its most vulnerable is a full recognition of human dignity. The Catholic tradition acknowledges that there are limits on human freedom to decide when one's life will end, along with limits on the pursuit of care. It requires people to go beyond asking "What do I want?" or even "What does my grandmother want?" to accepting that finitude, vulnerability, and dependence on community do not undermine but rather uphold human dignity.

Finitude

To accept finitude is to know that death will come but need not be feared. As Joel Shuman and Brian Volck argue in their book *Reclaiming the Body*, "Because we come from God, belong to God, and are destined finally to return to God, we need not fight without restraint to control all the circumstances of our existence, or to preserve our lives as they near their end, or to control absolutely the circumstances of our dying."[12] Instead, we can embrace living and dying "within the bounds of our creatureliness" and "receive as gifts all that flows from being embodied, including our frailty, our dependence, and finally, our mortality."[13] Because Christ has conquered death, we are freed from fear, we can look forward to eternal life with God and the Communion of Saints, and we can be present and receive the presence of others.[14] No matter how close to the end of life we are, life is still meaningful, because even in our frailty, we are still called by God and are able to respond to God's love with "gratitude, humility, and obedience."[15]

The acceptance of human finitude shapes Catholic thinking about medical care at the end of life. To refuse disproportionate treatment is, according to Pope John Paul II, to accept the human condition in light of the concrete situation of a particular person. He claims: "There is a moral obligation to care for oneself and to allow oneself to be cared for, but this duty must take account of concrete circumstances. It needs to be determined whether the means of treatment available are objectively proportionate to the prospects for improvement. To forgo 'extraordinary' or disproportionate means is not the equivalent of suicide or euthanasia; it rather expresses acceptance of the human condition in the face of death."[16]

The "real situation of the patient" is the best criterion for determining whether treatments are ordinary and required or are extraordinary and optional. Care for "the sick person" is more important than "a precarious and burdensome prolongation of life."[17]

However, respecting the good of the person can include foreseeing but not intending death. Using pain relievers, "even when result is decreased consciousness and a shortening of life," is licit because "death is not willed or sought, even though for reasonable motives one runs the risk of it" and the ideal is still to keep patients as alert as possible until their death, so that they can "prepare in a fully conscious way for their definitive meeting with God."[18] Seeking death, however, is viewed as a failure to recognize and respond in love to the dying person. "True 'compassion' leads to sharing another's pain; it does not kill the person whose suffering we cannot bear."[19]

Though this tradition is sometimes viewed as legalistic, John Berkman argues that the Catholic distinctions between "ordinary" and "extraordinary" care were always defined relative to the patient. There is an absolute duty not to take life, but also a relative duty to preserve it. In determining whether a treatment is licit, the relevant factors to be considered include debt that would constitute hardship for one's family, excessive pain, amputation, and having to move far away.[20] The patient's quality of life and his or her ongoing ability to pursue the spiritual purpose of life are also key.[21] This flexible method for evaluating treatment options is designed not to provide a set of rules but to provide criteria for moral discernment that give due consideration to the dying patient's physical, emotional, and spiritual needs and capacities. Embracing this method entails valuing life while accepting the limits of the human condition.

Vulnerability

Vulnerability is perhaps more difficult for many to accept than finitude. We tend to see the best life and the best death as those in which our dependence on others and suffering are minimal. Yet to be human is, as John Kavanaugh writes, to be "not full, not complete, not finished, not secure, not self-sustaining, not self-insuring. This lack is poverty, but a poverty which is blessed, pronounced good with all created being."[22] To accept this vulnerability of ours is "to enter into the mystery of our own unmanageable humanity."[23] When we are weak and fragile, Kavanaugh insists, we are at our most beautiful, our most human.

Even if dementia comes, stealing memory and cognitive function, human life retains its dignity. Those who are suffering may forget family and friends, but "those surrounding them do not forget. We are called to remember for them, . . . [for] we as a Christian community are one body and are accountable to narrate each other's lives faithfully."[24] The decline of cognitive ability and memory challenges our ideas about what it means to be human. Is the person who cannot remember who he or she is still a person? Stanley Hauerwas, however, suggests that this is not the most important question, because we care for others not because they are "persons" but because "they are my Uncle Charlie, or my father, or a good friend."[25] To deny the humanity of those whose capacities are diminished would be to call into question the humanity of all those with disabilities or mental illness, instead of recognizing their "perduring dignity."[26]

Community

Those who lift up the value of the end of life must affirm the "unique place of suffering and dependency in the Christian picture of the good life."[27] Christians have a story in which suffering and dependence are central and an understanding of human dignity that allows for reliance on community. In this context, pain and deterioration do not necessarily lead to a loss of meaningful life or relationships. Instead, both the dying and their caregivers can offer the time of dying as form of service to and "participation in the broken Body of Christ."[28] A Christian theology that emphasizes the inalienable nature of human dignity claims that despite finitude, brokenness, and the need for care, human persons retain their inestimable worth.[29]

Is a Christian Vision of Dignity a Conversation Stopper?

Many people argue that because the Christian narrative differs so markedly from the more prominent cultural narrative about self-sufficiency, it may be impossible for Christians to find common ground with those who value autonomy above all else. If it is impossible to make a compelling argument for relying on the care of others, for living with diminished capacities, and for accepting death when it comes without speaking of foundational Christian beliefs, then perhaps Christians should instead focus on practices to form their own people rather than on entering public conversations about dying with people who bring very different commitments to the table. Are finitude, vulnerability, and dependence on community uniquely Christian values?

Accepting death may be seen as un-American because the culture is relentlessly optimistic, and this fuels a desire to never give up on life. In the bioethicist Ezekiel Emanuel's recent essay telling why he wants to die at the age of seventy-five years, he notes the influence of the "American immortal," a type who wants life expectancy to continue to increase.[30] The influence of this mentality can clearly be seen in the problem of overtreatment that was referenced above. Yet Ezekiel is not alone in asserting a desire to accept death at a reasonably old age. He does not seek euthanasia, but he wishes to avoid medical treatment (including, admittedly, some that the Catholic tradition would likely term "ordinary") so that he does not prolong the dying process. Many doctors seem similarly convinced of the benefits of accepting finitude.[31] Not everyone wants to live forever. Here there is some common ground upon which to build.

Though more challenging for many people, a vision of human life that values vulnerability is not completely countercultural. For instance, affirmation of people with disabilities has become mainstream. The Americans with Disabilities Act (1990) reified and extended the growing acceptance of disabilities and the acknowledgment of the rights of the disabled to participate in American society.[32] Portrayals of disability as a death sentence are increasingly challenged, both by the disabled and by their friends and caregivers. Diminished capacity is more complicated at the end of life, especially when necessary pain medication limits conscious awareness and mental abilities that once were central to a person's identity have faded away. Still, it is possible to draw on what many affirm about the value of individuals of differing capacities to make the argument for honoring the dignity of human life, even at its most vulnerable stage.

Finally, some theologians who affirm the Christian value of giving and receiving care from others have noted a widespread reluctance by many people to do either. Charles Camosy worries about vulnerable elderly people, who so often feel badly about burdening others with their care, and he asks why our culture is so fearful of caregiving.[33] John Berkman, too, upholds Christian advocacy of the corporal works of mercy while noting the strangeness of this practice within "a culture that emphasizes autonomy and self-mastery," where "we should not be surprised to see the spiritual pathology of the refusal to receive hospitality."[34] Many theologians who celebrate the giving and receiving of care see their views as standing in tension with the prevailing cultural wisdom.

Some versions of the Christian affirmation of caregiving overlook the very real burdens of care and rightly elicit concern from critics. Thomas Shannon notes that "financial questions are much more critical and pressing than recent magisterial statements by Rigali and Lori, among others, suggest. And these financial realities are morally relevant to the question of what kind of treatment to provide in general, not just to the specific issue of [artificial nutrition and hydration]. As difficult as it is to acknowledge, cost of treatment can constitute a genuine burden and become disproportionate to the outcome desired and, therefore, cause an intervention to become extraordinary."[35]

Recent Magisterial statements on euthanasia suggest that "to act to end life because life itself is seen as a burden, or imposes an obligation of care on others, would be euthanasia," but the tradition of ordinary and extraordinary means has always allowed for consideration of financial burdens on a family.[36] Caregiving can, in fact, be burdensome on a family. It can be especially burdensome on women, who tend to be caregivers for both children and elders.[37] No one is obligated to pursue treatment that would unduly burden his or her relatives if the outcome of such treatment would be disproportionate to the total costs of time, energy, and money. It is important for advocates of caregiving who seek common ground to acknowledge that it can be virtuous to consider the needs of a family, as long as the needs of its most vulnerable members are not neglected.

However, even with this corrective, those who advocate caregiving for the dying are rightly concerned about the countercultural nature of their views. In fact, Christians may have particular insights about the interdependence of human beings that underline the goodness of caring for the vulnerable. This means that we have the duty to "show our fellow citizens that, in many if not all situations, solidarity is an effective and appropriate response to suffering. By standing with those who suffer, we can potentially help them reconstruct their identities, find a new wholeness in their lives, and ultimately transcend the loss of their previous integrity."[38]

In witnessing to solidarity, Christians can connect with widely shared insights about the importance of community and family. Though advocates of caregiving for the vulnerable can sometimes draw stark contrasts between their views and American individualism, in fact narratives lifting up the value of shared work, celebration, and suffering are also part of the fabric of American identity.[39] The tension between autonomy and community is quintessentially American; individualism does not go unchallenged. When Christians speak the language of community and uphold the practice of caregiving, they call others back to a story that is central to American culture and values.

Though Christian arguments for the dignity of the dying can be countercultural, claims about the value of community, vulnerability, and finitude are not completely alien. It is possible to articulate the wisdom of the Christian tradition about the end of life in a compelling way and to bring into public conversation important insights about the end of life for those who may have diminished capacities but are nonetheless worthy of care and respect.

AUTONOMY AND CONTROL

Cultural Narratives of Death

Most Christian theologians writing about end-of-life care make arguments like those reviewed in the last section. However, not just outside the Christian community but also inside it, people are asking questions about how long we must wait for death. Though not unsympathetic to claims about human finitude, vulnerability, and dependency, some theologians assert the validity of claims of autonomy and control. These claims have clear cultural resonance. Recall that in the movie *Amour*, a husband fully embraced his duty to care for his wife as her disease progressed. She, in turn, reluctantly but lovingly accepted his care. The audience witnesses his patient remembering of her love for music and his attempts to adapt to her decreasing capacities. For a long while, he carries on for her; but in the end, it becomes too much for one person to bear. Though the audience does not hear his reasoning, it seems that he must have concluded that in certain situations, no one can care or remember well enough to carry on. Even though he loves his wife with all his heart, he comes to a point at which he feels that he has no choice but to end her life and his own.

Some might argue that the husband acted as virtuously as he could alone, but he still lacked the support of a community and a larger narrative within which to locate suffering and vulnerability. The movie portrayed compassion in a world limited to two lovers. Only he could understand her, and only he could bear to see her deteriorate. No family members, students, or caregivers proved themselves capable or worthy of accompanying the two on their painful journey.

Was theirs a great love story, as the movie's title implies? Perhaps, though it may not be a fully Christian love story. The husband and wife are alone in the world with their love, which ultimately cannot bear the weight of her decline. Outside a religious context, their suffering seems to have no point. They "cannot situate this life with its suffering in any ongoing story carried by a community that can make this suffering person's life its own."[40] However, if Christians have important insights about finitude, vulnerability, and community that stem from theological understandings of the human person, they also share many widely held concerns about autonomy in the dying process.

Christian Wrestling with Autonomy Claims

Undoubtedly, certain aspects of the cultural conversation about dying raise troubling questions for Christians. Some are bold enough to ask if there is "a duty to die."[41] However, even those who would affirm the importance of finitude, vulnerability, and community raise questions about how far we must go to honor these fundamentally important values. Cathleen Kaveny rightly calls the question of meaning in the dying process "fundamental."[42] She takes suffering seriously as a threat to identity, noting that for some, "suffering is such a wrenching experience because it disintegrates previously autonomous persons, cleaving them from the plans and purposes with which they have defined themselves as past authors of their own lives."[43] She acknowledges that pain can be so severe that it drains all energy, makes it impossible to pursue life goals, reduces the world and the dying person to the pain, and "unmakes the self as an agent by destroying the ability to reflect upon and to articulate one's experiences."[44] Though she holds out solidarity as the ordinary answer to pain and a loss of identity, she leaves open the possibility of exceptions and refuses to characterize advocates of autonomy as unrepentant individualists.[45]

In noting the complexity of the problem in light of the competing goods of autonomy and solidarity, Kaveny is not alone. Lisa Sowle Cahill, though arguing in favor of palliative care and a noninterventionist approach that makes euthanasia much less necessary, allows for some weighing of conflicting goods in very difficult situations.[46] Like many theologians who believe that war is much less necessary than the vast majority of Americans would believe, yet hold out the possibility of just wars, these theologians believe that there are cases in which waiting for death may not be morally required. Still, most theologians who hold this as a moral possibility hesitate to support legalized PAS because of the many practical difficulties associated with giving human beings, let alone doctors, the power to kill.[47]

Yet some theologians are not willing to rule out the legal, active seeking of death on the basis of fears of abuses and a slippery slope. In a recent case study on PAS, the authors attempt to respond to arguments for finding dignity and meaning in suffering at the end of life.[48] The subject of the case is a scholar who has previously spoken out against PAS. But when faced with her own father's decision to end his life with the assistance of a doctor before brain cancer renders him mentally incapacitated, she wavers. Her father claims that his faith in God and the resurrection of the body will help him to go to his death with confidence. He seeks the good death so valued by other Christians, but he believes that he needs consciousness and the ability to remember and relate to his wife and adult children in order to have it. With his family, he constructs a beautiful farewell service, in which he affirms his love for them and for God. If theologians who affirm human dignity encourage Christians to testify to their faith by welcoming death as a friend when it comes rather than fighting death as an enemy, the dying man in this case study sees his solution as a more direct way of welcoming death before disease renders him unable to testify to anything. The case study suggests that faithful Christians need not be rampant individualists in order to seek death; nor must they oppose the legislation that makes this option a realistic possibility for more people.

Others, though not going quite this far, also raise questions about whether a strong faith necessarily rules out seeking death. Hans Küng questions those who say that Christians must respect God's sovereignty, and thus wait for death instead of deciding for themselves when it is best to die. He likens their claims to the arguments of opponents of contraception who counsel Christian spouses to trust in God's providence. In contrast, he argues that at both the beginning of life and the end, God leaves to us "the responsibility for making conscientious decisions."[49] Because human beings are not simply creatures obeying God's will but also co-creators of their lives, "an ethic of responsible shaping of life" is more in keeping with human dignity than an ethic of submission.[50] Moreover, a loving God would not want us to languish in misery. Faith and "unshakeable trust in God, who is not a sadist" can give us hope and confidence to seek death when we believe our time has come.[51]

If actions such as smothering someone with a pillow (as in *Amour*) or prescribing medication that will certainly lead to death (as in the case study discussed above) lie on the extreme edges of Christian conversations, Christine Gudorf suggests that Christians should at least consider whether distinctions between accepting death and seeking death are crystal clear.[52] She notes that Christians do not hold life to be the greatest good; we celebrate heroes and martyrs who accept death for the sake of others. To value one's own life less than the lives of others can be saintly, as in the story of Saint Maximilian Kolbe, who volunteered to die in a concentration camp in the place of a married man with children. How much does it matter that others/enemies caused the death of the martyr, she asks. Is it not possible to aim virtuously at death?[53] In the context of modern medicine, people can be kept alive way past the time when they would have died in previous eras. May we now claim the freedom to die, if not with a physician's assistance, then at least by refusing food and water or ordinary medication aimed at keeping us going?[54]

Gudorf suggests that the stories of those like her one-hundred-two-year-old great aunt must be taken seriously: "Rose was content to wait until God called her, but she refused to force herself to eat and drink. She would have us ask if a will to live is a Christian moral requirement and its absence sinful."[55] Gudorf points to the necessity of "updat[ing] the traditional happy death, faced with medicalized deathbeds and so many intervention options—often more than the human spirit can endure.[56] She claims that though those who persist in receiving all ordinary care until the bitter end may be heroes, the tradition should also have a place for ordinary people who make a less-than-ideal choice and "accede to the shortening of their lives . . . in the face of suffering that is both unavoidable and permanent, and that seems to us unbearable."[57]

Christian conversation about end-of-life care cannot ignore questions like these. Claims upholding human dignity at all stages of life—accepting finitude, insisting on the value of persons with a variety of capacities, and decrying the fear of dependence—are absolutely crucial to any Christian discussion of end-of-life care. They are central to the ethical work of virtually all theologians who address death and dying. However, some theologians take these claims quite seriously yet still see blurry lines between an appropriate welcoming of death and an inappropriate pursuit of death. They wonder if we can really sort out the many complex intentions that accompany treatment decisions, and confidently characterize acts as "active" or "passive." They remind us of the agency of human beings, who are not only creatures but also co-creators of their lives. They push us to think about whether traditional categories are adequate in the context of modern medicine.

Finding common ground solutions to the problems of end-of-life care will require sustained conversation between those on different sides of the divide described above. It may be possible to find a greater overlap outside the boundaries of politics and academia, in the local realm. In order to find common ground solutions, however, we first need to understand more about how people die and why progress seems so elusive.

UNDERSTANDING THE SOCIAL CONTEXT

The current social context presents new problems for those seeking a good death—longer periods of living with disease and weakness, along with uncertainty about when death will finally come. This situation gives rise to legitimate fears about euthanasia on one hand and overtreatment on the other hand. Yet conversations about dying come too late, when they come at all. The strong valuing of autonomy leads to difficulties in providing and relying on care, along with an inability to make sense of finitude, suffering, and vulnerability. By aiming at autonomous choice and by acting with compassion for those we love, we often end up with less-than-ideal situations at the end of life and an impasse in conversations about end-of-life care.

Longer Periods of Illness and Dying

For most of human history, death followed a brief illness, and doctors and patients could see clearly when nothing more could be done. However, today, according to Dr. Atul Gawande, "Swift catastrophic illness is the exception; for most people, death comes only after long medical struggle with an incurable condition—advanced cancer, progressive organ failure (usually the heart, kidney, or liver), or the multiple debilities of very old age. In all such cases, death is certain, but the timing isn't. So everyone struggles with this uncertainty—with how, and when, to accept that the battle is lost."[58]

Despite hopes for a "compression of morbidity" (i.e., a shortened length of time during which people would be living with chronic illness), vulnerability at the end of life appears to be increasing. According to a recent comprehensive study, "When mortality declines because people survive longer with a disease rather than because people were less likely to get a disease, there will be an expansion of disease morbidity," which means a "life with disease and mobility functioning loss."[59] Though some still hope for breakthroughs, "we are making little headway in defeating various kinds of diseases. Instead, our main achievements today consist of devising ways to marginally extend the lives of the very sick."[60] This is not to say that there has been no progress. We do live longer, with less pain and more options for treating illnesses, but all this does not diminish the reality of increases in chronic illness and incapacity among the elderly.[61]

Fears: Too Much Care or Not Enough?

As our capacity to treat illness increases, our concepts of what it means to provide "ordinary" care or to "do everything" evolve. The level of care that medical institutions in the United States can provide at the end of life differs markedly from what was possible only fifty years ago, and from what is available even today in much of the developing world. Yet more resources do not always ensure better deaths. Gawande cautions that "the medical system knows how to do expensive treatment, but no one is good at knowing when to stop."[62] Television shows tell stories of emergency room miracles in which impossible odds are overcome and those in critical condition are brought back to life. Many patients have a sense that everyone can be saved and see the cessation of treatment as an indication that they have given up on life, on God, on loved ones, and on themselves. For some, the cultural push to keep going is strong, and the medical system keeps coming up with more things that can be done without pointing to graceful ways to say "enough."

For others, however, the prospect of overtreatment is so worrisome that legalizing PAS seems like a logical next step. PAS accounts for a small number of deaths in Oregon and Washington State, and many who request the required medication die of natural causes before they use it. Some claim that just knowing they have access to this option reassures people and gives them the sense of control they seek.[63] In practice, others argue, it is difficult to honor autonomy while allowing suicide. PAS may look like respect for autonomy; however, "in a consumerist, youth-worshipping culture, giving older persons the choice to kill themselves makes them anything but free."[64] Camosy worries about a lack of transparency and a failure to impose strict standards in Oregon, saying, "there is little reason to expect that even the formal limit will stay at six months. Indeed, if it is 'my body' and 'my choice,' how could Oregon limit the practice at all? Who is the government to tell me what I can or can't do with my body and my life?"[65] Even theologians who see a theoretical argument for PAS as an exception often hesitate to support its legalization. Thus Nigel Biggar claims that it is important to ignore seemingly autonomous requests for PAS, because in most cases what the patient really wants is not death but relief from excessively burdensome treatment and pain control, and affirmation from family and friends.[66] Others dispute this claim, arguing that the predicted slippery slope has not materialized, while the small percentage of Oregonians who do seek PAS tend to be white males, not women or people of color.[67] It is not yet clear that pressure on the vulnerable is leading to overuse or abuse in Oregon and Washington, though limited access to data continues to hinder the public's ability to properly assess this experiment, and what we do know should cause some worry.

Kaveny argues that the Supreme Court's decisions in *Washington v. Gluckberg* and *Vacco v. Quill* (1997) struck the right balance in asserting no constitutional right to PAS yet finding no constitutional impediment to states' experimentation with the practice.[68] Though some worry about a slippery slope, in her view, "exceptions do not necessarily erode a legal rule; in fact, recognition of a true exception can function as a 'safety valve' that enables the rule to maintain its force in the vast majority of cases."[69]

Is the exception narrow enough to prevent the slippage that worries so many? Kaveny believes it is. The Supreme Court did not affirm a broad-based right to take one's own life in times of suffering. Nor did it place the dying in a special category, implicitly valuing their lives less than those of other persons. Rather, in refusing to treat the dying differently from others, the Court shows solidarity with the dying who are "still among the living," affirms a special interest in protecting them from prejudice, and situates exceptions to the general rule against killing in this context, rather than highlighting or denying the worst cases.[70] Respect for the dying has been preserved, because the Court has carved out a very narrow exception for extreme cases of unbearable pain while refusing to consider claims to PAS on the basis of loss of dignity.[71]

The difficulty is that though the law might strike the right balance, emerging data from Oregon and Washington suggest that those seeking PAS rarely cite unbearable pain as the reason for their decisions. Though cases of failure to relieve pain certainly exist, most dying patients seek PAS because they feel that their autonomy, dignity, and ability to live mean-ingful lives are threatened.[72] They want death with dignity, and they can-not envision dignity without consciousness and control.[73] Many may be better served by palliative care that would mitigate feelings of suffering and despair. The number of deaths from PAS may be low, but the practice could still be slippery, leading to legitimate fears about eroding respect for the dying. Because of the prevalence of fears of overtreatment on one side and insufficient respect for life on the other, dialogue and common ground on end-of-life care can be hard to imagine.

The Conversation Gap

Current conversations about choices in end-of-life care are both contro-versial and insufficient. The debate over what some have called "death panels," which were originally proposed in the Affordable Care Act, gives evidence of widespread fears about a formal conversation about dying. The good news is that doctors "are having more conversations now about what patients want for the end of their life, by far, than they have had in all their lives to this point. . . . The problem is that it's way too late."[74] According to Gawande, the costs of the lack of conversation are huge: "People have concerns besides simply prolonging their lives. Surveys of patients with terminal illness find that their top priorities include, in addition to avoiding suffering, being with family, having the touch of others, being mentally aware, and not becoming a burden to others."[75] Conversations adequate for the complex process of dying are needed, and the health care system simply does not provide most people with the resources to have them.[76]

Conversations are also impaired by insufficient knowledge. According to Dr. Angelo Volandes, many people agree to treatment they would not want if they were fully informed.[77] To remedy this problem, Volandes has devoted his career to making short videos of patients in the later stages of chronic illnesses. Overtreatment in a context of "medical maximalism" and a "war on death" is extremely difficult to avoid.[78] Even when patients are asked what they want, their lack of familiarity with death leaves them nearly helpless. One of Volandes's patients told him that when he had reviewed options with her, she "understood the words" but "didn't know what you meant. It's not what I imagined. It's not what I saw on TV."[79] With the aid of his videos, which are designed to be as objective as possible, more patients choose comfort or limited care over "doing everything," because "when people get good communication and understand what's involved, many, if not most, tend not to want a lot of the aggressive stuff that they're getting."[80] Volandes's intent is to make the use of videos routine in order to open doors to the kind of informed conversation about death that most people simply are not having. He is not invested in trying to change the law. A doctor who uses his videos says that "the change will come locally, not nationally."[81] It will come when people know more about dying than they currently do.

Doctors are a key source of knowledge. What we know about how doctors die is instructive. Unlike many of their patients, who are unfamiliar with futile medical care that ultimately disrespects persons, they do not ask their own doctors to "do everything."[82] They know more about what treatment at the end of life looks like, are more likely to have advanced directives or living wills, and are more willing to forgo aggressive treatment. Some argue that doctors can show others the way, especially by modeling how having "a little more time being me and not being somebody else" might be preferable to a longer life with limited ability to interact with others.[83] Doctors "know enough about death to know what all people fear most: dying in pain, and dying alone," and because of this knowledge they rarely ask for "everything."[84] Instead, they are much more likely to refuse interventions that will only extend the dying process while seriously compromising their quality of life.

However, doctors do not know everything about dying, and thus they cannot handle the necessary conversations alone. Gawande writes, with honest confusion: "'Is she dying?' one of the sisters asked me. I didn't know how to answer the question. I wasn't even sure what the word 'dying' meant anymore."[85] The medical questions are complicated, but the philosophical and theological ones are even more complex. How are life and death to be defined? When does treatment become futile? What constitutes an adequate quality of life? What is the difference between accepting death and seeking it? None of these questions admit of easy answers; they transcend the limits of science and medicine, and seem to push those on both sides further apart.

In the current context, we face longer periods of illness and lessened capacity, leading to fears about overtreatment on one hand and calls for PAS on the other hand. Conversation seems as elusive as agreement. Meanwhile, reports of the problematic status of end-of-life care continue to multiply.[86] In this context, Catholics could continue to primarily work on one side of a difficult political battle, or they could turn to the local sphere, where slowly spreading changes may be more possible.

BUILDING UP AN ALTERNATIVE CONTEXT

I have argued that though there is a very real tension between those emphasizing the dignity of the dying, even in their vulnerability, and those emphasizing the importance of autonomy and some control over the dying process, there is also unacknowledged common ground. If Christians turn some of their attention away from political battles and instead focus at the local level, more progress can be made. In a cultural context where good deaths prove more and more elusive, this work is all the more important. Building communities of discernment and solidarity to support "good deaths" is a common ground strategy with power to bring together those who may disagree about exceptional cases but who nonetheless share many of the same hopes and desires about living meaningful lives until the very end. To this end, I suggest cultivation of a complex understanding of human persons, a richer vision of dying, a socially conscious method of making treatment decisions, and better conversations about death.

Bridging the Anthropology Divide

Some theologians place the blame for the current context on problematic individualist understandings of the human person. They worry that when people understand themselves primarily as autonomous individuals, they fear that their lives will make no sense when they can no longer think and do things for themselves. When they lack a strong community of friends and family to whom they can turn for care and support, they will fear being unable to take care of things on their own. These fears lead to an understandable need to control the dying process, either by opting out before it gets too complicated or by doing everything possible to hang onto life. According to Shuman and Volck, the need for control leads us to distance ourselves from death, and this is exemplified by the reality that death is now concentrated in hospitals and nursing homes.[87] We seek control in order to avoid the vulnerability of a dying process that we cannot reconcile with how we understand ourselves or our lives.

Although the desire to be in control of one's mind and body, and thus even of life and death, is sometimes characterized as wholly problematic, it is a valid, widely shared concern. One need not be an unrepentant individualist to fear dementia and physical incapacity or to want not to burden friends and family with caring duties that can sometimes last for years. Many people can imagine a point at which suffering would be unbearable both to themselves and their loved ones. Kaveny writes that severe physical pain can be so overwhelming that it requires a person to use all his or her mental resources just to make it go away, leaving little energy for living.[88] The desire for control is not simply an illustration of the flawed anthropology of mainstream culture. Rather, in the context of nearly unlimited medical options and longer periods of morbidity, many rightly worry about the possibility of holding onto the selves they know while making a graceful and purposeful exit. If a good death involves, as Pope John Paul II claims, being able to "prepare in a fully conscious way for their definitive meeting with God," it can seem more and more elusive.[89]

It is incumbent on Christians to commit to caregiving in their communities in order to help others to see that the uniqueness of each person can be respected, even in the face of diminished capacity. It is incumbent upon them to show that "in many if not all situations, solidarity is an effective and appropriate response to suffering. By standing with those who suffer, they can potentially help them reconstruct their identities, find a new wholeness in their lives, and ultimately transcend the loss of their previous integrity."[90] Instead of dismissing real concerns about autonomy that are particularly salient in the context of contemporary medical care, concerns that dominate all other discourse about dying save our own, Christians should take these concerns seriously. Through providing care for the elderly and dying, Christians can also bear witness to the dignity of dying persons.

In a short story illustrating the power of solidarity to restore person-hood, the writer Nathan Poole portrays a man struggling with the early stages of Alzheimer's disease.[91] The lines of his memory are beginning to blur. Things that used to be second nature (e.g., the maps of local rivers that his father made, the streets of his hometown) are sometimes hard to recall. His wife has died, and his daughter is married. He lives alone. From time to time, there are incidents that suggest he will need more care, and this frightens him. At the end of the story, however, his daughter is moving home with her two small children in order to get away from an abusive husband. His home will be a refuge for her, and she, with her familiar presence and memories of the life of their family, will help the blurry lines come clear, at least from time to time. In the last scene, the man is shown "lowering his face into her palm" and seeing the rivers he used to know "[rush] into his mind, culminating like a prayer that forms high up in the Seed Lake watershed of early spring, bright and clean and harmless, and comes barreling down after the rain with irresistible power, now heavy and now full of salt in the low country."[92] In the giving and receiving of care, he will become more himself again, even as he gradually eases into dying. It seems clear that his daughter, too, will find a lost part of herself in healing her relationship with her father. Community and individuality are revealed as intertwined. If Christians want to encourage better end-of-life care, this is the vision of what it means to be human that Christians will need to narrate.

Envisioning a Good Death

To build communities that can support virtuous dying, it will also be necessary to help people think more broadly about death and dying. Theologians who know the realities of clinical settings can contribute to new ways of thinking. Berkman's treatment of artificial nutrition and hydration

(ANH) is a great illustration. Berkman upends the typical ethical debate on ANH by raising questions about its clinical usefulness and its relation to Christian understandings of feeding. First, he claims that it is not always clear that ANH extends life because of its associated medical complications. Alternatives—such as finding a more appropriate diet, more appetizing food, or food of the right consistency—are sometimes more effective, and all offer the advantage of human contact.[93] Noting the ANH can often signal the end of attention to a patient, he advocates placing eating in the context of the Christian life, avoiding the "alienation" of ANH whenever possible, and finding better ways to truly care for patients.[94]

Berkman looks to the reality of clinical care in order to assess practices and consider the theological vision from which they flow. With understanding and compassion for patients, he emphasizes the futility of some treatments that may seem obligatory, while encouraging alternatives that may provide a higher quality of life for the dying without shortening life as often as some may fear. His work points to the need for developing medically sound practices that will help people visualize a good death when it is their turn to be among "the dying."

In my survey of the current theological conversation about end-of-life care, I noted two dominant trends in the category of "vision." The more dominant side of the conversation emphasizes finitude, solidarity, and vulnerability, in contrast to excessive individualism and problematic desires to be in total control of one's life and death. The other side emphasizes the depth of suffering many experience as meaningless and upholds human autonomy, including, in rare cases, the right to choose death. If Christians want to be true to the best of their own tradition and to have an impact on the way people die, it will be necessary to draw from both sides of this divide.

Revival of the tradition of virtuous dying is central to one side of the theological conversation. Christopher Vogt's work, among others, recalls medieval beliefs in the need for developing the virtues of patience, humility, and compassion throughout one's life and on one's deathbed.[95] Contrary to the cultural wisdom emphasizing the dignity found in independence and control, the Christian tradition, these thinkers emphasize, values submission to God and reliance on others. This is our understanding of what it means to be human. It is not about choice, freedom, or personal desires. Lydia Dugdale exemplifies this way of thinking when she writes, "The deathbed must again become a place of community, a place for the dying to forgive and to receive forgiveness, to bless and to receive blessing, and a place for the attendants to anticipate and prepare for their own deaths."[96] Therese Lysaught, too, calls Christians to look to the heart of their tradition, to Jesus's journey through Holy Week, a journey involving submission to God's will, great physical suffering, and mental anguish—all endured for the sake of a greater good.[97] This story, not cultural narratives that praise the willingness to end one's life on one's own terms, should be definitive for Christians. With these narratives in hand, Christians can cultivate the virtues necessary to "grow old in Christ."[98]

This vision, though powerful, is complicated by our current context, where loss of one's full mental capacity, control, and even consciousness is becoming more and more common. The tradition envisions pain and suffering accompanied by a conscious preparation for death, which is why it urges caution in the use of morphine, even while approving it.[99] However, today, people often experience years of physical and mental decline before reaching death, and pain medication limiting consciousness is becoming more necessary. The opportunities to grow in virtue as one endures suffering, accepts care, reconciles with family and friends, and prepares for death—all so central to the traditional visions—can be elusive. It is important to balance the call for submission to God with an affirmation of the role of the individual in discerning treatment options.

In ecclesial contexts, the witness of those who die well is fundamental to our vision. Typically, we look to the saints and holy people who freely entered into the dying process. Lysaught tells the story of Joseph Cardinal Bernardin, emphasizing how his willingness to let go of the life he knew, to accept his suffering, and to make prayer his work was born of his many years of daily prayer, through which he learned to stop trying to be in control.[100] Kaveny, too, looks to Bernardin, who "viewed the purpose of his whole life as learning to subordinate his own will to God's will," assumed there was meaning in the dying process, and understood the gift of being cared for by others.[101]

These stories of submission are important. People need role models to make it plausible to approach dying as a time to let go. However, stories about submission to God are not the only stories worth telling. Küng's insistence on human responsibility and creativity is also crucial. It is important to tell more active stories, to talk not only about suffering but also about deciding when it is time to leave the hospital in order to go

home or into a hospice, to remember decisions about forgoing futile treatment and choosing to live the time one has left with as much normalcy
as possible. Even Bernardin not only submitted his will to God's will but
also engaged in an active process of "discerning from all the facts and circumstances confronting him that God was drawing his life to a close."[102]
If Christian narratives of role models are to counter powerful stories of
those who actively seek death and honor the insights of both sides of the
theological divide, they must attend to the active decision making and the
desire for consciousness that often accompany good deaths.

Adapting the Framework for Treatment Decisions

Another key way to bridge the divide from below is to develop traditional
Catholic thinking about accepting and refusing treatment. The right to
refuse treatment is a part of the tradition that involves ascertaining when
to stop fighting and let go. This decision requires strength, self-knowledge,
and a willingness to decide for oneself (with the aid of family and friends)
when it is time to welcome death. God's sovereignty is acknowledged, but
so, too, is human agency.

The tradition on ordinary and extraordinary care must be extended in
light of current health care realities. Daniel Daly proposes the category
of "unreasonable means," that is, care options where the burdens to the
patient and the community would outweigh the benefits to the patient and
would limit ordinary care for others.[103] When the categories of ordinary
and extraordinary care were originally developed, health care was a local
reality. Benefits and burdens were understood in reference to the patient
and his or her family, though community concerns could be occasionally
invoked for important people in the community.[104] Today, we can use a
similar common good argument, along with broad sensibilities about how
disproportionate our medical options are when viewed in light of "global
suffering and death due to a lack of access to basic medical care."[105]
Because end-of-life care is extraordinarily expensive and there is almost
always something more to be done, we should be able to categorize some
care as not only "not obligatory" but also unreasonable. The tradition
could aim to help patients, particularly in Catholic health care contexts,
"preferentially opt for other people's basic medical care before one's own
superextraordinary medical needs."[106]

Combined with an emphasis on the individual patient's right to decide to refuse treatment, the category of unreasonable means respects both autonomy and community. If it were to be integrated into Catholic health care settings, it could answer some worries about long periods of decline and help more people balance respect for their own autonomy with concern for the lives of others. It would help decrease the number of cases in which Catholic teaching about the value of life until the very end is difficult to accept.

Tools for Encouraging Better Conversation

In addition to practicing caregiving in order to bridge the divide about personhood, forging a vision of good death, and extending the tradition on ordinary and extraordinary means, those who wish to shape supportive communities for virtuous dying will need to encourage better conversations about death. We need earlier and better conversations about what it means to honor life as an important but not absolute value and to accept death without giving up on life. Though movements to encourage conversation have begun, there is evidence that religious scholars, health care workers, and the staffs of community organizations could play important roles in furthering their reach.

Dr. Susan Block, a prominent expert on palliative care, notes that doctors cannot do what is needed on their own. Doctors tend to focus on facts and viable options. They ask, "What do you want?" However, people need help working through their anxiety about death, fears of suffering, worries about loved ones and finances, and assistance in figuring out what is most important to them. As Block puts it, "I need to understand how much you're willing to go through to have a shot at being alive and what level of being alive is tolerable to you."[107] This kind of conversation takes hours, not minutes, and requires reflection on issues of suffering and meaning that lie outside doctors' area of expertise.

Today, doctors generally keep treating until patients say stop, but patients are not equipped to make these kinds of decisions either. They need the experience that doctors and nurses have because often they have no experience of their own to draw upon; but they also need to talk with people who are able to address the deeper issues involved. Discerning what each of us wants is only part of virtuous dying.

Block founded the Conversation Project in order to encourage better conversations that doctors often are not able to provide. Another project, Death over Dinner, encourages people to talk about their desires over a meal with extended family.[108] Callahan and Nuland also affirm that though institutional and political change are essential, so too are better conversations, because "substantial shifts will be needed in the way our culture thinks about death and aging" and conversation is a way to help people think differently.[109]

The Catholic tradition is well suited to this kind of work. It has a rich moral framework that is not widely known, even among Catholics. This framework at its best respects both sides of the theological divide. It can speak to concerns about autonomy and community, and most people have both. Venues for conversations could include parishes, high schools, community health centers, nonprofits, and hospitals. For instance, a Catholic Charities center in my city included a conversation on advanced directives in the agenda for a weekly meeting of mothers in a poor neighborhood. Though the instruction was quite simple, it gave the women a chance to talk about their faith, experiences, fears, and hopes in relation to death and dying; and it sent them home with materials to share with their families. It drew upon their experiences, both positive and negative, and asked them to think about their wishes. These women are now better equipped than many for the tough conversations that are surely ahead. A better-designed program presented by someone with grounding in the tradition would be even more helpful.

"CHANGING THE WORLD"

In chapter 3 I highlighted the work of the sociologist James Davidson Hunter, who shows the importance of localized strategies for social change and calls on people of faith to consider alternatives to politics, which has claimed too much of their hope and energy. In this chapter I have applied his theory to end-of-life care, arguing that Christians from both the right and left should come together to build up better care for the dying.[110] Hunter challenges not only an overemphasis on political involvement but also idealistic hopes of changing the world one person at a time. Instead, he advocates working through social networks and institutions to advance an agenda, moving it so far inside the culture that opposing views become nearly unthinkable.[111] Advocates should work in multifaceted ways with people and networks that are capable not just of convincing one or two more souls to be "fools for Christ" but also of convincing an entire generation to embrace a radically different viewpoint.[112] Hunter believes that Christians who want "to change the world" must become more knowledgeable about how social change happens. If they want to be not only faithful but also effective, they must learn to use powerful social and cultural tools, as other successful groups have done.

Hunter's realism is critical for effectively responding to the problem of how we die. Most Christian theological responses to the problem examined in this chapter advocate better palliative care. Though proponents of PAS note the limits of such care, they, like their opponents, nearly always agree that more could be done to help people walk away from futile treatment, make people more comfortable in their last days, provide better pain relief, provide more social support, assist doctors in learning how to care rather than cure when appropriate, and assist dying people to find meaning in their diminishment and suffering. These concerns are also shared by many secular writers.

If so many people affirm the need for better palliative care, why is it so elusive? The Project on Death in America (1994–2003) set out to answer this question and to provide a road map for transforming the way Americans die.[113] Researchers cited the following obstacles: a lack of training among medical professionals in pain management and patient support, a lack of institutional commitment, funding issues, research gaps, and a lack of good instruments with which to measure the quality of care.[114] Project leaders wanted to "change the culture of medicine in hospitals and nursing homes, where almost 70 percent of Americans die."[115] They targeted professionals in medicine in clinical and academic settings who could instigate change from the inside and trained them to be role models and share information. In the second phase of the project, the board expanded its scope to include "interfaith, community-based, and school-based programs and programs for special groups such as incarcerated youth or union home health care workers—to support individual and community bereavement."[116] They were concerned to make an impact on current practices, research in the field, and the larger culture. As the project ended in 2003, the board committed its last resources to palliative care and left advice for future funders to carry on the work they had begun.[117] Their final report notes that "nobody is against us—nobody thinks it's a bad idea to improve care for the dying. But not many people can face the fact that someday they will actually be one of 'the dying' themselves."[118]

Changing the culture involves making the unthinkable thinkable. What many people say they want is control, consciousness, nondependence on the care of others, and the ability to continue doing what is important to them. From the perspective of the Christian tradition, "what I want" is not the only question, though it is one important question. Those who would influence the way people die need to honor desires for conscious control of the dying process. Yet the tradition also has compelling ways of speaking about welcoming death, respecting the value of life at its most fragile, and honoring the bonds of community. As the experience of the movement for palliative care has shown, those who seek social change need to work hard to move their vision into local institutions. But the work of changing the culture requires a mixture of vision and practices. By moving some energy from politics to practices in local communities, Christians can help more people see things differently—to realize how their desires for authentic selfhood intersect with what the tradition teaches about finitude, vulnerability, and community. Some aspects of the Christian tradition will be stumbling blocks to many. Undeniably, the story of love portrayed in the movie *Amour* has wide appeal. However, through the work of vision, narrative, moral reasoning, and conversation, we can connect with the commonly held values of autonomy and community in order to help more people embrace a deeper understanding of love and move toward the good deaths they deserve.

NOTES

1. Dan Gorenstein, "How Doctors Die: Showing Others the Way," *New York Times*, November 19, 2013, http://www.nytimes.com/2013/11/20/your-money /how-doctors-die.html. Most still die in hospitals or nursing homes, but there has been a shift. Fewer people are dying in hospitals, more palliative care is being offered, and the hospice movement is growing.

2. Eugene F. Diamond, MD, "The Right to Pain Control," *National Catholic Bioethics Quarterly*, Summer 2013, 240–41.

3. Pew Research, "Views on End-of-Life Medical Treatment," November 21, 2013, http://www.pewforum.org/2013/11/21/views-on-end-of-life-medical -treatments/.

4. Charles C. Camosy, *Peter Singer and Christian Ethics: Beyond Polarization* (Cambridge: Cambridge University Press, 2012), 77–79.

5. Atul Gawande, "Letting Go: What Should Medicine Do When It Can't Save Your Life?" *New Yorker*, August 2, 2010, http://www.newyorker.com/magazine/2010/08/02/letting-go-2; and Gorenstein, "How Doctors Die."

6. M. Therese Lysaught, "Love Your Enemies: Toward a Christoform Bioethic," in *Gathered for the Journey: Moral Theology in Catholic Perspective*, ed. David Matzko McCarthy and M. Therese Lysaught (Grand Rapids: William B. Eerdmans, 2007), 307–28.

7. Ian Lovett, "California Legislature Approves Assisted Suicide," *New York Times*, September 11, 2015, http://www.nytimes.com/2015/09/12/us/california-legislature-approves-assisted-suicide.html?_r=0.

8. Pew Research, "Views on End-of-Life Medical Treatment," November 21, 2013, http://www.pewforum.org/2013/11/21/views-on-end-of-life-medical-treatments/.

9. Andrew Dugan, "In US, Support Up Doctor-Assisted Suicide," Gallup, May 27, 2015, http://www.gallup.com/poll/183425/support-doctor-assisted-suicide.aspx.

10. Nigel Biggar, *Aiming to Kill: The Ethics of Suicide and Euthanasia* (London: Darton, Longman, and Todd, 2004).

11. Pew Research, "Views on End-of-Life Medical Treatment." A total of 31 percent say doctors should always "do everything." Minorities are much more likely than whites to hold this view; see Cathy Lynn Grossman, "Black, Hispanic End-of-Life Views Rooted in Faith, Family—and Mistrust," Religion News Service, November 21, 2013, http://www.religionnews.com/2013/11/21/black-hispanic-end-life-views-rooted-faith-family-mistrust/.

12. Joel Shuman and Brian Volck, MD, *Reclaiming the Body: Christians and the Faithful Use of Modern Medicine* (Grand Rapids: Brazos, 2006), 123.

13. Ibid.

14. Ibid., 124.

15. Autumn Alcott Ridenour, "Coming of Age: Curse or Calling?" *Journal of the Society of Christian Ethics* 33, no. 2 (2013): 15.

16. John Paul II, *Evangelium Vitae* (Washington, DC: US Council of Catholic Bishops, 1995), no. 65.

17. Ibid.

18. Ibid.

19. Ibid.

20. John Berkman, "Medically Assisted Nutrition and Hydration in Medicine and Moral Theology: A Contextualization of Its Past and a Direction for Its Future," *The Thomist* 68 (2004): 81.

21. Ibid., 82–83.

22. John F. Kavanaugh, *Faces of Poverty, Faces of Christ* (Maryknoll, NY: Orbis, 1991), 99.

23. Ibid., 100.

24. Keith G. Meador and Shaun C. Henson, "Growing Old in a Therapeutic Culture," in *Growing Old in Christ*, ed. Stanley Hauerwas, Carole Bailey Stoneking, Keith G. Meador, and David Cloutier (Grand Rapids: William B. Eerdmans, 2003), 109. See also Carole Bailey Stoneking, "Modernity: The Social Construction of Aging," in *Growing Old in Christ*, ed. Hauerwas et al., 63–89.

25. Stanley Hauerwas, "Must a Patient Be a Person to Be a Patient?" 1975, http://www.tandfonline.com/doi/abs/10.1300/J095v08n03_13.

26. Justin F. Rigali and William E. Lori, "Human Dignity and the End of Life," *America*, August 4, 2008, http://americamagazine.org/issue/663/article/human-dignity-and-end-life.

27. David Cloutier, "The Pressures to Die," in *Growing Old in Christ*, ed. Hauerwas et al., 249.

28. Ibid., 256.

29. For an alternative perspective, see Ezekiel Emanuel, "Why I Hope to Die at 75," *The Atlantic*, September 17, 2014, http://www.theatlantic.com/features/archive/2014/09/why-i-hope-to-die-at-75/379329/.

30. Ibid.

31. See, e.g., Dan Gorenstein, "How Doctors Die: Showing Others the Way," *New York Times*, November 19, 2013, http://www.nytimes.com/2013/11/20/your-money/how-doctors-die.html; and Timothy Quill, "Physician-Assisted Death in the United States: Are the Existing 'Last Exits' Enough?" *Hastings Center Report* 38, no. 5 (2008): 17–22.

32. Cathleen Kaveny, *Law's Virtues: Fostering Autonomy and Solidarity in American Society* (Washington, DC: Georgetown University Press, 2012), 34–37.

33. Camosy, *Peter Singer*, 70–71.

34. Berkman, "Medically Assisted Nutrition," 103–4.

35. Thomas A. Shannon, "'Unbind Him and Let Him Go' (Jn 11:44): Ethical Issues in the Determination of Proportionate and Disproportionate Treatment," *Theological Studies* 69, no. 4 (2008): 912.

36. Ibid., 908. See also Daniel J. Daly, "Unreasonable Means: Proposing a New Category for Catholic End-of-Life Ethics," *Christian Bioethics* 19, no. 1 (2013): 40–59.

37. See Julie Hanlon Rubio, Barbara Hilkert Andolsen, Rebecca Todd Peters, and Cheryl Kirk-Duggan, "Women Scholars in the Society of Christian Ethics: The Impact and Value of Family Care," *Journal of the Society of Christian Ethics* 27, no. 2 (2007): 31–54.

38. Kaveny, *Law's Virtues*, 173.

39. See, e.g., Robert N. Bellah, Richard Madsen, William M. Sullivan, Ann Swidler, and Steven M. Tipton, *Habits of the Heart: Individualism and Commitment in American Life* (New York: Harper & Row, 1985).

40. Stanley Hauerwas, *God, Medicine, and Suffering* (Grand Rapids: William B. Eerdmans, 1990), 2.

41. John Hardwig, "Is There a Duty to Die?" *Hastings Center Report* 27, no. 2 (1997): 34–42.

42. Kaveny, *Law's Virtues*, 142.

43. Ibid., 153.

44. Ibid., 154.

45. Ibid., 173.

46. Lisa Sowle Cahill, "A 'Natural Law' Reconsideration of Euthanasia," in *On Moral Medicine*, ed. Stephen E. Lammers and Allen Verhey (Grand Rapids: William B. Eerdmans, 1987), 451. Cahill's more recent work emphasizes the need to work for the Christian vision of a good death through practices such as hospice care, though she holds that "it may be difficult if not impossible" to formulate precise arguments for "indirect" killing and against "direct" killing. See Lisa Sowle Cahill, *Theological Bioethics: Participation, Justice, Change* (Washington, DC: Georgetown University Press, 2005), 117. See also David F. Kelly, *Medical Care at the End of Life: A Catholic Perspective* (Washington, DC: Georgetown University Press, 2007), 118–32.

47. See, e.g., Biggar, *Aiming to Kill*.

48. James B. Martin-Schramm, "Death, Duty, Dignity," in *Christian Ethics: A Case Method Approach*, 4th edition, ed. Laura A. Stivers, Christine E. Gudorf, and James B. Martin-Schramm (Maryknoll, NY: 2012): 309–29.

49. Hans Küng, "A Dignified Dying," in *On Moral Medicine*, 3rd edition, ed. M. Therese Lysaught and Joseph J. Kotva Jr. (Grand Rapids: William B. Eerdmans, 2012), 1096.

50. Ibid., 1091.

51. Ibid., 1097.

52. Christine Gudorf, "Heroes, Suicides, and Moral Discernment," *Journal of the Society of Christian Ethics* 29, no. 1 (2009): 87–108.

53. Ibid., 95.

54. Ibid., 97.

55. Ibid., 97–98.

56. Ibid., 99.

57. Ibid., 101.

58. Gawande, "Letting Go."

59. Eileen M. Crimmins and Hiram Beltran-Sanchez, "Mortality and Morbidity Trends: Is There Compression of Morbidity?" *Journal of*

Gerontology: Social Sciences 66B, no. 1 (2011): 83. The authors analyze four diseases and find increases in length of illness and mobility functioning from 1998 to 2008.

60. Daniel Callahan and Sherwin B. Nuland, "The Quagmire: How American Medicine Is Destroying Itself," *New Republic*, June 9, 2011, 16.

61. Ibid.

62. Gawande, "Letting Go."

63. Timothy Quill, "Physician-Assisted Death in the United States: Are the Existing 'Last Exits' Enough?" *Hastings Center Report* 38, no. 5 (2008): 17–22.

64. Camosy, *Peter Singer*, 75.

65. Ibid., 78–9.

66. Biggar, *Aiming to Kill*.

67. Martin-Schramm, "Death, Duty, and Dignity," 316–18.

68. Kaveny, *Law's Virtues*, 163.

69. Ibid., 169.

70. Ibid., 167–69.

71. Ibid., 172.

72. Jaime Joyce, "The Evolving State of Physician-Assisted Suicide," *The Atlantic*, July 16, 2012, http://www.theatlantic.com/health/archive/2012/07/the-evolving-state-of-physician-assisted-suicide/259862/.

73. This is discussed by Daniel Callahan, "Organized Obfuscation: Advocacy for Physician-Assisted Suicide," *Hastings Center Report* 38, no. 5 (2008): 30–32. A recent example is by Brittany Maynard, "My Right to Death with Dignity at 29," CNN, November 2, 2014, http://www.cnn.com/2014/10/07/opinion/maynard-assisted-suicide-cancer-dignity/.

74. Gawande, "Letting Go."

75. Ibid.

76. Gorenstein, "How Doctors Die."

77. Jonathan Rauch, "How Not to Die: Angelo Volandes's Low-Tech, High-Empathy Plan to Revolutionize End-of-Life Care," *The Atlantic*, April 24, 2013, http://www.theatlantic.com/magazine/archive/2013/05/how-not-to-die/309277/.

78. Ibid.

79. Ibid. Much of end-of-life care and decision making are much more ordinary than television shows would have us imagine. See Louise Aronson, "Weighing the End of Life," *New York Times*, February 2, 2013, http://www.nytimes.com/2013/02/03/opinion/sunday/weighing-the-end-of-life.html.

80. Rauch, "How Not to Die."

81. Ibid.

82. Gorenstein, "How Doctors Die."

83. Ibid.

84. Ken Murry, "How Doctors Die: It's Not Like the Rest of Us, but It Should Be," *Zocalo*, November 30, 2011, http://www.zocalopublicsquare.org/2011/11/30/how-doctors-die/ideas/nexus/.

85. Gawande, "Letting Go."

86. One of the most recent is by the Committee on Approaching Death, *Dying in America: A Report on Improving Quality and Honoring Individual Preferences Near the End of Life* (Washington, DC: Institute of Medicine, 2014), http://www.nap.edu/openbook.php?record_id=18748.

87. Shuman and Volck, *Reclaiming the Body*, 124, 126.

88. Kaveny, *Law's Virtues*, 154.

89. John Paul II, *Evangelium Vitae*, no. 65.

90. Kaveny, *Law's Virtues*, 172–73.

91. Nathan Poole, "A Map of the Watershed," *Image* 81 (2014): 7–29.

92. Ibid., 21.

93. Berkman, "Medically Assisted Nutrition," 96–98.

94. Ibid., 99–101.

95. Christopher P. Vogt, *Patience, Compassion, Hope, and the Christian Art of Dying Well* (Lanham, MD: Sheed & Ward, 2004).

96. Lydia Dugdale, "The Art of Dying Well," *Hastings Center Report* 40, no. 6 (2010): 23.

97. Lysaught, "Toward a Christoform Bioethic," 315–17.

98. Hauerwas et al., *Growing Old in Christ*.

99. John Paul II, *Evangelium Vitae*, no. 80.

100. Lysaught, "Toward a Christoform Bioethic," 317–22.

101. Kaveny, *Law's Virtues*, 149.

102. Ibid., 151.

103. Daly, "Unreasonable Means," 40–59.

104. Ibid., 42.

105. Ibid., 46.

106. Ibid., 53.

107. Susan Block, *The Conversation Project*, http://theconversationproject.org/about/susan-block-md/.

108. See http://deathoverdinner.org/.

109. Callahan and Nuland, "Quagmire," 18.

110. In advocating practices, I build on the work of Lisa Sowle Cahill, who argues in *Theological Bioethics* that theological bioethics must not be purely theoretical but should also focus on "middle axioms," or the actions of Catholic health care organizations that can instantiate values that are central to Catholic health care ethics.

111. James Davidson Hunter, *To Change the World: The Irony, Tragedy, and Possibility of Christianity in the Late Modern World* (New York: Oxford University Press, 2010), 32–47.

112. Robert Putnam and David Campbell point out that liberal views on homosexuality have risen rapidly and are currently the single most important factor influencing the movement of young adults away from organized religion. Robert D. Putnam and David E. Campbell, *American Grace: How Religion Divides and Unites Us* (New York: Simon & Schuster, 2010), 129.

113. Open Society Institute, *Transforming the Culture of Dying: The Project on Death in America: October 1994–December 2003* (Washington, DC: Open Society Institute, 2004), https://www.opensocietyfoundations.org/publications/transforming-culture-dying-project-death-america-1994-2003.

114. Ibid., 16.

115. Ibid., 18.

116. Ibid., 20.

117. Ibid., 32–61.

118. Mary Callaway, ME, associate director of the Project on Death in America, quoted in *Transforming the Culture of Dying*, by Open Society Institute, 29.

Conclusion

Francis and Ferguson

The argument of this book is that division in the church is problematic, but common ground is possible to find in "the space between" the personal and the political. I have tried to show that conservative and liberal Catholics agree about more than they think they do, and that they could find even more to talk about and build upon if they stepped out of their polarized debates and into this other space. I have sought to begin imagining what could be done about social problems if Catholics were to join together and form partnerships with others in their communities who share their concerns, if not their politics. In these final pages, I try to briefly summarize my major claims and answer the concerns of readers who may wonder if now is precisely the wrong time for this sort of book. In the era of Pope Francis and in the aftermath of events in Ferguson, Missouri (just a few miles from my home), and in many other US cities that are drawing attention to the realities of social inequality and institutional racism, is there not more justification than ever to push for structural change? Why not seize this social justice moment?

The desire for common ground solutions arises from my experiences—as a political science major who gradually came to have less faith in politics, as a member of two diverse extended families whose members have been known to argue about politics, as a parent who raised children in the heart of the culture wars, as a teacher trying to reach a diverse student body, as a member of academic professional societies pained by ongoing division, as a speaker who is often asked to negotiate polarized Catholic audiences, as a theologian who tries to remember that those for whom I write are both faithful and diverse, and as a Catholic who wants Catholic Social Teaching (CST) to be something that all believers can affirm and act upon.

In part I of this book, I tried to clear some space for the kind of conversations I want to encourage by highlighting some of the limits of politics and lifting up the potential of the local sphere. I also attempted to recover and extend the language of cooperation with evil in order to underline the reality of our interconnectedness to others and the gravity of choices connecting us to social structures for which we bear some responsibility. The idea was not to burden readers with guilt but to bring attention to the reality that everyday actions do matter. In considering the import of choices, I was also talking about the reality of social sin and the obligation to work to lessen it. Although the traditional use of the concept of cooperation with evil certainly has its limits, I utilized it because it captures something important about solidarity and makes CST inescapably personal.

Part II of the book tackled four controversial issues, which were chosen to illustrate the difficulties and possibilities of common ground approaches: marriage, poverty, abortion, and end-of-life care. In each case, I described the current divide and suggested ways of moving past it. I insisted that though personal conversion is necessary, it is far from sufficient. Although I affirmed that politics is indispensable, I argued that far too much energy goes into politics and that finding agreement here is often extraordinarily difficult. There is much to gain from focusing more attention on the local sphere—to strengthen marriage through education and better job opportunities, to empower those who live in poor communities, to help young adult men and women avoid abortion and bring unexpected pregnancies to term, and to enable better choices at the end of life using the wisdom of Catholic teaching.

Focusing on the local entails a willingness to shift some energy away from politics—from legal battles over same-sex marriage, government policy designed to provide more services for the poor or reduce barriers to economic growth, action to strengthen or weaken existing abortion laws, and efforts to increase or restrict access to assisted suicide. It also entails shifting some energy away from the personal, for though our interactions with family and friends, along with efforts to evangelize individuals, are important manifestations of Christian commitment, we are called to take more responsibility for others. Neither a whole-scale retreat from politics nor a rejection of efforts at personal conversion is necessary. Rather, I suggest focusing more energy on a neglected space, where instead of fighting each other, Catholics can participate more, agree on more, and, consequently, build up more.

Is Pope Francis leading a different kind of movement? Some Catholics would hold that this pope, unlike John Paul II and Benedict XVI, places social justice at the center of the church's agenda. Others would claim that he places Jesus at the center, as when he famously said that "the church sometimes has locked itself up in small things, in small-minded rules. The most important thing is the first proclamation: Jesus Christ has saved you."[1] Francis's genius may be that he does both. This is possibly why his approval ratings are so high.[2] He is pushing Catholics to see the import of both the structural causes of poverty and their lifestyles. Defining poverty as a life issue, he insists that an economy that does not value human life "kills"; that ours is a "throwaway culture" that treats some as "the outcast, the 'leftovers'"; that we are almost "incapable of feeling compassion at the outcry of the poor"; and that "the culture of prosperity deadens us."[3] He is loved because he gives an authentic witness of Christian discipleship, as evidenced by his lifestyle choices and his ministry to outcasts. He is loved because he dares to name inequality as the key scandal of our times.

Along with Pope Francis's prophetic words, the events in Ferguson and other US cities raise questions about arguments pointing away from politics. When Michael Brown was shot by the police on August 9, 2014, protests erupted. Attention was brought not only to Brown's case but also to similar cases in many other cities in the United States in which unarmed black men have been shot by police officers. Though activists have been talking about problems of police violence and mass incarceration for years, Ferguson and the other cases brought the issue to national prominence. People began asking questions about why Ferguson (and other similar small towns in suburban Saint Louis County and elsewhere) were poor, racially segregated, plagued by unemployment, and saddled with failing schools. A thorough analysis shows that towns like Ferguson developed the way they did because of government policies related to zoning, transportation, public housing, municipal services, and urban renewal. Thus, as one important report concludes, "The conditions that created Ferguson cannot be addressed without remedying a century of public policies that segregated our metropolitan landscape. Remedies are unlikely if we fail to recognize these policies and how their effects have endured."[4] Along with everything detailed in this report, the broken court system in Saint Louis County also bears part of the blame for the tensions between the police and poor citizens (particularly African Americans), which are linked to problems of overzealous fee collection, sentencing disparities, and mass incarceration.[5]

None of these problems will be solved quickly or easily, but there may now be an opening that was not present before August 9, 2014. There has been some movement on police reform.[6] Efforts to simplify and reform the court system are in process.[7] Political work on these important issues will likely continue for years, if not decades. Of course, much of this work is controversial, and much of it will be difficult because of the political divisions in Missouri between the state's more conservative rural and more liberal urban populations. The significance of this work is difficult to underestimate. Yet we can still ask, "What else can we do?"

In fact, important things are happening in Ferguson at the community level to complement the long-term work of political reform. ONE Ferguson was created in the aftermath of the Michael Brown case.[8] The organization is committed to providing space for conversations between black and white residents that were avoided for years. They advocate police reform, encourage economic development, and create safe spaces for children. At a spring festival in 2015, group members videotaped interviews with anyone who wanted to talk about their hopes for the community. They plan to use the videos in future public conversations and to make them available at the local public library. A 5-/10-kilometer race a week later drew large crowds from the local community, as well as supporters from throughout the area who want to see Ferguson thrive. Outside funding for civic institutions and private businesses is becoming available. Some larger chain stores are coming to town. Local universities are responding with initiatives of their own, including increasing their efforts to recruit and retain African American students and serve youth in neighborhoods near their campuses.[9] None of these initiatives in the space between can replace the necessary structural reform, but the city cannot afford to wait for the day when just policies are in place. There is plenty of other work that can be done, and much of it is work anyone can do. This is participatory CST at its best.

CST is not an "either/or" proposition. We will always need both politics and personal conversion. But the space between is crucial, too, and it has been neglected. Beyond the "both-and" of politics and personal conversion, this is what CST has to offer: a strong vision of the importance of communal, civic, ecclesial, and neighborhood life.[10] This vision is closely tied to our anthropology, which insists that people are inherently social—that is, made for relationships, not just in marriage and the family but also in local communities. This anthropology links each of us to everyone, both living and dead ("we are all responsible for all"), and it should inspire a commitment in us to participate in and support national and international organizations. But it also recognizes that human beings are finite and that therefore, practically speaking, we can only be in relationship with so many people. This vision is inclusive, in that those with both "red" and "blue" politics can see the import of action here while maintaining their commitments in other spheres. Finally, it is hopeful, in that it allows us to see the possibility of progress, without being naive.

For those who worry that this book is giving up on the potential of the "Francis moment," I want to emphasize that Pope Francis is so loved because he opens his arms wide in welcome. He calls Christians to "proclaim the Gospel without excluding anyone."[11] He asks us to strive to see the good in people without "grow[ing] impatient at the weeds."[12] He draws from liberation theology the theme of "accompaniment," which he uses to talk about going to those who "thirst for God" but stand outside the church, as well as to characterize ministry to those inside the church who are growing in virtue.[13] Accompaniment, he says, requires us "to remove our sandals before the sacred ground of the other."[14] In countless ways, he has been a witness of profound respect for the other.

All this is well known to those who follow the pope closely, though most stress that he is talking about accompanying the unbeliever or the less-than-perfect Catholic. Yet near the end of Evangelii Gaudium, in a section that has received much less attention, he clearly links accompaniment to our journey with those within the church who differ from us. We only need to think of the 2014–2015 Synod on the Family to know that Pope Francis is serious about bringing people together and having them frankly talk through their differences. The theological rationale for doing so had already been laid out in Evangelii Gaudium, where he talks about the need to deal honestly with conflict. Facing conflict differs from ignoring it or being imprisoned by it. Peacemakers find fruitful ways to deal with conflict. They are able "to build communion amid disagreement" because they are "willing to go beyond the surface of a conflict and to see others in their deepest dignity."[15] This kind of profound solidarity allows for "a resolution to take place on a higher plane and preserves what is valid and useful on both sides."[16] Conversation across lines of difference is possible, the pope says, "when we live out a spirituality of drawing near to others and seeking their welfare. . . . Whenever we encounter another person in love, we learn something new about God. Whenever our eyes are opened to acknowledge the other, we grow in the light of faith and knowledge of God."[17] Seeking common ground is worth it because in encounter, growth happens. If we are to make progress, we need to be challenged by those who disagree with us. We have seen Pope Francis living out this vision in his interactions with the church's different factions. Still, so far, he has managed to hold nearly everyone together.

With respect to each of the issues treated in this book, my hope is that Christians of differing views will all feel implicated by the existence of the social evil to which they are connected and will thus be motivated to seek ways to alleviate it. Though Catholics retain commitments to both politics and personal conversion, our tradition also offers other ways of decreasing cooperation with evil and increasing cooperating with good. In political debates, we are often just as divided and unhelpful as everyone else; but at the local level, there is untapped potential for collaboration and creative problem solving. If Catholics can get this right, we can bring to the table our strong sense that society is rich and complex, and thus that there are many avenues to social change.

It would not be right to give up all hope in either politics or personal conversion. The important work on structural change being done by committed theologians, Catholic organizations, and politicians can and must continue, just as evangelization efforts aimed at individuals and families should always flourish. However, in the face of impasses on marriage, poverty, abortion, and end-of-life care, it would be prudent to move some energy to a different social space. Possibly, in joining together in community efforts, we will build up goodwill, come to a better understanding of social issues, and work our way toward greater agreement on issues of structural change. In the meantime, this book is a call to build up "the space between," where people of differing views may find it easier to come together in trying to transform the world, beginning with the part of it that they can see. In this space, we can join with Pope Francis, who claims as his mission "being in the heart of the people" and asks us "to regard ourselves as sealed, even branded, by this mission of bringing light, blessing, enlivening, raising up, healing and freeing."[18] In the search for common ground and in shared efforts to respond to suffering, we can begin to heal the Body of Christ.

NOTES

1. Antonio Spadaro, SJ, "A Big Heart Open to God," *America*, September 30, 2013, http://americamagazine.org/pope-interview.

2. Pew Research Center, "In US, Pope's Popularity Continues to Grow," March 5, 2015, http://www.pewforum.org/2015/03/05/in-u-s-popes-popularity-continues-to-grow/. A total of 86 percent of Catholics and 70 percent of all Americans view the pope favorably. His high ratings are consistent across gender, ethnic, and political divisions. Catholics who attend Mass more often and those who identify as conservative rate him higher than do other Catholics.

3. Pope Francis, *Evangelii Gaudium*, 2012, nos. 53–54, http://w2.vatican.va /content/francesco/en/apost_exhortations/documents/papa-francesco_esortazione -ap_20131124_evangelii-gaudium.html.

4. Richard Rothstein, "The Making of Ferguson: Public Policies at the Root of Its Troubles," Economic Policy Institute, http://www.epi.org/publication /making-ferguson/#_note91.

5. See Better Together, *Municipal Courts Report*, http://www.bettertogether stl.com/studies/public-safety/municipal-courts-report.

6. Matt Apuzzo and John Eligon, "Ferguson Police Tainted by Bias, Justice Department Says," *New York Times*, March 4, 2015, http://www.nytimes .com/2015/03/05/us/us-calls-on-ferguson-to-overhaul-criminal-justice-system .html.

7. Koran Addo, "ArchCity Defenders Saw Problems with Municipal Courts before Ferguson Turmoil," *Saint Louis Post Dispatch*, April 15, 2015, http://www .stltoday.com/news/local/metro/archcity-defenders-saw-problems-with-municipal -courts-before-ferguson-turmoil/article_f1493907-7c8c-55af-a68b-6e36df0c2 cae.html.

8. See ONE Ferguson, www.oneferguson.com.

9. For new initiatives at Saint Louis University and Washington University, see Saint Louis University, "University Marks Progress on Clock Tower Accords," January 27, 2015, http://www.slu.edu/pestello-clock-tower-accords-update-126; and Washington University in Saint Louis, "WashU Voices: Ferguson and Beyond," https://voices.wustl.edu/.

10. Recent social science is also confirming the importance of the local sphere. See, e.g., the discussion of the important findings of researchers who studied the "Moving to Opportunity" project and found evidence of the importance of neighborhoods by David Leonhardt, Amanda Cox, and Claire Cain Miller, "An Atlas of Upward Mobility Shows Paths out of Poverty," *New York Times*, May 4, 2015, http://www.nytimes.com/2015/05/04/upshot/an-atlas-of-upward-mobility-shows-paths-out-of-poverty.html; and Robert D. Putnam, *Our Kids: The American Dream in Crisis* (New York: Simon & Schuster, 2015), who stresses the need to move beyond "red" and "blue" strategies in figuring out how to rebuild community and address the problem of increasing inequality.

11. Pope Francis, *Evangelii Gaudium*, no. 15.

12. Ibid., no. 24.

13. Ibid., no. 169.

14. Ibid.

15. Ibid., no. 228.

16. Ibid.

17. Ibid., 272.

18. Ibid., 273.

INDEX

abortion: abstinence education and, 174–76, 179–80; adoption vs., 160, 170, 176–77, 181–82; agency and, 165–68; contraception and, 160, 172–74, 189n87; cooperation with evil and, 33, 35, 165–68; culture against, 179–82; demographics, 159; health and, 177–78; law and, 161–65; limits of traditional strategies on, 172–78; public opinion and, 161–65; reasons for, 159–60, 168–69; social welfare and, 177–78; as tragedy, 169–70; vulnerability and, 165–67; women's perspectives in, 168–72

abstinence education (AE), 174–76, 179–80

adoption, 160, 170, 176–77, 181–82

Affordable Care Act: contraception and, xiv, 48; cooperation with evil and, xiv, 27, 35; end-of-life care and, 194–95; prudence and, 35; US Conference of Catholic Bishops and, 3–4

agency, abortion and women's, 165–68

Albrecht, Gloria, 183

alienation, 68–69, 94, 131

American Grace: How Religion Divides and Unites Us (Putnam & Campbell), 11

Americans with Disabilities Act, 7, 17, 58, 200

Amour (film), 193–94, 202

Andolsen, Barbara Hilkert, 41

Aquinas. *See* Thomas Aquinas

artificial nutrition and hydration (ANH), 213–14. *See also* end-of-life care

asset accumulation, 138–39

asset mapping, 135–36

autonomy, 195, 196, 199, 202–6, 208, 211, 213, 217,

Before Sunrise (film series), 88, 92–93, 112

Benedict XVI, Pope, 5; on alienation, 68–69; on charity, 19; on consumption, 101; on economic activity, 67–68; on globalization, 72; on gratuity, 147; on lifestyles, 60, 133; on love of neighbor, 58, 67; Pope Francis vs., 229; on solidarity, 130

Berkman, John, 54n92, 200–201, 213–14

Bernardin, Joseph Cardinal, 215–16

Berry, Wendell, 63, 68

Obamacare: contraception and, xiv,
48; cooperation with evil and,
xiv, 27, 35; end-of-life care and,
194–95; prudence and, 35; US
Conference of Catholic Bishops
and, 3–4
O'Connell, Maureen, 65, 126
O'Malley, Timothy, 176

parishes, 142–44
parochialism, 67, 70
participation, 132–33
partisanship, xvii
Partners in Health (PIH), 130, 137
patience, 214
Pecknold, C. C., 20
personal transformation, 71–74
Pertman, Adam, 177
Pfeil, Margaret, 40, 42
physician-assisted suicide (PAS), 194,
195, 204, 208–9. *See also* end-of-
life care
Pius XI, 61, 130–31
place, 71
Planned Parenthood, 163
pluralism, 12–15, 35, 36
politics: cooperation with evil and,
32–36; as insufficient, 67–70;
moving from faith to, 5–11; opting
out of, 15–16; poverty and, 34–35,
126; "space between" and, 57;
suspicion of religious involvement
in, 11–12
Pope Benedict XVI, 5; on alienation,
68–69; on charity, 19; on consumption, 101; on economic activity,
67–68; on globalization, 72; on
gratuity, 147; on lifestyles, 60, 133;
on love of neighbor, 58, 67; Pope
Francis vs., 229; on solidarity, 130
Pope Francis, 229, 231, 232–33

Pope John Paul II, 6; on alienation,
131; on death, 212; on economic
activity, 62; on end-of-life care,
197; on greed, 37, 44; on participation, 132–33; Pope Francis vs., 229;
on poverty, 73; on solidarity, 129
Pope Pius XI, 61, 130–31
poverty: adaptation of contemporary
responses to, 139–46; alienation
and, 131; asset accumulation
and, 138–39; asset mapping and,
135–36; "both-and" approach
to, 126; in Catholic Social Teaching, 125; charity and, 125, 126,
131–32; in conservative thought,
100; cooperation with evil and,
34–35; decline in, 127–28; effectiveness of current programs on,
139–42; frugality and, 133–35, 145;
individual steps against, 125–26;
internalization of, 103; job creation
and, 137–38; job training and,
137–38; in liberal thought, 100;
living wage and, 101–2; marriage
and, 99–100, 117n47; microfinance
and, 137–38; minimum wage and,
102; needs assessment and, 136;
in New Monasticism, 73; participation and, 132–33; persistence
of, 127–28; politics and, 34–35,
126; reduction, 126–27; reduction principles, 129–35; reduction
strategies, 135–39; relationship
building and, 136–37; Saint Vincent de Paul Society and, 136–37,
139–40, 142; savings and, 139, 145;
social ethics and, 59; solidarity and,
129–30; subsidiarity and, 130–32,
139; unemployment and, 102–3;
in United States, 128–29; wisdom
from past on, 142–44